Promoting Positive Behavior

Guidance Strategies for
Early Childhood Settings

Suzanne K. Adams
University of Colorado at Denver

Joan Baronberg
University of Colorado at Denver

Merrill
Prentice Hall

Upper Saddle River, New Jersey
Columbus, Ohio

Library of Congress Cataloging-in-Publication Data

Adams, Suzanne K.
Promoting positive behavior: guidance strategies for early childhood settings / Suzanne
K. Adams, Joan Baronberg.
p. cm.
Includes bibliographic references.
ISBN 0-13-140809-7 (pbk.)
1. Behavior modification—United States. 2. Early childhood education—United States. 3.
Socialization—Study and teaching (Early childhood)—United States. I. Baronberg, Joan. II.
Title.
LB1060.2.A33 2005
370.15'28—dc22   2004040023

Vice President and Executive Publisher:
Jeffery W. Johnston
Publisher: Kevin M. Davis
Development Editor: Julie Peters
Editorial Assistant: Amanda King
Production Editor: Sheryl Glicker Langner
Design Coordinator: Diane C. Lorenzo

Photo Coordinator: Kathy Kirtland
Cover Design: Jim Hunter
Cover Image: Corbis
Production Manager: Laura Messerly
Director of Marketing: Ann Castel Davis
Marketing Manager: Autumn Purdy
Marketing Coordinator: Tyra Poole

This book was set in Times Roman by Carlisle Communications, Ltd. It was printed and bound by R. R.
Donnelley & Sons Company. The cover was printed by Phoenix Color Corp.

Photo Credits: Mark Herlinger, pp. 11, 19, 35, 51, 65, 79, 99, 111; Anthony Magnacca/Merrill, p. 123;
Barbara Schwartz/Merrill, p. 137; Anne Vega/Merrill, p. 1.

Pearson Education Ltd.
Pearson Education Singapore Pte. Ltd.
Pearson Education Canada, Ltd.
Pearson Education–Japan

Pearson Education Australia Pty. Limited
Pearson Education North Asia Ltd.
Pearson Educación de Mexico, S.A. de C.V.
Pearson Education Malaysia Pte. Ltd.

10 9 8 7 6 5 4 3 2 1
ISBN: 0-13-140809-7

PREFACE

Promoting Positive Behavior: Guidance Strategies for Early Childhood Settings is designed as a text for college courses at the two- and four-year levels to prepare teachers and other professionals to work with young children and their families in early care and education settings of all kinds. This book can also serve as a resource for practicing early childhood teachers, caregivers, and administrators. The primary goal of this text is to articulate a variety of guidance strategies designed to promote the emotional well-being of young children, reduce problem behaviors, and enhance children's social competence.

The concepts and guidance strategies presented in *Promoting Positive Behavior* are based on current research, evidence-based practice, and the authors' experience with the ECE-CARES Project, a teacher-training program for early childhood educators housed at the University of Colorado at Denver. Five constructs synthesized from research on young children's social/emotional development form the core of CARES Strategies:

- Caring and cooperative early childhood settings
- Assertiveness (self-esteem and mastery)
- Relationship skills
- Emotional regulation and reactivity
- Self-control

Since its inception in 1994, the ECE-CARES Project has trained over 2,000 early childhood educators and implemented CARES Strategies in early care and education settings serving over 20,000 children and their families. In a series of research studies, children in settings practicing CARES Strategies demonstrated significantly higher rates of prosocial skills than children in control classrooms, showing more positive peer interactions, improvements in emotional regulation, and use of peaceful conflict resolution.

Promoting Positive Behavior presents real-life examples specific to the needs of adults working with toddlers, preschoolers, and primary-grade children. The vignettes, insights, and strategies described in this book represent a collection of knowledge and experiences gathered from hundreds of care and education professionals with whom we have worked. The guidance strategies presented are designed to be woven into the fabric of typical routines and learning activities of any care and education setting.

Text chapters include research and practical skills designed to give care and education providers a factual knowledge base and an integrated set of guidance strategies for use in professional practice. In general, chapters follow this sequence:

- **Opening vignette** presents a real-life scenario focusing on the content in the chapter
- **Presentation of concepts, research, and strategies** to enable early care and education providers to guide young children and promote positive behavior
- **Ideas for involving families** either interspersed throughout or in a separate section at the end of the chapter
- **Key terms and concepts** to define important terminology used in the chapter
- **Learning in action** provides small-group activities and field assignments that allow students in college courses to observe, practice, and apply concepts and strategies; designed to be carried out independently or under the direction of the instructor
- **Children's books** that relate to the chapter theme
- **Suggested reading and resources** to provide additional sources of information and assistance
- **References** that direct readers to sources of information cited in the text

We have tried to adopt an informal, comfortable writing style to make the book easy to read and follow. To avoid the awkwardness of "he or she," we have called a child *he* in the odd-numbered chapters and *she* in the even-numbered chapters. The choice of masculine or feminine pronoun does not imply an exclusive reference to the particular gender indicated.

ACKNOWLEDGMENTS

When we first started the ECE-CARES training project, we were guided by our formal educational backgrounds, our own experiences as teachers of young children and mentors of practitioners in the field, work with college students preparing for professions in the field of early childhood education, and our own experiences as mothers. As workshop presenters and on-site mentors in early childhood settings, we have been privileged to work with hundreds of early childhood care and education providers. Our teacher training program has been improved and enhanced through their enthusiastic participation, sensitivity, ideas, and experiences. This book reflects these dedicated professionals in so many ways. We thank them and the children and families they work and play with for helping educate us, for keeping our feet firmly planted in the real world, and for all they contribute to the betterment of children's lives.

We want to extend special thanks to Kristen Klaassen who has led ECE-CARES workshops and mentored early childhood providers in school districts and community programs throughout Colorado using the guidance strategies recommended in this book. Kristen has also added to our knowledge and experiential base by bringing up her own child with all the CARES Strategies—which seem to be working really well! We are also grateful to Bill Wride, Margie Marshall, Becky Keigan, and Gail Boekhoff for sharing their outstanding educational practices and for their support of CARES.

We are indebted to our editor Kevin Davis who had both the larger vision of this book and the ability to look at details. He provided suggestions and encouragement at every step of the way. We thank our production editor, Sheryl Langner, for her attention and prompt responses.

Our deep appreciation is extended to our photographer Mark Herlinger and to Julie Sitleret and her dedicated staff at Highland Early Learning Center for allowing us to take photographs in their classrooms. They truly demonstrated the essence of the CARES Model with the patience and cooperation they extended to us. The text is also enhanced by the drawings of Katy Strascina. We are grateful to have such a talented friend.

The suggestions and comments of the following reviewers were invaluable: Russ Andaloro, University of Arizona; Gholam Reza Azarmi, City College of San Francisco; Maryann Baumann, Community College of Denver; Ginny Buckner, Montgomery College; Donna Cohn, Pima Community College; Garrett Albert Duncan, Washington University, St. Louis; Joanne Greata, Nova Southeastern University; Kathy Hamblin, Aims Community College; Mary Hanrahan, Northern Virginia Community College; Laura Mason, Santa Monica College; and Patricia Weaver, Fayetteville Technical Community College.

Together we have four children and two husbands, whose understanding of our hours spent attached to the computer and whose support of the importance of our work meant so much. We extend special thanks to Loren Gollhardt for the many hours he spent in assistance with formatting.

ABOUT THE AUTHORS

Suzanne Adams, Ph.D., is an Assistant Research Professor at the University of Colorado at Denver, where she is also the Early Childhood Program Coordinator. In addition, Dr. Adams is the Director of the ECE-CARES Project, a unique training and mentoring program for early childhood teachers and related service professionals. The focus of this program is to help early childhood personnel respond constructively to the complex influences on young children's lives, promote children's emotional well-being, reduce disruptive classroom behavior, and enhance children's social competence.

Dr. Adams has coordinated several teacher training grants funded by the U.S. Department of Education, the U.S. Department of Justice, the Colorado Department of Education, the State of Colorado Youth Crime Prevention and Intervention Initiatives, and Safe and Drug-Free Schools and Communities. She has served in a variety of service capacities through professional organizations and currently sits on the governor-appointed Colorado Interagency Coordinating Council.

Dr. Adams has presented many workshops on a variety of topics, including promoting social competence in young children, developmentally appropriate practice, intervention strategies, behavioral challenges, family-centered approach, and teacher mentoring. She has published in the areas of conflict mediation with young children, social competence, early literacy development, and is the co-producer of the video, "The CARES Model: Building Social Skills and Reducing Problem Behaviors in Early Childhood Classrooms."

Joan Baronberg, M.A., has worked in the field of early childhood education for over 25 years. She assisted in the development and evaluation of urban education demonstration projects for the U.S. Office of Education and in the early development of Project Head Start for the U.S. Office of Economic Opportunity in Washington, D.C. Before joining the ECE-CARES Project, Ms. Baronberg worked in the field of child abuse prevention and developed programs and curricula for use by children and families. Ms. Baronberg has taught children and teachers, led workshops throughout the state of Colorado, and mentored early childhood providers. She is the co-producer of the video, "The CARES Model: Building Social Skills and Reducing Problem Behaviors in Early Childhood Classrooms."

Ms. Baronberg received her Master's Degree from Bank St. College of Education in New York City. Her Master's thesis, "Black Representation in Children's Books," was published by the ERIC Information Retrieval Center. She later authored "The Eight Week Nurturing Program for Children" published by Family Focus, Inc., a child abuse prevention agency in Colorado.

Ms. Baronberg sat on the development board for the newest Denver Public Schools elementary school, is a member of the National Association for the Education of Young Children, and is the founder and coordinator of a 250 member Internet genealogy group.

CONTENTS

Chapter 1   Complex Influences on Children's Lives   1
Vignette   2
Stressful Influences on Children's Lives   2
The Importance of Social Competence for Young Children   4
A Model for Enhancing Social Competence   5
    Caring and Cooperative Early Childhood Settings   5
    Assertiveness: Self-Esteem and Mastery Skills   6
    Relationship Skills: Initiating and Maintaining Relationships   6
    Emotional Regulation and Reactivity   6
    Self-Control: Managing Aggression and Conflict   7
Key Terms and Concepts   7
Learning in Action: Small Group Activities and Field Assignments   7
Suggested Reading and Resources   8
References   8

Chapter 2   Building Social Competence: Class Meetings and Family Involvement   11
Vignette   12
Class Meetings   12
    What Is a Class Meeting?   12
    What Makes a Class Meeting Successful?   13
    How Do I Schedule Class Meetings?   14
    What Are Appropriate Topics for Class Meetings?   14
Class Meetings as a Guidance Strategy   15
Importance of Family Involvement   15
Key Terms and Concepts   16
Learning in Action: Small Group Activities and Field Assignments   17
Suggested Reading and Resources   17
References   18

Chapter 3   Structuring the Physical Environment to Enhance Social Development   19
Vignette   20
Structuring Space and Materials   20
Environmental Elements That Enhance Children's Well-Being and Reduce Stress   21
    The Cozy Corner   21
    Space and Time for Active Play   23
    An Organized Environment   25
    A Relaxing and Personal Environment   26
    A Predictable School Environment   28
Key Terms and Concepts   31
Learning in Action: Small Group Activities and Field Assignments   31
Related Children's Books   31
Suggested Reading and Resources   32
References   33

Chapter 4   Creating a Caring Emotional Environment   35
Vignette   36
Safety as a Primary Need   36
Introducing the Safety Rule to Children   36
Introducing the Safety Rule to Families   39
Discipline to Promote Positive Social Skills   39
Positive Guidance Techniques   40
Use the Safety Rule   40
Use Positive Verbal Guidance   40
Model the Behavior You Want a Child to Follow   41
Reinforce Appropriate Behavior   41
Ignore Non-Disruptive Inappropriate Behavior   43
Offer Choices   43
Redirect and Offer Acceptable Substitutes   43
Facilitate Problem Solving with Children   43
Use Logical Consequences   44
Extreme Behavior Intervention Methods   44
Time Out from Reinforcement   45
Holding an Out-of-Control Child   46
Sequence of Response   46
Families and Child Guidance   47
Key Terms and Concepts   47
Learning in Action: Small Group Activities and Field Assignments   48
Suggested Reading and Resources   49
References   49

Chapter 5   Identifying and Expressing Emotions   51
Vignette   52
Emotional Literacy in the Early Childhood Setting   52
Ability to Identify and Name Emotions   53
Helping Children Identify and Label Emotions   53
Ability to Recognize the Emotions of Others   57
Helping Children Identify Emotions of Others and Practice Empathy   58
Understanding the Situations or Reactions That Produce Emotional States   59
Managing Emotions (Emotional Regulation)   59
Handling Relationships   60
Key Terms and Concepts   60
Learning in Action: Small Group Activities and Field Assignments   61
Related Children's Books   61
Suggested Reading and Resources   62
References   63

Chapter 6   Enhancing Prosocial Skills   65
Vignette   66
Why Are Prosocial Skills Important?   66
Why Are Some Children Not Developing Prosocial Skills?   67
Teaching Prosocial Skills   67
Show We Value Prosocial Behavior   68

       Be Very Specific When Encouraging Prosocial Behavior   68
       Help Children Use Prosocial Skills Throughout the Day   68
       Facilitate Friendship Skills   69
       Teach Group Entry Skills and Play Partner Behaviors   69
       Integrate Concrete Props When Teaching Prosocial Skills   69
       Select Books with Prosocial Themes   70
       Plan Fun Activities that Highlight Prosocial Skills   70
       Promote Acceptance and Respect for Diversity   71
       Replace Competitive Games with Cooperative Activities   72
       Develop a Sense of Group Association and Belonging   72
       Invite Community People to Speak to Children   72
   Supporting Peer Interaction Skills for Children with Special Needs   72
   Including Families in Teaching Prosocial Skills   73
   Key Terms and Concepts   75
   Learning in Action: Small Group Activities and Field Assignments   75
   Related Children's Books   75
   Suggested Reading and Resources   76
   References   77

Chapter 7   Peaceful Problem Solving   79
   Vignette   80
   Kinds of Conflict in Early Childhood Classrooms   80
   A Peaceful Problem-Solving Model   82
   Teaching the Problem Solving Steps to Young Children   84
       Facilitating Regular Class Meetings   84
       Using Puppet Role-Plays   84
       Using Children's Literature   85
       Using Pictures and Posters as a Stimulus   85
       Creating a "Solution List"   86
       Acting-Out Make-Believe Role Plays   86
       Telling Stories   88
       Creating Problem Cards   88
       Developing a Class Meeting Agenda   88
   Examples of Conflict Familiar to Children in School   88
   Introducing Problem-Solving in Your Early Childhood Setting   89
   Problem Solving at Work   89
   Situations in Which the Problem Solving Process Can Be Used   90
       Negotiating Routine Interpersonal Conflicts   90
       Negotiating Responses to Behavior Problems with an Individual Child   91
       Sharing Power over Classroom Decisions   91
   Problem Solving with Toddlers   91
   Modifications for Children with Special Needs   92
   Benefits to Teachers and Classrooms   92
   Including Parents in Teaching Problem Solving   93
   Key Terms and Concepts   96
   Learning in Action: Small Group Activities and Field Assignments   96
   Related Children's Books   97
   Suggested Reading and Resources   97

References   98

Chapter 8   Anger Management and Calming Down   99
Vignette   100
What Is Anger?   100
Strategies to Reduce Children's Anger   101
    Assertiveness Skills as an Anger Prevention Tool   103
Calming-Down Steps   104
Dealing with Anger in the Early Childhood Setting   105
Including Families in Teaching Anger Management   107
Key Terms and Concepts   108
Learning in Action: Small Group Activities and Field Assignments   108
Related Children's Books   109
Suggested Reading and Resources   109
References   110

Chapter 9   Stress Reduction   111
Vignette   112
What Is Stress?   113
Signs of Stress in Children   113
Can Stress Be Reduced?   114
Practices That Reduce Stress in the Early Childhood Setting   114
Teaching Stress Reduction Strategies   115
    Difference Between Feeling Tense and Feeling Relaxed   115
    Teach Children How to Visualize   115
    Practice Slow Breathing   116
    Introduce Children to Simple Massage and Back-Rubs   116
    Teach Yoga Stretches and Yoga Exercises   117
    Design Movement Activities and Dramatics   117
    Practice Feather Painting   117
    Use Stress Reduction Techniques Throughout the Day   118
Including Families in Stress Management   118
Key Terms and Concepts   119
Learning in Action: Small Group Activities and Field Assignments   119
Related Children's Books   119
Suggested Reading and Resources   120
References   120

Chapter 10   Emotionally-Responsive Curriculum Planning   123
Vignette   124
What Is An Emotionally Responsive Curriculum?   124
    Observe Themes in Children's Spontaneous Play   124
    Gain Knowledge of Children's Developmental Histories and Life Experiences   125
Planning Themes with a Social-Emotional Focus   127
Using Children's Literature   132
Key Terms and Concepts   132
Learning in Action: Small Group Activities and Field Assignments   133
Related Children's Books   134

Suggested Reading and Resources   135
References   136

Chapter 11 Intervention for Children with Behavior Challenges   137
Vignette   138
What Is Challenging Behavior?   138
Basic Preventive Practices and Teaching Strategies   138
Understanding Functions of Challenging Behavior   139
Creating a Positive Behavior Support Plan   141
ABC Analysis Examples   141
Modifying the Environment to Prevent Problem Behaviors   142
Teaching Replacement Skills   142
A Positive Response to Challenging Behavior   144
Behavior Support Plans in Action   144
Function for Child Is to Obtain an Outcome   144
Function for Child Is to Avoid or Escape   146
Monitoring Effectiveness of Behavior Support Plans   146
When to Seek Assistance   148
Working with Families to Use Positive Behavior Support   148
Key Terms and Concepts   149
Learning in Action: Small Group Activities and Field Assignments   150
Related Children's Books   151
Suggested Reading and Resources   151
References   152

Appendices
Appendix A: Lesson Plans for "Friends" Theme   154
Appendix B: Problem Solving in Action   156
Appendix C: Lesson Plans for "Beginning of School" Theme   158
Appendix D: Lesson Plans for "Bullying" Theme   160
Appendix E: Getting Started in Your Classroom   162
Appendix F: Blank Lesson Planning Forms   164
Appendix G: Basic Classroom Preventive Practices   166
Appendix H: Social Skills Inventories   168

Index   171

Note: Every effort has been made to provide accurate and current Internet information in this book. However, the Internet and information posted on it are constantly changing, so it is inevitable that some of the Internet addresses listed in this textbook will change.

Discover the Companion Website Accompanying This Book

The Prentice Hall Companion Website: A Virtual Learning Environment

Technology is a constantly growing and changing aspect of our field that is creating a need for content and resources. To address this emerging need, Prentice Hall has developed an online learning environment for students and professors alike—Companion Websites—to support our textbooks.

In creating a Companion Website, our goal is to build on and enhance what the textbook already offers. For this reason, the content for each user-friendly website is organized by topic and provides the professor and student with a variety of meaningful resources. Common features of a Companion Website include:

For the Professor—
Every Companion Website integrates **Syllabus Manager**™, an online syllabus creation and management utility.

- Syllabus **Manager**™ provides you, the instructor, with an easy, step-by-step process to create and revise syllabi, with direct links into Companion Website and other online content without having to learn HTML.

- Students may logon to your syllabus during any study session. All they need to know is the web address for the Companion Website and the password you've assigned to your syllabus.

- After you have created a syllabus using **Syllabus Manager**™, students may enter the syllabus for their course section from any point in the Companion Website.

- Clicking on a date, the student is shown the list of activities for the assignment. The activities for each assignment are linked directly to actual content, saving time for students.

- Adding assignments consists of clicking on the desired due date, then filling in the details of the assignment— name of the assignment, instructions, and whether or not it is a one-time or repeating assignment.

- Adding assignments consists of clicking on the desired due date, then filling in the details of the assignment—name of the assignment, instructions, and whether or not it is a one-time or repeating assignment.

- In addition, links to other activities can be created easily. If the activity is online, a URL can be entered in the space provided, and it will be linked automatically in the final syllabus.

- Your completed syllabus is hosted on our servers, allowing convenient updates from any computer on the Internet. Changes you make to your syllabus are immediately available to your students at their next logon.

For the Student—

- **Introduction**—General information about the topic and how it will be covered in the website.
- **Web Links**-A variety of websites related to topic areas.
- **Timely Articles**—Links to online articles that enable you to become more aware of important issues in early childhood.
- **Learn by Doing**—Put concepts into action, participate in activities, examine strategies, and more.
- **Visit a School**—Visit a school's website to see concepts, theories, and strategies in action.
- **For Teachers/Practitioners**—Access information you will need to know as an educator, including information on materials, activities, and lessons.
- **Current Policies and Standards**—Find out the latest early childhood policies from the government and various organizations, and view state, federal, and curriculum standards.
- **Resources and Organizations**—Discover tools to help you plan your classroom or center and organizations to provide current information and standards for each topic.
- **Electronic Bluebook**—Paperless method of completing homework or essays assigned by a professor. Finished work can be sent to the professor via email.
- **Message Board**—Virtual bulletin board to post and respond to questions and comments from a national audience.

To take advantage of these and other resources, please visit the *Promoting Positive Behavior: Guidance Strategies for Early Childhood Settings* Companion Website at

www.prenhall.com/adams

Educator Learning Center:
An Invaluable Online Resource

Merrill Education and the Association for Supervision and Curriculum Development (ASCD) invite you to take advantage of a new online resource, one that provides access to the top research and proven strategies associated with ASCD and Merrill—the Educator Learning Center. At **www.EducatorLearningCenter.com** you will find resources that will enhance your students' understanding of course topics and of current educational issues, in addition to being invaluable for further research.

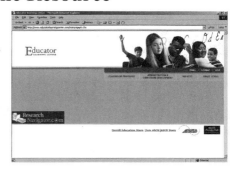

How the Educator Learning Center will help your students become better teachers

With the combined resources of Merrill Education and ASCD, you and your students will find a wealth of tools and materials to better prepare them for the classroom.

Research

- More than 600 articles from the ASCD journal *Educational Leadership* discuss everyday issues faced by practicing teachers.

- A direct link on the site to Research Navigator^{TM} gives students access to many of the leading education journals, as well as extensive content detailing the research process.

- Excerpts from Merrill Education texts give your students insights on important topics of instructional methods, diverse populations, assessment, classroom management, technology, and refining classroom practice.

Classroom Practice

- Hundreds of lesson plans and teaching strategies are categorized by content area and age range.

- Case studies and classroom video footage provide virtual field experience for student reflection.

- Computer simulations and other electronic tools keep your students abreast of today's classrooms and current technologies.

Look into the value of Educator Learning Center yourself

A four-month subscription to Educator Learning Center is $25 but is FREE when used in conjunction with this text. To obtain free passcodes for your students, simply contact your local Merrill/Prentice Hall sales representative, and your representative will give you a special ISBN to give your bookstore when ordering your textbooks. To preview the value of this website to you and your students, please go to www.EducatorLearningCenter.com and click on "Demo."

CHAPTER 1

COMPLEX INFLUENCES ON CHILDREN'S LIVES

Since her parents' recent separation, 4½-year-old Laura's behavior has become increasingly disturbing. At times, Laura just sits with a distant stare, not attending to anything in particular. At other times, she interacts with her classmates but suddenly lashes out at them without provocation—yelling, shoving, or pulling hair. She often talks about her father and the fact that he doesn't come home anymore. She worries that her mother will leave her too.

After one month at Head Start, Jamani continues to distress the children and adults with his aggression and inability to relate well to adults or children. During free playtime, Jamani is typically preoccupied with guns, fighting, and "bad guys." He is careless, often outright destructive with toys. At circle time, he resists sitting down. If made to sit in the circle, he bothers the children next to him and interrupts the teacher's attempts to read a story and talks about his cousin Deon, who is a member of a gang. During naptime, Jamani pokes and heckles the child in the cot next to him. He rejects attempts by the staff to rub his back and help him quiet down to rest. With adults, Jamani maintains an "I am tough style," never admitting to feeling afraid or sad, even when his facial expression clearly reflects those feelings.

STRESSFUL INFLUENCES ON CHILDREN'S LIVES

Laura and Jamani are both reacting to negative circumstances in their lives. The task of growing up in today's world is complex. Young children are faced with mastering typical developmental tasks related to building a healthy sense of competence and self-esteem, maintaining positive relationships with friends and family members, expanding self-regulation in the expression of emotions and conflict resolution, and adapting to child-care or school settings. Many are faced with additional stressors including working parents juggling family and job responsibilities, single-parent households, divorce, stepparents and blended families, poor-quality child care, demands of inappropriate educational expectations and pressure to perform, and high mobility contributing to disruption of family social supports. Some children are born to young, single parents who may be lacking in parenting skills.

Some children experience severe family disruption due to substance abuse, parental mental illness, incarceration of a parent, or foster care placement. Some families' ability to meet the basic physical and emotional needs of young children may be impaired due to unemployment, poverty, or homelessness.

Today's children are increasingly exposed to violence in the media through TV, movies, video games, and music. The portrayals of catastrophic events such as terrorist attacks, riots, or war on television make many children feel helpless and frightened. Some children witness violence personally because they live in a neighborhood where gang and other criminal activities are prevalent. Other children directly experience violence in their homes due to domestic violence or child abuse.

In addition to the trauma associated with experiencing or witnessing violence, each year in the United States more than 4 million children experience some extreme traumatic event, including natural disasters, motor vehicle accidents, life-threatening illness or injury, sexual assault, or the sudden death of a parent.

FIGURE 1.1

Selected Facts Related to Stressful Influences on Young Children's Lives

- 25% of young children live in a single-parent household at any given time; 50% will live in a single-parent family at some point in their childhood.[1]

- Each year more than 1 million children experience the divorce of their parents.[6]

- 20% of all children live in a blended family (with a stepparent) before the age of 18.[6]

- 20% of newborns are born to a mother who did not graduate from high school; 12.5% are born to a teenage mother.[1]

- 1 out of every 20 children under 18 is being raised by grandparents.[5]

- 1 out of every 50 children has a parent in prison.[1]

- 60% of preschoolers and 79% of school-age children have mothers in the workforce.[1] While this fact alone need not be a negative influence (if the child receives quality care by caregivers other than the mother), studies have shown that 86% of child-care centers provide child care that is poor to mediocre; 40% of infant and toddler centers provide care that could jeopardize children's safety and development.[2]

- 16.1% of children younger than 18 live in poverty.[1]

- 14% of young children lack health insurance.[1]

- The average child has witnessed more than 100,000 acts of violence on TV by the time he has completed elementary school.[4]

- There were 879,000 substantiated cases of child abuse and neglect in 2000[3]; children whose parents abuse drugs and alcohol are almost three times more likely to be abused and more than four times more likely to be neglected.[7]

- Over 3 million children each year witness domestic violence in their home.[1]

Sources:
(1) Children's Defense Fund (2002)
(2) Cost, Quality, and Child Outcomes Study Team (1995)
(3) National Clearinghouse on Child Abuse and Neglect (n.d.)
(4) Center for Media Education (1997)
(5) Child Trends (2000)
(6) Hetherington (1999)
(7) Jaudes & Voohis (1995)

THE IMPORTANCE OF SOCIAL COMPETENCE FOR YOUNG CHILDREN

To successfully interact with others and cope with the complexities, stress, and expectations of modern life, it is vital that all children acquire social competence. **Social competence** is the ability to recognize, interpret, and respond appropriately in social situations.

During the last two decades, researchers have presented a convincing body of evidence to indicate that unless children achieve minimal social competence by about the age of six years, they have a high probability of being at risk throughout life (Katz & McClellan, 1997). Long-term risks of early challenging behavior include delinquency and conduct disorders in childhood and adolescence and social and emotional difficulties in adulthood including substance abuse and psychiatric illness (Campbell, 1995; Huffman, Mehlinger, & Kerivan, 2000; Kupersmidt & Coie, 1990; Vitaro, Tremblay, Gagnon, & Pelletier, 1994). Adults who failed to achieve minimal social competence as children are more likely to commit violent crimes against others. Girls may be at risk for early pregnancy, single parenthood, and a lack of parenting skills—potentially "mothering the next generation of children with challenging behaviors" (Kaiser & Rasminsky, 1999, p. 12).

Young children need a minimum level of social and emotional competence to function in a group and benefit from the learning environment of the school setting. School success is not predicted by a child's fund of facts or a precocious ability to read so much as by emotional and social measures. A child's readiness for school depends on the most basic of all knowledge, that is, how to learn—with seven crucial capacities: confidence, curiosity, intentionality, self-control, relatedness, capacity to communicate, and cooperativeness (National Center for Clinical Infant Programs, 1992). School success requires understanding of other people's feelings and viewpoints, cooperating with adults and peers, emotional self-control, and the ability to resolve conflicts constructively (Thompson, 2002). This social and emotional school readiness is critical to successful kindergarten transition and success in the early grades (Peth-Pierce, 2001). Children who have difficulty paying attention, following directions, getting along with others, and controlling negative emotions perform less well in school, despite the ability to master academic material (McLelland, Morrison, & Holmes, 2000; Slavin & Madden, 2001).

Children do not outgrow behavioral challenges. Without intervention, behavior problems tend to worsen over time. Lower levels of social acceptance in kindergarten are predictive of deficits in classroom social skills, work habits, and lower academic performance as assessed by grades and standardized achievement test scores in the first and second grade (Parke, Harshman, Roberts, Flyr, O'Neil, Welsh, & Strand, 1998).

Clearly, promoting positive social behavior in young children should be a priority in early childhood education. The cost of failure to intervene early is far too high a price to pay when predictable negative outcomes can be prevented (Center for Human Investment Policy, 2000).

A MODEL FOR ENHANCING SOCIAL COMPETENCE

The guidance strategies presented in this book are designed to assist early childhood care and education providers to respond constructively to the complex influences on young children's lives, promote children's emotional well-being, reduce disruptive classroom behaviors, and enhance children's social competence. Specific classroom strategies are based upon an extensive review of research on young children's social/emotional development and risk and protective factors.

Risk factors are situations and characteristics that are thought to contribute to the likelihood that a child will have difficulty coping with life or experience emotional and behavioral problems (Peth-Pierce, 2001). Individual risk factors include prenatal exposure to drugs or alcohol, low birth weight, medical problems, difficult temperament, and early behavior and adjustment problems. Family disruption, family conflict, and poor parenting practices are family risk factors. School and community risk factors include lack of services for children and families, poor quality child care, poor relationships with teachers, and low socioeconomic status (Peth-Pierce, 2001).

Protective factors are characteristics within individuals, families, and communities that are thought to reduce the risk of negative outcomes, support recovery from stress, and foster healthy development. Easygoing temperament and engaging personality are individual protective factors. Nurturing and supportive parents, a stable and predictable family environment, high-quality child care, warm and open relationships with teachers, and higher socioeconomic status are protective factors at the family, school, and community level. Researchers have found that protective factors can moderate or buffer the negative effects of stress and provide resilience. **Resilience** is the term used to describe a set of qualities that foster a process of successful adaptation despite risk and adversity (Benard, 1993; Peth-Pierce, 2001; Werner, 1982).

A review of research on young children's social/emotional development has been synthesized here into five constructs. The authors present guidance strategies based upon these constructs throughout this book in such a way that they can be integrated naturally throughout the school environment and daily activities and routines to support positive classroom management while promoting prosocial behavior and development in all domains.

Caring and Cooperative Early Childhood Settings

To create a caring and cooperative environment in an early childhood care and education setting, teachers and caregivers thoughtfully:
- Design the physical environment and select and organize materials
- Provide a private space known as the Cozy Corner
- Create a safe and caring emotional environment through the use of a classroom Safety Rule, positive guidance techniques, and class meetings
- Provide a predictable daily schedule, routines, and transitions

Long-term reduction of problem behaviors requires that children be taught alternative positive social behaviors. Using responsive adult/child interactions, carefully designed props and themes for child-selected play, class meetings, books, puppets, and role plays, teachers help children learn to:
- Consider others' needs
- Identify "helpful" (prosocial) vs. "hurtful" (antisocial) actions

- Engage in prosocial skills such as helping, giving, comforting, sharing, and showing empathy
- Use the classroom Safety Rule to decide on appropriate behavior for themselves and others

Assertiveness: Self-Esteem and Mastery Skills

For children to assert themselves in positive ways and develop self-worth and a sense of mastery, educators help children:
- Feel capable and competent
- Become decision makers and trust their own ideas
- Set goals independently
- Assert their own point of view appropriately
- Become motivated to learn

Children who experience chronic stress may develop a sense of helplessness and low self-esteem. Children with a positive sense of self-worth and mastery are persistent and energetic in their efforts to solve challenging tasks.

Relationship Skills: Initiating and Maintaining Relationships

The most important factor contributing to resilience against stress is establishing a strong caring relationship with one or more key persons. To enhance children's abilities to form positive relationships with adults and peers, teachers help children learn skills to:
- Separate appropriately from primary caregivers
- Attach appropriately to teacher as a surrogate caregiver
- Develop a sense of association and belonging
- Engage in play with peers
- Initiate social contact and join a group
- Develop friendships

It is within caring relationships that children experience and learn empathy, which is a prerequisite for all other prosocial behavior.

Emotional Regulation and Reactivity

Children's abilities to control their emotions, demonstrate a range of emotions, and react in appropriate ways to emotional situations is an indicator of emotional well-being. Teachers help children learn to:
- Label, validate, and express feelings
- Control impulses and self-regulate
- Monitor, evaluate, and modify emotional reactions
- Practice stress reduction and tension relief

Emotional regulation includes modifying emotional reactions to appropriately accomplish one's goals. To do this, children must identify their own emotions and express them appropriately while recognizing and respecting the feelings of others.

Self-Control: Managing Aggression and Conflict

Early intervention in the antecedents of problem behavior can reduce the risk of habitual patterns. Teachers help children acquire skills concerning:

- Social problem solving (conflict resolution)
- Anger management and alternatives to aggression
- Recognition of responsibility and consequences of one's actions

Young children's abilities to think of multiple solutions to social problems and choose the most appropriate among these is the key to social success. Children can be taught to "rethink" situations and change their own "self talk" in order to arrive at new solutions for themselves. With facilitation from an adult at first, children can learn problem-solving steps and ways to control anger.

KEY TERMS AND CONCEPTS

Social competence: the ability to recognize, interpret, and respond appropriately in social situations in order to interact effectively with people

Risk factors: situations and characteristics that are thought to contribute to the likelihood that a child will have difficulty coping with life or experience emotional and behavioral problems

Protective factors: characteristics within individuals, families, and communities that are thought to reduce the risk of negative outcomes, support recovery from stress, and foster healthy development

Resilience: a set of qualities that foster a process of successful adaptation despite risk and adversity

LEARNING IN ACTION: SMALL GROUP ACTIVITIES AND FIELD ASSIGNMENTS

1. Early childhood educators need to be able to connect stressed families with local community resources. Locate an agency in your community that could be helpful to a family experiencing the following examples of stressors:
    - A family member is being physically or emotionally abusive.
    - The parents were recently separated and are considering divorce.
    - A teenage mother expresses concern about her parenting abilities.
    - The father recently became unemployed and the family needs resources for housing, food, or utilities.
    - Someone in the family has a substance abuse problem.
    - The mother is suffering from postpartum depression.
    - The 4-year-old was recently diagnosed with ADHD (attention deficit hyperactivity disorder).
2. Consider Laura and Jamani from the opening vignette. What factors in their lives do you think might be influencing their behavior?

3. Children today can have complicated schedules. They may spend over 8 hours per day between school and child care settings, get picked up at 6:00 p.m. by mom and brother, grab dinner at a fast-food restaurant, rush to the local YMCA to watch big brother's basketball game, and finally get home at 9:00 p.m. With three or four of your classmates, discuss the kinds of difficulties that may confront families today related to "the hectic pace of modern life" and the impact these difficulties may have on young children.
4. Discuss the protective factors enhanced by an early childhood program with which you are familiar (a setting where you work or where your child attends).

SUGGESTED READING AND RESOURCES

Benard, B. (1991). *Fostering resiliency in kids: Protective factors in the family, school, and community.* San Francisco: Far West Laboratory for Educational Research and Development.

Garbarino, J. (2000). *Lost boys: Why our sons turn violent and how we can save them.* Garden City, NY: Anchor.

Levin, D. (1998). *Remote control childhood? Combating the hazards of media culture.* Washington, DC: National Association for the Education of Young Children.

Luthar, S. S., & Zigler, E. (1991). Vulnerability and competence: A review of research on resilience in childhood. *American Journal of Orthopsychiatry, 61,* 6–22.

Novick, R. (1998). The comfort corner: Fostering resiliency and emotional intelligence. *Childhood Education, 74,* 200–204.

Werner, E., & Smith, R. (1992). *Overcoming the odds: High-risk children from birth to adulthood.* New York: Cornell University Press.

REFERENCES

Benard, B.(1993). Fostering resiliency in kids. *Educational Leadership, 51*(3), 44–48.

Campbell, S. B. (1995). Behavior problems in preschool children: A review of recent research. *Journal of Child Psychology and Psychiatry and Allied Disciplines, 36,* 113–149.

Center for Human Investment Policy. (2000). *Colorado survey of incidence of mental health problems among children in early childhood programs.* Denver, CO: Graduate School of Public Affairs at the University of Colorado and the Colorado Department of Human Services.

Center for Media Education. (1997). *TV violence and children.* Retrieved April 20, 2003 from http://www.cme.org/children/kids_tv/c_and_t.html

Child Trends. (2000). *Family structure and living arrangements.* Retrieved April 20, 2003 from http://www.childtrendsdatabank.org/demo/family/59Family Structure.htm

Children's Defense Fund. (2002). *The state of children in America's union: A 2002 action guide to Leave No Child Behind.* Washington, DC: Author.

Cost, Quality, and Child Outcomes Study Team. (1995). *Cost, quality, and child outcomes in child care centers* Public Report (2nd ed.). Denver: Economics Department, University of Colorado at Denver.

Hetherington, E. M. (1999). *Coping with divorce.* Hillsdale, NJ: Erlbaum and Associates.

Huffman, L. C., Mehlinger, S. L., & Kerivan, A. S. (2000). Risk factors for academic and behavioral problems at the beginning of school. In *Off to a good start: Research on the risk factors for early school problems and selected federal policies affecting children's social and emotional development and their readiness for school* (pp. 1–94). Chapel Hill: University of North Carolina, FPG Child Development Center.

Jaudes, P., & Voohis, J. (1995). Association of drug abuse and child abuse. *Child Abuse and Neglect, 19*(9), 1065–1075.

Kaiser, B., & Rasminsky, J. S. (1999). *Meeting the challenge.* Ottawa, Ontario: Canadian Child Care Federation.

Katz, L. G., & McClellan, D. E. (1997). *Fostering children's social competence: The teacher's role.* Washington, DC: National Association for the Education of Young Children.

Kupersmidt, J. D., & Coie, J. D. (1990). Preadolescent peer status, aggression, and school adjustment as predictors of externalizing problems in adolescence. *Child Development, 61,* 1350–1362.

McClelland, M. M., Morrison, F. J., & Holmes, D. L. (2000). Children at risk for early academic problems: The role of learning-related social skills. *Early Childhood Research Quarterly, 15,* 307–329.

National Center for Clinical Infant Programs. (1992). *Head Start: The emotional foundations of school readiness.* Arlington, VA: National Center for Clinical Infant Programs.

National Clearinghouse on Child Abuse and Neglect. (n.d.). *National clearinghouse on child abuse and neglect data system: Summary of key findings from calendar year 2000.* Retrieved April 20, 2003 from http://www.calib.com/nccanch/pub/factsheets/canstats.cfm

Parke, R. D., Harshman, K., Roberts, B., Flyr, M., O'Neil, R., Welsh, M., & Strand, C. (1998). Social relationships and academic success. *Thrust for Educational Leadership, 28*(1), 32–34.

Peth-Pierce, R. (2001). *A good beginning: Sending America's children to school with the social and emotional competence they need to succeed.* Monograph from the Children's Mental Health Foundations and Agencies Network(FAN). Bethesda, MD: National Institute of Mental Health.

Slavin, R. E., & Madden, N. A. (2001). *One million children: Success for all.* Thousand Oaks, CA: Corwin Press.

Thompson, R. A. (2002). The roots of school readiness in social and emotional development. In *Set for success: Building a strong foundation for school readiness based on the social-emotional development of young children.* Kansas City, MO: The Ewing Marion Kauffman Foundation.

Vitaro, F., Trembley, R. E., Gagnon, C., & Pelletier, D. (1994). Predictive accuracy of behavioral and sociometric assessments of high-risk kindergarten children. *Journal of Clinical Child Psychology, 23,* 272–282.

Werner, E. (1982). *Vulnerable but invincible: A longitudinal study of resilient children and youth.* New York: McGraw Hill.

Chapter 2

BUILDING SOCIAL COMPETENCE: CLASS MEETINGS AND FAMILY INVOLVEMENT

Marisa's class of 3-year-olds seemed able to create a make-believe gun out of almost any material in the classroom. Tinker toys™, Legos™, bristle blocks, and crackers all became weapons in many of the children's hands. Marisa tried "outlawing" guns, explaining to the children why even toy guns weren't safe, and redirecting them to other activities or materials. Nothing was helping. Finally, she said to the children, "We need to sit down and talk about this at a class meeting."

Bill, a Head Start teacher of 4-year-olds, was preparing his group to welcome two new children into the classroom. During a class meeting the day before the new children arrived, Bill took out the flannel board and told a little story about joining a class in the middle of the year. He asked the children how a new child might feel. Some of their ideas were "shy" and "scared." Bill asked his group how they might help new children feel welcome and less scared. The children responded thoughtfully. "Ask them to play." "Give them a toy." "Sit by them at snack table." "Show them how to clean up." Bill wrote down all of their ideas and encouraged his class to try these positive behaviors the next day when the new children came to class.

The next day, Bill introduced the children to the class during a class meeting. He watched the children throughout the day and noticed they indeed made many efforts to make the new arrivals feel welcome and help integrate them into the classroom routines.

These classroom vignettes depict children gaining emotional understanding and practicing social skills during class meetings.

CLASS MEETINGS

What Is a Class Meeting?

A **class meeting** is a group get-together. Class meetings differ from "circle times" or regular "large group" times because they focus on real issues going on in the classroom and in children's lives. The purpose of class meetings is for adults and children to discuss issues, listen to each other, make choices, and solve problems together. Class meetings also provide a means for building a caring classroom community—what one kindergarten teacher calls "the kindergarten family" (Adams & Baronberg, 2001).

The role of the care and education provider in a class meeting is to create an atmosphere in which children feel that their ideas and feelings will be respected, acknowledged, and protected. The goal for children is to gain a better understanding of their own feelings and behaviors, learn to express those feelings and ideas, develop a heightened sensitivity for the feelings and perspectives of others, and improve their group social skills (Adams & Baronberg, 2001; Harris & Fuqua, 2000; McClurg, 1998). Class meetings are times to talk and solve problems, providing a forum for children and teachers to gather to discuss issues, practice prosocial skills, and make decisions about the ways they want their class to be (Developmental Studies Center, 1996; DeVries & Zan, 1994).

What Makes a Class Meeting Successful?

Plan in advance.
Care and education providers need to determine the topic, focus, and goals of the class meeting; the processes to help children become and stay engaged; the appropriate time of day; and a comfortable place in which to meet. Conscious decision making about the size and composition of the group is important as well. Class meetings work best with a small group of five to eight children, especially when introducing new skills or discussing more difficult issues.

Use staff appropriately.
When the class meeting includes the whole group of children, roles for the leader of the class meeting and the assistants should be clear. Will some children need special help? How can the assistant reduce distractions? Many teachers prefer to divide the class in half and have one adult lead a class meeting while the other adult leads another activity (possibly art) with the other children. Later in the day or the next day, children who have participated in the class meeting do the alternative (art) activity while the second group does the class meeting.

Establish ground rules.
Set ground rules with children and review them often. Ensure that no one person talks for a lengthy period of time. Practice listening skills. Some teachers use a tangible reminder of whose turn it is to talk, such as a "talking stick" held as a microphone.

Ask questions and talk about consequences.
"What do you think would happen if ...?" "How would you feel?" "What should we do if ...?"

Use visual aids and props.
Plan for this in advance. Photographs (particularly of young children), puppets to act out situations, dolls, books, and other age-appropriate props all help keep children's attention and make the topics more concrete.

Promote reading readiness and literacy by writing as much as is age-appropriate.
Keep a large pad of paper available for writing questions or children's ideas and suggestions. Use only a few words. For preschoolers, two or three words per line are appropriate, and for primary children, a short sentence. Add an illustration by using a picture cut from a magazine, making a simple line drawing, or incorporating children's drawings.

Include a physical or musical activity.
Children are more likely to pay attention and learn a new concept or skill when they have an opportunity to practice through movement, songs, or games.

Try different discussion approaches.
To give all children a chance to speak without needing to wait for each child to have a turn, try "partner chats." These are opportunities for children to talk in pairs. Introduce this idea by raising a simple question such as: "What is your favorite flavor ice cream? Where do you go to eat it? Talk with your partner about ice cream."

Plan for repetition of important topics.
Each of the strategies suggested in this book can be introduced at one class meeting, revisited at a subsequent class meeting, and practiced at yet another class meeting.

Provide for special needs.
Will some children need language translations, special seating, or augmentive communication devices?

Congratulate everyone at the end of the class meeting.
Use this as an opportunity to create a sense of belonging and community. Acknowledge that class meetings are new for both the adults and the children and that everyone needs time and practice to get used to them.

Be sensitive to family and cultural differences.
Some children and families are not used to discussing feelings or talking about problems outside the context of the family. Communicate with families about your purpose for class meetings and invite them to observe a class meeting in action. Ask parents for ideas to make class meetings more comfortable and useful for their child.

How Do I Schedule Class Meetings?

The appropriate length of a class meeting is determined by the age and developmental level of the children involved, the size of the group, and the time of the year. A class meeting should last only as long as children are interested and involved. For very young children (3 and under), for children with special needs, or for children just getting used to class meetings, the total time should be 5 to 10 minutes. Four- to 6-year-olds or children who have more experience with class meetings may remain engaged for 10 to 20 minutes.

Teachers and caregivers plan class meetings as a regular part of their daily schedule. Class meetings should be held a minimum of two or three times per week. Once children become used to class meetings, they often ask for a class meeting themselves. Other times, class meetings are called spontaneously when the need arises (for example, following a playground squabble).

What Are Appropriate Topics for Class Meetings?

Suggestions for class meetings are described for teaching each of the skills designed to enhance social competence presented in this book:
- Vocabulary used to describe feelings, identifying the feelings of self and others, and expressing emotions appropriately (Chapter 5)
- Prosocial skills such as helping, sharing, taking turns, and comforting (Chapter 6)
- Five-step process for peaceful problem solving (Chapter 7)
- Anger management and calming down (Chapter 8)
- Stress reduction techniques (Chapter 9)

At first, teachers and care providers take the lead in planning for and leading class meetings. As children learn to express their thoughts and ideas, class meetings change to have less focus on the adult's leadership and more participation and management by the children. As children become used to participating in class meetings, they may even suggest topics. Primary-grade teachers can keep a large piece of easel paper or a writing board "open" for children to write down topics they would like addressed at a class meeting. One kindergarten teacher uses this technique successfully: "As kids encounter problems or difficulties during the day, they write them on what we call our 'agenda.' Later in the day when we have a class meeting, I consult the 'agenda' and try to cover what the kids wrote down. It really makes them feel empowered."

CLASS MEETINGS AS A GUIDANCE STRATEGY

Class meetings are one of many guidance strategies. **Guidance** includes "everything adults deliberately do and say, either directly or indirectly, to influence a child's behavior" (Hildebrand, 1994, p. 4). Early childhood care and education providers guide children's behavior and influence children's social competencies in many ways. Indirect and direct guidance strategies to enhance protective factors for young children and to build social competence will be emphasized in this book. The discussion below summarizes these concepts and indicates the chapters in which they will be covered.

Indirect guidance does not include specific interactions with children but involves behind-the-scenes work and planning such as:

- Organizing the physical environment (Chapter 3)
- Planning a daily schedule and establishing routines (Chapter 3)
- Planning **developmentally appropriate curriculum** responsive to the ages, experiences, and needs of the group (Chapter 10)
- Involving families in all aspects of the early childhood program

Direct guidance includes the physical, verbal, and affective techniques used to influence children's behavior. **Physical guidance** takes many forms: proximity to child, body language, modeling, removing, or restraining (Chapter 4). **Verbal guidance** includes providing reminders, stating limits and rules clearly, reinforcing appropriate behavior, offering choices, redirecting, teaching problem-solving techniques, and using logical consequences (Chapter 4). **Affective guidance** is embedded in adult/child interactions and includes physical affection, focused attention, smiles, and praise. Using affective guidance, adults set the tone of the emotional environment, actively listen to children, respond in a sensitive manner, and label and validate children's feelings (chapters 4 and 5).

Although direct guidance through class meetings is an effective means for teaching new skills, the ultimate goal is for children to be able to use new skills in real-life situations (sometimes called "transfer of training"). Teachers and caregivers can do many things to embed opportunities to practice social skills throughout the day in an early childhood setting. Each chapter will present ideas for reinforcing and practicing social skills in the course of normal adult/child interactions, taking advantage of **teachable moments**.

IMPORTANCE OF FAMILY INVOLVEMENT

Parents and families have the most direct and lasting impact on children's learning and development of social competence. When parents are involved, students achieve more, exhibit more positive attitudes and behavior, and feel more comfortable in new settings. Early childhood providers need to reach out to families in order to build the kind of relationships that engage them as active partners early in their children's education (National Dropout Prevention Center/Network, 2003).

Families are crucial partners in promoting positive social skills. Home visits, parent visitation to child care or school setting, telephone conversations, newsletters, informal notes, bulletin boards, workshops, and regular face-to-face communication can be used to keep families informed about the specific social skills being focused on in the early childhood setting and for care providers to learn about what families are doing at home.

If guidance strategies are to be truly effective, parent involvement and support are crucial. Early care providers need to engage parents as soon as their child is enrolled in the program and ask for assistance in understanding the child's background and the family's goals for the child. Sensitivity to family and cultural differences is crucial and can be heightened by the care provider's ability to listen and encourage communication. Acceptance of differences in families is essential for each child and parent to feel a sense of belonging in early childhood programs. Mutual respect, cooperation, shared responsibility, and negotiation of differences in opinion between parents and care and education professionals are necessary to achieve shared goals related to the guidance and education of young children.

According to the National Association for the Education of Young Children (1998) Code of Ethical Conduct, professionals' ethical responsibilities to families most related to guidance strategies include:

- Develop relationships of mutual trust with families we serve
- Acknowledge and build upon strengths and competencies as we support families in their task of nurturing children
- Respect the dignity of each family and its culture, language, customs, and beliefs
- Respect families' child-rearing values and their right to make decisions for their children
- Help family members improve their understanding of their children and enhance their skills as parents

As our nation's population becomes more and more diverse in terms of race, ethnicity, and language, early child care providers may need to learn about cultures and family child-raising styles that are different from their own. Families participating in their programs can help them do so. Parents become a respected source of information and are accorded another meaningful role in their child's education. Establishing dialogue and trust is the first step in this process and should include: expressing a desire to learn from the parent, asking for parents' opinions, discussing ways to support the family's values and customs, and acknowledging that there are many points of view on a topic (Sturm, 2003).

KEY TERMS AND CONCEPTS

Class meeting: a gathering of children and adult(s) that provides a forum for discussing issues, practicing prosocial skills, making decisions as a group, and solving classroom problems

Guidance: words and actions used by adults to influence a child's behavior

Indirect guidance: guiding children's behavior through behind-the-scenes work and planning rather than direct interactions with children

Direct guidance: the many forms of physical, verbal, and affective techniques used to influence children's behavior

Physical guidance: techniques that employ physical contact, actions, or proximity intended to influence behavior of children

Verbal guidance: using words to influence children's behavior

Affective guidance: interaction between adults and children focused on expression of genuine feelings and positive regard

Developmentally appropriate curriculum: curriculum planning that takes into account children's ages, their individual needs, and the context in which children live

Teachable moment: an unplanned opportunity to reinforce or teach a concept or skill

LEARNING IN ACTION:
SMALL GROUP ACTIVITIES AND FIELD ASSIGNMENTS

1. Identify the key elements of a class meeting. Discuss how a class meeting is different from a traditional circle time.
2. Develop a class meeting for the beginning of the school year. Use the topic of helping children get to know one another. Define your age group, how many children will be at the class meeting, and how you will use an assistant in the class meeting. Describe how you will introduce the topic, what props you will use, and what problems you foresee and how you might handle them.
3. In small groups, discuss the ethical responsibilities of professionals to families as presented in the text. What do these mean to you?

SUGGESTED READING AND RESOURCES

Charney, R. S. (2002). *Teaching children to care: Problem-solving class meetings* .Retrieved August 10, 2003 from http://www.responsiveclassroom.org/PDF_files/Teaching%20 Children%20to%20Care/8908ch13.pdf

Couchenour, D., & Chrisman, K. (2000). *Families, schools, and communities.* Albany, NY: Delmar.

Gonzales-Mena, J. (2000). *Multicultural issues in child care* (3rd ed.). Mountain View, CA: Mayfield.

Halaby, M. (2000). *Belonging: Creating community in the classroom.* Newton Upper Falls, MA: Brookline Books.

Hudson, S. J. (2000). Using circle time to teach the social curriculum. *Journal of Early Education and Family Review, 7*(5), 29–32.

Lynch, E., & Hanson, M. J. (1998). *Developing cross-cultural competence: A guide for working with children and their families.* (2nd ed.). Baltimore, MD: Paul H. Brookes.

REFERENCES

Adams, S. K., & Baronberg, J. (2001). *The CARES model: Building social skills and reducing problem behaviors in early childhood classrooms.* Denver, CO: Western Media Products. (Instructional videotape depicting six class meetings in early childhood classrooms.)

Developmental Studies Center. (1996). *Ways we want our class to be: Class meetings that build commitment to kindness and learning.* Oakland, CA: Developmental Studies Center.

DeVries, R., & Zan, B. (1994). *Moral classrooms, moral children: Creating a constructivist atmosphere in early education.* New York: Teachers College Press.

Harris, T. T. & Fuqua, J. D. (2000). What goes around comes around: Building a community of learners through circle times. *Young Children, 55*(1), 44–47.

Hildebrand, V. (1994). *Guiding young children.* New York: Macmillan College Publishing Company.

McClurg, L. G. (1998). Building an ethical community in the classroom: Community meeting. *Young Children, 53*(2), 30–35.

National Association for the Education of Young Children. (1998). *Code of ethical conduct: Guidelines for responsible behavior in early childhood education.* Washington, DC: Author.

National Dropout Prevention Center/Network. (n.d.). *Family involvement overview.* Retrieved April 2003 from http://www.dropoutprevention.org/effstrat/familyinv/famover.htm

Sturm, C. (2003). Creating parent-teacher dialogue: Intercultural communication in child care. In C. Copple (Ed.), *A world of difference: Readings on teaching young children in a diverse society* (pp. 69–73). Washington, DC: National Association for the Education of Young Children.

Chapter 3

STRUCTURING THE PHYSICAL ENVIRONMENT TO ENHANCE SOCIAL DEVELOPMENT

Jovan comes into preschool the first few mornings with a frown on his face. When the teachers greet him good morning, he scowls at them. If the other children come close to him, he pushes them away. He refuses to join greeting circle time and tries to distract the other children either by acting like a comedian or being combative with the adults.

On the third day of school, Jovan's teacher, Anita, approaches him as he arrives. She gently reminds Jovan about the Cozy Corner, a special "alone place" in the classroom. She asks him if he would like to go to the Cozy Corner instead of coming to circle time. Jovan says "Yes."

Jovan continues to choose to go to the Cozy Corner every day when he comes to school. In the Cozy Corner, he plays with the toys, lies down and rests, and frequently watches what is happening in circle time. When he emerges from the Cozy Corner, he is in a much better mood. The amount of time Jovan spends in the Cozy Corner slowly decreases, and he joins circle time for longer periods each day.

STRUCTURING SPACE AND MATERIALS

Young children's social and emotional development can be promoted through careful planning of their physical environment. The impact of the environment is sometimes underrated by practitioners but has been demonstrated to have a powerful impact on children's behavior and development (Greenman, 1988; Slaby, Roedell, Arezzo, & Hendrix, 1995). As adults, experience shows us that the physical environments in which we live and work affect our own moods, outlooks, ability to concentrate, motivation to engage in relationships, readiness to interact with others in a positive way, and even our health. This is naturally true for children as well.

Well-designed space and thoughtful selection of materials promotes self-control and positive social behaviors and reduces problem behaviors. Changing the environment can actually change behavior (Katz & McClellan, 1997).

Following are widely accepted guidelines for arranging furnishings and equipment and selection of materials:

- Clearly define activity areas and pathways using furnishings and low room dividers to create observable boundaries. Clear physical boundaries inhibit running, reduce intrusions into another child's play space, and structure safe pathways for children to move throughout the room (Kostelnik, Whiren, Soderman, Stein, & Gregory, 2000).
- Eliminate large open spaces and interrupt long pathways that might encourage running.
- Separate areas that encourage noisy play (block building, dramatic play) from areas that are used for quiet activities (reading, writing).
- Set up messy activities (painting, water, snack) on hard surface floors.
- Select materials suited to the age and various competence levels of the group of children. Materials that are too advanced lead to frustration; materials lacking challenge often lead to boredom and destructive handling. Consider potential choking hazards for toddlers.

- Store materials so that they can be reached easily and independently by young children.
- Provide quantities appropriate to the age and number of children to promote some sharing. Be aware that conflict arises when there are so few materials that children must either compete with each other or wait with nothing to do (Slaby et. al., 1995).
- Select equipment and furnishings appropriate to the size of children to increase comfort and decrease fatigue. Provide child-sized sinks, toilets, and drinking fountains or build platforms around adult-sized equipment. Arrange adaptations for children with special needs.
- Consider sturdiness, durability, craftsmanship, and composition of materials to maximize safety. Inspect materials frequently to ensure that they are safe, intact, and usable. Missing pieces or incomplete materials can lead to failure and frustration.
- Maintain cleanliness of all materials and equipment on a regular basis.

ENVIRONMENTAL ELEMENTS THAT ENHANCE CHILDREN'S WELL-BEING AND REDUCE STRESS

Planning for children in today's complex world entails adding other elements to these regularly accepted guidelines. Educational environments need to be purposefully structured to respond to the stresses all children face in modern life and to build the protective factors that help children cope with these stresses, build resiliency, and learn positive responses.

> **Risk Factor:** Child lives in a crowded home situation; child experiences hurried life style or is in group care for long periods of time
> **Protective Factor:** Space and time to be alone; space and time for active play

The Cozy Corner

To help children become resilient to the risks created by living in crowded situations, participating in a hurried lifestyle, being part of a stressed society, and sometimes being in institutional care for very long periods of time, teachers and caregivers can provide an alone space for children. We call this alone space the Cozy Corner. A **Cozy Corner** is a small space where a child may go to feel safe, be somewhat private, and have a physical area all to himself. The Cozy Corner is a refuge where the child has a respite from the pressures of group noise, group crowding, group decision making, and where the need to share toys and attention is absent. The Cozy Corner is appropriate for children of all ages, even the toddler for whom seclusion represents a space for onlookers and quiet, solitary play. Children use this time and space to "regroup," to relax, to re-set their emotional equilibrium—or even to nap.

A Cozy Corner is *not* a time-out space. It is chosen by the child (not by the teacher). A child may choose to spend time in the Cozy Corner for a variety of reasons. Some children like to go to the Cozy Corner when they are tired or sad; others like to use the Cozy Corner to play with a toy or read a book all by themselves; still others use the Cozy Corner as a time to calm down after a spat with another child or a problem at home.

Adults introduce children to the idea of a Cozy Corner during class meetings and explain and model examples of its use through puppet role-plays or stories. Adults make the Cozy

Corner idea attractive to the children by talking about it at various times of the day, asking children who have used the Cozy Corner to tell what it was like, and even using it themselves. One teacher introduced the Cozy Corner this way:

> I told the children that now we have a place in our room to go to help yourself feel better. I told them that on some days I get a little irritable having to handle too many problems and that I need a little time by myself. Now I can go to our own Cozy Corner to be alone for a while. I asked them if they ever need a place to go to help themselves feel better. One little boy told me right away that sometimes he doesn't feel like coming to preschool, and he would like it if he could go someplace and not have to talk to anybody!

Since the Cozy Corner can be used by only one child at a time, it need only be a very small space. It can be set up in a corner of the room, behind a couch, or under a shelf. It should be located in a quiet part of the room and have clear boundaries and a sense of privacy (while being arranged in a way that allows adults to monitor). Soft material—such as a padded mat, pillows, a bean bag, flowers, or a plant—set the tone. A few simple materials keep the space interesting but uncluttered: one or two children's picture books, a stuffed animal (that can be laundered), two or three small manipulative materials that help children focus such as an Etch-A-Sketch,™ small squares of fabrics with different textures, or a magnet set (for older children). These materials should be changed a few times a month. Figure 3.1 depicts a simple Cozy Corner that fits under a desk or shelf in the classroom.

FIGURE 3.1

Cozy Corner

Occasionally, the Cozy Corner may already be occupied when another child desires to have some private time. In this case, teachers may help the child make a choice—to sign up for a turn in the Cozy Corner as soon as it is available, or to find another area of the room that is not currently busy. ("Nathan, I see that no one is in the book nook right now. Would you like to have some quiet time over there?")

Cozy Corners are very successful in helping children identify how they are feeling and work out what to do when they are upset. One teacher described it this way:

> Since setting up the Cozy Corner, the children have used it every day. At first, it drew many children because of the new toys there, but now the children use it as a place to get away from their peers for a while. Sometimes we will suggest, "You look angry (or sad or tired). Would you like to go to the Cozy Corner until you feel better?" but almost always the children will initiate its use by themselves. One little girl said, "I need to go to the Cozy Corner to make my body get quiet." Several parents have asked about it, saying that their children told them about the Cozy Corner. Three different moms have told us that their child wants them to make a Cozy Corner at home.

Space and Time for Active Play

Almost all early childhood programs schedule a set time each day for active play. This is generally outdoors but when weather does not permit, large motor play is accommodated in the regular classroom or in another designated indoor space. Many children would benefit from even more time to stretch their muscles and "let off steam."

Large muscle activities can play a significant part in reducing children's tension and preventing problems which result from children's naturally high activity level. Staff need to create opportunities for large muscle play during the regular course of the school day and in addition to outdoor playtime. Such active play may involve taking a small group of children to another room for a short activity period or setting up an obstacle course or indoor climbing equipment in a large motor area in the room. Manipulative activities such as pounding clay, sand and water play, block building, or woodworking also provide large muscle movement. Toddlers should have a specified area in the room where large motor play is always available with equipment such as climbers, slides, tunnels, push and pull and riding toys, and lightweight blocks (Lowman & Ruhmann, 1998).

For kindergarten and primary grade children, the current emphasis on academic skills often results in fewer physical education classes and restrictions on unstructured free play or recess periods. Because primary age children are continuing to develop motor skills, they need daily participation in physical activities to develop coordination and body strength. Physical activity and games also provide an important means for peer interaction and practice of social skills and contribute to a sense of well-being (Wortham, 2002).

Regular outdoor play is important for children of all ages. "Because their physical development is occurring so rapidly, young children through age 8 need daily outdoor experiences to practice large muscle skills, learn about outdoor environments, and experience freedom not always possible indoors" (Bredekamp, 1987, p. 8). Outdoor play also helps reduce children's stress and gives them opportunities for both time alone and social experiences in a group.

Outdoor learning is supported by the appropriate physical environment. "Play spaces for children of all ages need to be more than playgrounds. They should be 'habitats'" (Rivkin,

2000, p. 4). Using the words "habitat" or "play space" reminds us to think about the quality of the experiences we are offering outdoors for children. These spaces can be so much more than "playgrounds." They can be valuable learning places where children can run, climb, jump, slide, balance, build, dig, dance, sing, pretend, relax, relate to nature, talk, draw, watch, and wonder.

Many early childhood programs inherit outdoor play spaces that were originally planned for other uses. Fortunate are the programs that have the financial and other resources to redesign or remodel these spaces. Care providers often have to compromise on what they would like ideally for young children's outdoor play space and what actually exists. Burgeoning rules and regulations intended to keep children safe have also led to "concern that the emphasis on playground regulation has literally sapped the life from many play areas" (Hampton, 2003, p. 2).

Staff planning to face all these issues is crucial. Creativity is needed to make the best of limited resources; to accommodate regulations; and to design, remodel, or maintain attractive space to promote large muscle play, positive social interaction, curiosity, and fun. Following are guidelines to consider when planning outdoor play space:

- Safety is the most basic requirement for any outdoor environment. Regular monitoring includes checking for stability of equipment, missing or exposed pieces, rust, wood cracks or splintering, frayed ropes, sharp edges, slippery surfaces, standing water, and dangerous litter such as broken glass.
- Adequate and secure storage for moveable equipment and small playing parts should be developed.
- Outdoor play should allow for large muscle experiences, running, exuberant voices, and physical challenges. Traffic patterns should help to promote safety and positive social experiences.
- Equipment should be age-appropriate for the range of developmental abilities of the children in the program. Different age groups sometimes need to play in different areas of the playground. Toddlers and young preschoolers need to have space separate from older children.
- Children generally prefer and benefit from "equipment that does something (is moveable) or that is complex (offers several play options) and can be adapted to their play schemes," instead of stationary play structures that require children to adapt themselves to the limitations of the equipment (Ihn, 2002, p. 5).
- Formal climbing structures can be augmented by natural climbing opportunities. "Landscaping designed to create varied terrains, pathways, tunnels, and sensory discoveries will engage babies as they pursue their developmental themes" (Curtis & Carter, 2003, p. 101). Children of all ages benefit from similar movement and exploratory opportunities.
- Consider reducing the quantity of non-natural materials such as asphalt and plastic and increasing the amount of natural materials such as wood, trees, plants, flowers, and water. Curtis and Carter (2003) suggest planting fragrant herbs that spread quickly and can handle heavy traffic such as mint, lavender, rosemary, and creeping thyme. Besides providing beauty and a variety of textures to the outdoor environment, "bouquets can be brought inside for meal tables, bathrooms, and sensory investigation" (Curtis & Carter, 2003, p. 95). Expose children to the vegetation natural to their local and regional environments.

- Indoor equipment can often be moved outdoors. Easel painting and the sensory table are especially adaptable for outdoor play.
- Children with special needs should be given special consideration. Consistent with state and federal legislation for children with disabilities, outdoor environments should provide for equal and equitable access without segregating or stigmatizing any user. "Designing for equitable use means creating a design that is functional to a wide variety of users and one that allows for socialization between children. For example, in designing a water play element [we] chose to create a universal design of multi-height tables that would allow for an undertable or side approach by wheelchairs of various heights, walkers of various sizes and design, or standing children of various heights" (Stoecklin, 1999, p. 2).
- Create a single or several quiet places where children can play and adults can sit with them.
- Develop some space that is sheltered from intense sun and rain so that children can be outdoors on most days.
- Plan for outdoor learning experiences. For example, Hampton (2003) describes adding a bird blind where children can hide and observe birds attracted by feeders or planting a vegetable garden with colorful and interesting plants. Supplement children's interests by providing related materials such as collecting trays or magnifying glasses.

Risk Factor: Child lives in a chaotic or hectic environment; child must adapt to several environments, often all in one day (such as child care home, school, shared custody between two parents, playtime with extended family or friends)
Protective Factor: Organized environment; stable environment

An Organized Environment

To help children become resilient to the risks created by living in a chaotic, hectic, or frequently changing environment, early childhood providers need to make a planned effort to maintain a stable and organized environment. This shows the child that the world has order, an order than can be understood and managed even by small people. A stable and clearly organized environment also helps the child relax, become more independent, and feel more capable. Additionally, it can set a model for the development of a personal, internal sense of order.

The sense of order is made visually apparent by the room arrangement in the early childhood environment that keeps appropriate materials in designated areas (Gonzalez-Mena & Eyer, 1997). Often, this is a challenge for the teaching staff as many early childhood settings were not intentionally built for use by young children (Wellhousen, 1999). Staff need to allot time to plan how to overcome the difficulties of size and layout. Possible solutions to limited space include creating side-by-side wall-mounted easels, storing dress-ups and manipulatives in stackable see-through boxes, and using shoebags on hooks to keep small objects (such as tools to use in the sensory table and art materials) neat and organized.

In order for children (and substitute teachers and classroom visitors) to know where to find and return materials, both materials and shelves need to be clearly labeled. Signage on shelves and materials should be written in a combination of illustration and simple words that many children will be able to learn to read, and others will be able to recognize. Take care to minimize crowding and clutter since young children have difficulty selecting and returning materials on crowded shelves. Careful organizing of materials prevents frustration, interpersonal conflict, and loss or destruction of materials.

Attending to wall displays and decoration is well worth the effort as the sense of organization is undermined when wall displays are messy or cover every available space. At least one-third of all wall space should be kept empty, and displays should be put at the children's eye level. Consider rotating wall displays to reduce clutter or creating simple books to replace hanging charts.

Children's sense of stability is also enhanced when they are assured that the time they put into a project will be respected. We show this by saving their work—hanging up a painting or carefully storing it in their own portfolio, keeping a block building up overnight or taking a photograph of it, displaying a construction on a table top, or reading a child-made book aloud at story time.

Creating and maintaining age-appropriate **transitions** reinforces the sense of stability, helps children predict what will happen in their lives, reduces stress, and prevents many associated problems in early childhood settings.

- Limit the number of times all children have to transition between one activity. (Does every child have to wash hands at the same time? Could snack time be included as a center activity during child-choice time instead of requiring all children to sit at the same time?)
- Minimize wait time during transitions. Prepare materials in advance so that the next activity is clear and ready; handle "traffic flow" so that not everyone is waiting to do the same thing.
- Teach children about the expectations for transitions. Tell children in advance when a transition is to happen and what they are expected to do at that time. Use physical cues such as dimming the lights or singing a song.
- Provide children with something to do during transitions. Prepare a list of simple finger plays or short games to keep children engaged during any necessary waiting. Assign some children "chores" to keep them busy such as handing out paper towels, setting the table, holding the door, or carrying the sand toys to the playground.

> **Risk factor:** Child is highly stressed; child is away from home environment and family for large parts of the day
> **Protective Factor:** Relaxing, comfortable, personalized environment

A Relaxing and Personal Environment

Children's level of stress and sense of tension can be significantly reduced by a relaxing and comfortable environment. This environment should be as home-like as possible, with soft and individualized elements. Softening the room visually also helps to absorb and reduce noise which is another source of tension for some children. Reflections of their family and cultural backgrounds helps children feel more relaxed in their new and more institutional-like setting.

Hard, cold surfaces—such as those made of plastic—should be minimized. Soft furnishings (pillows with cases that can be removed and washed), cushioned furniture, rocking chairs (both adult and child-sized), attractive fabric used to cover tables or storage, and area rugs all add a soothing sense.

Photographs of children's families and objects that represent their cultures give a personal feeling. Display family photos in several activity areas, create scrapbooks of children at home and in school, and use small photos of individual children to identify their cubbies or to indicate that they are a class helper. Develop a bulletin board of "Who's Who in Our Class." Make homemade books with children's photos about themes such as "Grandparents" or "We Are Growing and Changing" or "We Are All Different." One teacher explained what she does:

> I like to keep my camera handy. I take photos of the children in the process of working. They quickly realize that I am just as interested in how they work together, how they concentrate and solve hard problems as I am in the products they produce. I also take a photo of each family member, specialist, or other visitor who comes to our room. I put the developed photos on one part of our central bulletin board. The children often go over to the board during the day and point to "our friends."

Books in the reading center or around the room should include several that reflect children's home languages and unique cultural backgrounds. Including multicultural materials helps promote a sense of individual pride, an acceptance of others who are different from you, and a feeling of belonging to the group. Lack of exposure to or knowledge about different cultures can perpetuate the belief that people who are different are appropriate targets for negative discrimination or aggression (Slaby et. al., 1995).

Collecting and displaying items from the school's natural environment (dried grasses, stones, flowering branches, pine cones) connects the classroom or home with its natural setting and gives children the chance to study nature and learn to arrange natural things as well as reinforcing the sense of the uniqueness of their own environment. One teacher in rural Colorado reported that:

> For some reason our school supervisor wanted us to study outer space. We had to explain to her that young children do not understand things remote from their own experience and need to start with topics relevant to their immediate environment. So we all rewrote the plan, creating a unit about the area surrounding our school.
>
> We took the children on walks—and asked their parents to do the same—and collected all sorts of things along the way. We brought these back to the classroom. Our natural environment here is full of hay and grasses and cows and horses. We didn't bring the cows back, but we did take pictures of them, and later children wrote stories about what they had seen. Then we went to the library and found books on horses and farming. Later we visited two of the children's farm homes. We talked to grandparents who have been running their farms for ages. We've done a lot of silly things and laughing. It's led us to all sorts of interesting projects, and it's been great fun for everyone.

Giving children many opportunities for individual self-expression also creates a sense of personal and group relaxation. Frustrations can be worked out by painting at the easel with large brushes and thick paints or using shaving cream on table tops. (Note: Water-color painting does not provide the same outlet as it is a small-muscle and precise activity.) Children can act out different roles and dramatize problem situations in the dramatic play/housekeeping area. Daily experience at the sensory table—with water, mud, rice, or grains—helps reduce anxiety and encourages peaceful social interaction.

Just as in adult environments, temperature, light, sound, and color all play an important part in creating comfort and reducing stress in children's environments. All children (and adults) are affected by these elements, and some are what has been termed "environmentally sensitive." These children may develop headaches, coughs, ear infections or nasal congestion and may become irritable, hostile, drowsy, unable to concentrate, or overactive as a result of environmental exposures (Rajhathy, 1999). Poor air quality, limited air circulation, and chemicals in building materials, paints, carpets, and perfumed products are the most significant culprits in environmental problems. There are several easy and practical remedies to reduce the effects of environmental pollution:

- Open windows as often as possible and air out rooms
- Utilize scent-free products (cleaning products, detergents, room sprays, markers) and avoid perfumes
- Eliminate children's exposure to idling buses and other vehicles or machines (including lawn mowers)
- Reduce use of foods with added coloring, preservatives, and other chemicals
- Check ventilation and heating systems regularly

Fluorescent lighting can be disturbing to some children, even creating sleep and eating problems. Prolonged exposure to artificial lighting has been linked to fatigue, hyperactivity, and decreased calcium absorption. Many of these lights also produce a hum and flicker that can increase stress, visual irritation, and even seizures (Rajhathy, 1999). Some fluorescent tubes emit a small amount of ultraviolet radiation. All fluorescent lighting in child care facilities should have plastic or glass diffusers covering the tubes. Where possible and safe, incandescent and lamp lighting should replace fluorescents. If fluorescent lighting must be used over children's resting areas, turn them off as often as possible, leaving on some other "zones" in the room. Always ensure that any breakage from fluorescent tubes is removed immediately, as tubes contain small amounts of mercury that might be ingested by children (Rajhathy, 1999).

Loud sounds or very high noise levels can be frightening to some children and over-stimulating to others. Avoid harsh and overly bright color schemes. Red, orange, and yellow energize a room and its inhabitants; blue, green, and violet cool things down and create a calmer, more serene atmosphere.

Risk factor: Unpredictable life style; busy schedule
Protective Factor: Predictable environment

A Predictable School Environment

The child who is involved in an unpredictable lifestyle sits on a roller coaster, never quite sure what will happen next. Sporadic or continual changes in a child's life without adequate explanation or preparation can be very disconcerting. Even with advance warning, children often cannot comprehend change and rely on repetition and ritual for their security. Early childhood caregivers can help reduce these stresses for children by making their school time consistent and predictable and less harried.

> By taking responsibility for determining the schedule and routines, adults convey to children that there is someone—larger and stronger than themselves—who will make sure their school world is a safe and predictable place where basic needs will be consistently met (Kaplow, 1995, p. 48).

In addition to reinforcing children's trust in the adult caregiver, consistency in the school day helps children predict for themselves what is going to happen and thus be better able to accomplish the behaviors expected of them. It frees them from the energy and strain spent on hypervigilance (constantly checking one's environment for danger). When changes to the regular schedule are made, children can be told in advance and often even involved in the planning for these changes.

Specific strategies for helping to create a predictable environment include:

- Post a **Pictorial Daily Schedule** with simple words and illustrations children can understand. (See Figure 3.2.) Refer to the schedule several times daily. "We have finished center time. What happens next? (Point to chart.) We go outside." Prepare the children in advance for any changes in the schedule.
- Establishing "rituals" for arrivals, departures, transitions, and separations (See Suggested Resources and Readings for book on structuring transitions.)
- Reading books about routines to children
- Putting books about routines on book shelves and in the Cozy Corner
- Acknowledging special emotional or physical needs of children who may need continuing reassurance about who will be picking them up from school and where they will be going then, that there is enough food to eat in school, or that rest time will be at the same time every day
- Involving children in choosing their own activities by using a **Choosing Chart** to put their names (or photos or patterns, for very young children) on the center where they want to play

One teacher described how the Choosing Chart works in her preschool class:

> My Choosing Chart has been a lifesaver. My morning class this year has nine very active boys who speak almost no English. When they first came to school, their attention spans were very limited, and they flitted from center to center. Then I made a Choosing Chart with photos of all the centers and four Velcro pieces next to each center to represent the number of children allowed to play there at one time. I glued a photo of each child onto a popsicle stick and put a piece of Velcro on the back of each stick. I keep these in a coffee can right next to the Choosing Chart.
>
> I think my Choosing Chart is so important that I've placed it on an easel right in the center of the classroom. I explained to the children over and over that they could choose the place they wanted to play by sticking their photo onto the Velcro next to the matching picture on the Choosing Chart. It took a few weeks, but now all those nine boys love the Choosing Chart. They feel really proud of deciding for themselves, and it helps them so much to focus. It's also worked to help them separate calmly from each other, as only four people can choose the same center at any one time. Sometimes, they will talk among themselves about who will get to play with the others "later but not now." My whole classroom is a more peaceful place for everybody—including me.

FIGURE 3.2

Pictorial Daily Schedule Chart

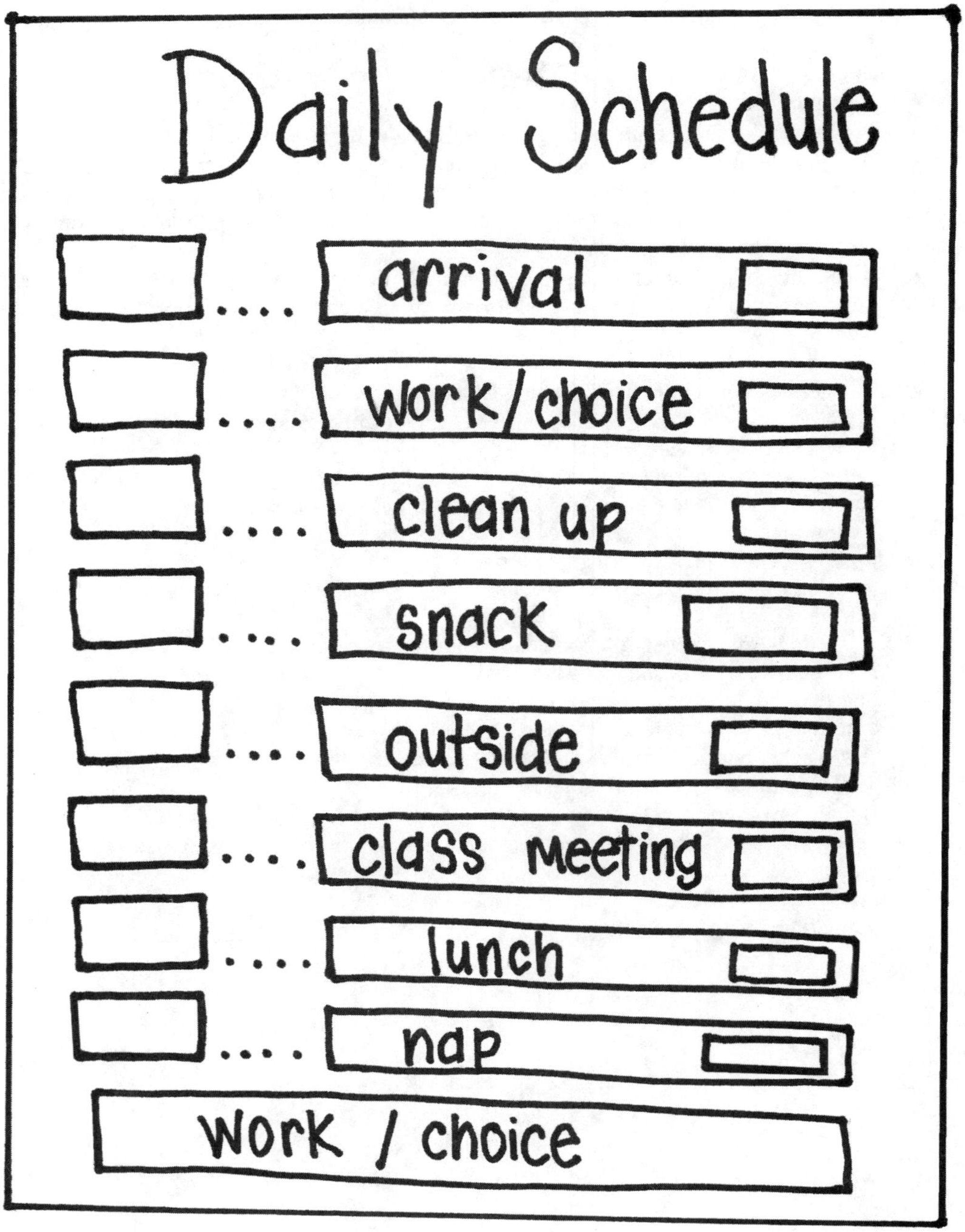

Daily Schedule

- arrival
- work/choice
- clean up
- snack
- outside
- class meeting
- lunch
- nap

work / choice

KEY TERMS AND CONCEPTS

Cozy Corner: an alone space where a single child can choose to go to make himself feel better

Transitions: those periods of time when children are moving from one activity to the next

Pictorial Daily Schedule: child-oriented poster with simple words and illustrations to show the sequence of the day's activities

Choosing Chart: child-oriented chart on which children can indicate their own choices for which center they want to play in

LEARNING IN ACTION:
SMALL GROUP ACTIVITIES AND FIELD ASSIGNMENTS

1. In small groups, discuss how the environment affects our mood and our ability to learn. Envision yourself on a crowded bus. It's a hot day, none of the windows are open, and the bus driver takes your money with a scowl. What "message" does that environment convey? How does it affect your mood, your ability to concentrate, your attitude toward others on the bus and toward the people you need to deal with after you get off the bus?
2. Plan a Cozy Corner for an early childhood setting. Draw your Cozy Corner on a piece of paper. Write down:
   - Where it will be located in the room
   - How you will establish physical boundaries
   - How you will make it "cozy"
   - What materials you will put in the Cozy Corner
   - How you will introduce the Cozy Corner to children
   - How you will explain the Cozy Corner to families
3. Create a Pictorial Daily Schedule or a Choosing Chart. Bring to class to share.
4. With a partner, plan a class meeting to talk with children about waiting. Give them a few examples of times during the day when they are asked to wait (for turns, to wash their hands, while another person is talking). Plan questions you will ask the children about how they feel about waiting, what they do when they have to wait, and what would be new ideas to help them wait.

RELATED CHILDREN'S BOOKS

Ancona, G. (1995). *El dia de Ricardo*. New York: Scholastic, Inc.
Berger, S., & Chanko, P. (1999). *SCHOOL*. New York: Scholastic, Inc.
Brown, M.W. (1995). *Buenas noches luna*. New York: Harper Trophy.
Erlich, A. (1989). *The story of Hanukkah*. New York: Penguin.
Hill, E. S. (1991). *Evan's corner*. New York: Penguin Group.
Kissinger, K. (1994). *All the colors we are*. St. Paul, MN: Redleaf Press.
Kuklin, S. (1992). *How my family lives in America*. New York: Simon & Schuster.

Lee, H. (1998). *At the beach*. New York: Henry Holt & Co.

Levine, E. (1989). *I hate English!* New York: Scholastic Inc.

Peters, R. (1994). *Regalia: American Indian dress and dance*. Littleton, MA: Sundance Publishers and Distributors.

Polacco, P. (1994). *Tikvah means hope*. New York: Bantam Doubleday Dell Books.

Rogers, F. (1985). *Going to day care*. New York: Penguin Putnam Books.

Simon, N. (1976). *Why am I different?* Morton Grove, IL: Albert Whitman and Company.

Smalls, I. (1997). *Beginning school*. Parsippany, NJ: Silver Press.

Waters, K., & Slovenz-Low, M. (1990). *Lion dancer: Ernie Wan's Chinese New Year*. New York: Scholastic Inc.

SUGGESTED READING AND RESOURCES

Alexander, N. (2002). *Maximizing outdoor play: Moving interest centers outdoors*. Retrieved October 6, 2003, from http://www.earlychildhood.com/Articles/index,cfm?FuseAction= Article&A=270

Bredekamp, S. (Ed.). (1990). *Developmentally appropriate practices in early childhood programs serving children from birth through age 8*. Washington, DC: National Association for the Education of Young Children.

Crosser, S. (1992). Managing the early childhood classroom. *Young Children, 47*(2), 23–29.

Feldman, J. (1997). *Wonderful rooms where children can bloom!* Peterborough, NH: Crystal Springs Books.

Feldman, J., & Jones, R. (1995). *Transition time: Let's do something different!* Beltsville, MD: Gryphon House.

Frost, J. L., & Wortham, S. (1988). The evolution of American playgrounds. *Young Children, 43*(5), 19–28.

Hudson, S. Thompson, D., Cechoa, C., & Mack, M. (2002). SAFE playgrounds: Recognizing risk factors. Retrieved October 6, 2003 from http://www.earlychildhood.com/ Articles /index.cfm?FuseAction=Article&A=128

Isbell, R. (1995). *The complete learning center book*. Beltsville, MD: Gryphon House, Inc.

Isbell R., & Exelby, B. (2001). *Early learning environments that work*. Beltsville, MD: Gryphon House, Inc.

Kielar, J. (1999). An antidote to the noisy nineties. *Young Children, 54*(5), 28–29.

Kritchevsky, S., & Prescott, E. (1997). *Planning environments for young children: Physical space*. Washington, DC: National Association for the Education of Young Children.

Moore, R., Goltsman, S., & Iascofano, D. (1992). *Play for all guidelines: Planning, design and management of outdoor play settings for all children*. Berkeley, CA: MIG Communications.

North Carolina State University. Natural Learning Initiative. (2003). Retrieved October 6, 2003 from http://www.naturallearning.org

Olds, A. R. (2000). *Child care design guide*. New York: McGraw-Hill.

Robles de Melendez, W., & Ostertag, V. (1997). *Teaching young children in multicultural classrooms: Issues, concepts and strategies*. Albany, NY: Delmar Publishers.

Saifer, S. (1990). Transitions: Structuring unplanned times. *Practical solutions to practically every problem: The early childhood teacher's manual*. St. Paul, MN: Toys `n Things Press.

Stoeklin, V. L. (2000). *Creating playgrounds kids love.* White Hutchinson Leisure and Learning Group. Retrieved October 6, 2003 from http://www.whitehutchinson.com/cgibin /printer.cgi?p=children/articles/playgrndkidslove

Sutterby, J. A., & Frost, J. L. (2002). Making playgrounds fit for children and children fit on playgrounds. *Young Children, 57(*3), 36–41.

Taylor, S. I., & Morris, V. G. (1996). Outdoor play in early childhood education settings: Is it safe and healthy for children? *Early Childhood Education Journal, 23(*3), 153–158.

Titman, W. (1994). *Special places, special people: The hidden curriculum of the school grounds.* Goldaming Surrey, UK: World Wide Fund for Nature/Learning Through Landscapes. (ERIC Document Reproduction Service. No. ED 430 384).

Vergeront, J. (1988). *Places and spaces for preschool and primary (outdoors).* Washington, DC: National Association for the Education of Young Children.

Vergeront, J. (1987). *Places and spaces for preschool and primary (indoors).* Washington, DC: National Association for the Education of Young Children.

REFERENCES

Bredekamp, S. (Ed.). (1987). *Developmentally appropriate practice in early childhood programs serving children from birth through age 8.* Washington, DC: National Association for the Education of Young Children.

Curtis, D., & Carter, M. (2003). *Designs for living and learning: Transforming early childhood environments.* St. Paul, MN: Redleaf Press.

Gonzalez-Mena, J., & Eyer, D. (1997). *Infants, toddlers and caregivers* (4th ed.). Mountain View, CA: Mayfield Publishing Company.

Greenman, J. (1988). *Caring spaces, learning places: Children's environments that work.* Redmond, WA: Exchange Press, Inc.

Hampton, N. (2003). Spaces for learning and fun. Perspectives on line, *The Magazine of the College of Agriculture and Life Sciences.* Retrieved October 6, 2003 from http://www.cals. ncsu.edu/agcomm/magazine/ spring03/spaces.htm

Ihn, H. (2002). *Analysis of preschool children's equipment choices and play behaviors in outdoor environments.* Retrieved October 8, 2003 from http://www. earlychildhood.com /Articles/index.cfm?FuseAction=Article&A=249

Ingham, V. (2001). *At home with color.* Des Moines, IA: Meredith Press.

Kaplow, L. (1995). *Unsmiling faces.* New York: Teachers College Press.

Katz, L. G., & McClellan, D. E. (1997). *Fostering children's social competence: The teacher's role.* Washington, DC: National Association for the Education of Young Children.

Kostelnik, M. J., Whiren, A. P., Soderman, A. K., Stein, L., & Gregory, K. (2000). *Guiding children's social development.* Albany, NY: Delmar.

Lowman, L., & Ruhmann, L. (1998). Simply sensational spaces: A multi-S approach to toddler environments. *Young Children, 53*(3), 11–17.

Rajhathy, J. (1999). Sick schools-sick kids. [Electronic version]. *Healthy Naturally*, October-November 1995. Retrieved October 10, 2003 from http://www. newworldpublishing.com /sickschools.html

Rivkin, M. S. (2000). *Outdoor experiences for young children.* ERIC Identifier ED448013. Retrieved October 6, 2003 from http://www.ericfacility. net/ databases /ERIC_Digests/ed 448013.html

Slaby R., Roedell, W., Arezzo, D., & Hendrix, K. (1995). *Early violence prevention: Tools for teachers of young children.* Washington, DC: National Association for the Education of Young Children.

Stoecklin, V. L. (1999). *Designing for all children.* White Hutchinson Leisure and Learning Group. Retrieved October 10, 2003 from http.www.whitehutchinson.com/cgibin/printer. cgi?p=/children/articles/designforall.shtml

Wellhousen, K. (1999). Big ideas for small spaces. *Young Children, 54*(6), 58–61.

Wortham, S. (2002). *Early childhood curriculum* (3rd ed.). Upper Saddle River, NJ: Merrill/Prentice Hall.

Chapter 4

CREATING A CARING EMOTIONAL ENVIRONMENT

After picking up a rock from the playground sand area and throwing it in the waste can, a 4-year-old proudly announced to his teacher, "I found something not safe on the playground and I throwed it away."

Kurtis, age 4, offered some sound advice on keeping safe. "Don't act silly when you're sitting on the toilet!"

SAFETY AS A PRIMARY NEED

In every early childhood care and education setting, every child must feel "I am safe here." With a sense of safety comes a sense of trust, one of the most basic developmental needs of all children and an essential part of the foundation on which all social, emotional, and intellectual development builds.

Abraham Maslow (1970) proposed an orderly progression of human needs. According to his hierarchy, basic physiological needs and a sense of physical and psychological safety must be achieved before one can achieve higher-level needs (belongingness, esteem, cognitive, aesthetic, or self-actualization). Therefore, if children do not feel safe, efforts to teach them positive social skills will be futile. Safety is necessary for children to feel empathy, develop relationships with others, and engage in social problem solving. Teachers need to make their classroom safe havens by preventing and stopping all hurtful actions within the classroom. Children need to feel safe about the adults, peers, and materials in their environment.

INTRODUCING THE SAFETY RULE TO CHILDREN

In classrooms and child care settings throughout the state of Colorado, the authors have assisted early childhood professionals to teach young children how to use a **Safety Rule** (adapted from Levin, 1994) to decide on appropriate behavior for themselves and others. As an easy, concrete way to present the Safety Rule, we teach it as having three parts:

- **We keep ourselves safe.**
- **We keep each other safe.**
- **We keep our things safe.**

Through many discussions, the teacher and children talk about what "we keep ourselves safe" means in terms of concrete behaviors surrounding the use of classroom materials, playground play, procedures on field trips, using the bathroom, and other common classroom behaviors.

The second part of the Safety Rule builds a sense of classroom community and responsibility towards others. "We keep each other safe" is clearly defined as no actions against someone which could hurt bodies (e.g., hitting, kicking, pushing, or other hurtful actions) or feelings (e.g., hurtful words, name-calling, teasing, swearing, or excluding others from play).

"We keep our things safe" includes caring for all classroom materials, the products children make (e.g., artwork, building structures) and anything that is brought from home. This portion of the safety rule is evoked often during clean-up times.

Teachers create a poster with pictures depicting each part of the Safety Rule (Figure 4.1). When possible, actual photographs of the children are used instead of graphics.

FIGURE 4.1

Sample Safety Rule Poster for a Classroom Using Graphics or Pictures Cut Out of Catalogs or Magazines

| We keep ourselves safe |
| We keep each other safe |
| We keep our things safe |

Sharla began an introductory class meeting on the Safety Rule by saying, "Today we're going to talk about how to stay safe at school. This poster will remind us of rules for the classroom that keep us safe. The first part says 'We keep ourselves safe' (Sharla points to each word as she reads it). There is a picture of a little girl on the swing. What are ways you can keep safe on the swing?"

Kali answers, "You don't jump off." "That's right," responds Sharla. "It would not be safe to jump off. To keep yourself safe on the swing you hold on tight until you stop swinging, then you get off."

Sharla repeats this for each picture under the "we keep ourselves safe" part of the Safety Rule. Then she asks the children if they have other ideas for keeping themselves safe at school. When they hesitate, she asks questions such as, "How do you stay safe with scissors?" "How do you keep yourself safe on the bus?"

For the first class meeting, Sharla only talks about the first line of the Safety Rule. Over the next few days, she conducts class meetings about the other parts of the rule. After the children begin to understand the concept of the Safety Rule, she makes up little stories for the children to judge, and teaches them to put thumbs up for a safe action and thumbs down for an unsafe action. "One day, a little boy named Jesus went down the slide with his head first. Show me with your thumbs—is that safe or not safe?" The children were excited to make "thumbs down" to show it was not a safe idea!

Besides discussions about the Safety Rule in class meetings, teachers may reinforce the Safety Rule while they introduce each learning center—what it means to be safe in the block area, the housekeeping area, the art area, etc. Sometimes teachers use puppets to role-play real classroom situations. Most importantly, teachers refer to the Safety Rule as a standard for behavior in their everyday interactions with children in the classroom as they go about their typical activities and routines. When a teacher observes a child climbing up on a chair, she might say, "Rebecca, is that keeping yourself safe?" When Steven refuses to share cooking utensils at the play dough table and grabs them away from another child, the teacher reminds Steven, "Grabbing toys is not safe." When a child carelessly throws the blocks on the shelf during clean up, the teacher asks, "Jasmine, is that keeping the blocks safe?" Similarly, teachers refer to the Safety Rule to reinforce positive behavior. "Yue Wan, you were really keeping Jesse safe when you helped him down the stairs."

In classrooms where a substantial number of children speak a language other than English, teachers include that language in the Safety Rule chart. A Spanish version might read:
1. Nosotros cuidamos de nosotros mismos.
2. Nosotros cuidamos de los otros.
3. Nosotros cuidamos de nuestras cosas.

INTRODUCING THE SAFETY RULE TO FAMILIES

Many early childhood programs have shared the Safety Rule with families, using various strategies:
- Presenting the Safety Rule during a Back to School event
- Creating a Safety Rule picture book to take home
- Including classroom anecdotes relevant to the Safety Rule in their monthly newsletter
- Creating a Safety Rule refrigerator magnet for each family to use at home

A simple refrigerator magnet can be made by printing the Safety Rule on tagboard, laminating it, and gluing a magnet strip to the back. See Figure 4.2 for the actual size of a refrigerator magnet used in one program.

FIGURE 4.2

Actual Size of Refrigerator Magnet Made by One Early Childhood Program in a Colorado School District

---

SAFETY RULE

We keep ourselves safe.

We keep each other safe.

We keep our things safe.

DISCIPLINE TO PROMOTE POSITIVE SOCIAL SKILLS

To support a safe environment and caring classroom, positive guidance techniques are an essential part of everyday classroom management and influence all adult/child relationships. **Discipline** is guidance and teaching. Discipline is discouraging undesirable behavior and encouraging desirable behavior. Discipline should not be demeaning, degrading, or harsh.

Positive guidance is constructive and instructive, teaching children to learn from their mistakes (Gartrell, 1998). Using a positive discipline approach, the focus is on strategies designed to prevent behavior problems rather than on punishment.

When addressing challenging behaviors, teachers should try to understand and analyze the underlying cause or motivation for the inappropriate behavior. (An extensive discussion of determining the probable cause and function of a behavior is included in Chapter 11.) Causes for troublesome behavior may include stress related to family disruption and traumatic experiences (as discussed in Chapter 1), chaotic schedules, illness, poor nutrition, lack of sleep, or a change in caregivers or routines. Behavior serves a function for the child who exhibits it. Problem behavior may be viewed as a form of communication—indicating what the child wants or does not want (Artesani, 2001).

Good discipline results from good planning. Children feel secure in an orderly environment and usually respond happily to appropriate and well-planned activities. The more appropriate fun things children have to do, the less likely they are to exhibit discipline problems. This means careful planning for activities that are suitable for the age and stage of the group, appropriately challenging, and thoughtfully scheduled. Discipline problems are more likely when children are bored or rushed, when they are frustrated due to excessive demands, when they have to wait, when they need attention, or when they are over-stimulated without time to unwind. Following a consistent schedule can do a great deal to avert undesirable behavior. Children feel comfortable when they know what they are going to do and understand procedures for transition times. (See Chapter 2 for more discussion on scheduling.)

To promote positive social skills in young children, care and education providers should provide discipline and guidance of children's behavior that is respectful, nurturing, positive, and promotes the development of self-control in young children (Bredekamp & Copple, 1997).

POSITIVE GUIDANCE TECHNIQUES

Use the Safety Rule

Basic rules and limits are necessary within the early childhood classroom. Children feel more secure if they know what behavior is acceptable and what behavior is unacceptable.

- Reasons for rules and expectations are respectfully explained on a routine basis so children understand their purpose.
- Children and teachers use the Safety Rule to decide on appropriate behavior for themselves and others.

Use Positive Verbal Guidance (Responsive Language)

Children often forget what constitutes appropriate behavior from one day to the next and from one situation to another (Kostelnik, Soderman, & Whiren, 1999). They need frequent reminders of the rules; if corrective action is necessary, adults should be clear but non-accusatory. **Responsive language** utilizes positive verbal guidance that is respectful towards children, labels and validates children's feelings, and clarifies rules and responsibilities. Responsive language gives reasons and explanations to children (Stone, 1993). Adults actively listen to children and respond in a sensitive manner.

State rules in positive terms.
Tell children what *to* do instead of what *not* to do. Try to eliminate "stop," "don't" and "no" from your statements to children (except to keep a child safe in an emergency).

"Please walk" rather than "Don't run."

"Eat your food" rather than "Don't play with your food."

"Sit down flat so other children can see" instead of "Don't stand up."

Make requests and give directions in respectful ways.
"When you are finished eating, please throw your napkin and cup in the trash can."

Validate children's feelings.
"I know that it is hard to wait for a turn. But other children want a turn too."

Clarify classroom rules and give reasons for the limits.
"Walk to the bus so that you stay safe and don't fall."
"Use a quiet voice in the hall so you don't disturb the other classes."

Model the Behavior You Want a Child to Follow

All young children benefit from a visual model of what to do, but this is especially important for children with developmental or language delays. Couple the **modeling** or demonstration of proper procedure, with direct explanation—otherwise children may not imitate the desired behavior themselves at a later time.

- Show the child exactly what you want while giving verbal directives.
- "Put your backpack under your seat like this."
- "After you dry your hands, throw away the paper towel right here."
- Verbal descriptions of desired behaviors are especially needed when the adult wants to model resisting temptation or delaying gratification.
- "It's really hard for me to wait for a turn on the swing. I want to run up there right now, but I will wait until Sarah is done."

Reinforce Appropriate Behavior

The most effective method of managing children's behavior is through the application of positive reinforcement. When teaching a new behavior, it is best to reinforce every time the behavior occurs. New behaviors require immediate and continuous reinforcement to be learned and maintained. For more complicated behavior, it is important to reinforce small steps. For example, to reinforce a child who is cleaning up the block area, which to her appears to have about a million blocks spread all over the floor, ask the child to put five blocks on the shelf, and then praise her. Don't wait until the entire job is completed.

- Behaviors that are followed by positive reinforcement are likely to be strengthened and repeated.
- Use **social reinforcers** (smiles, praise, pat on the back, wink, OK sign) and **activity reinforcers** (engaging in a special activity as a reward for desired behavior). **Tangible reinforcers** (stickers, stars, prizes) should be used only for short periods of time when other types of reinforcement fail to work with a particular child.
- Use **effective praise**: praise that is selective, specific, and positive.

Effective praise (called "encouragement" by Hitz & Driscoll, 1988) is more likely to provide meaningful feedback and foster healthy self-esteem. Ineffective praise may actually lower children's self-confidence, inhibit achievement, and make children depend on external praise (Katz, 1993; Kohn, 1993; Kohn, 2001). (See Figure 4.3.)

FIGURE 4.3

Comparison of Ineffective and Effective Praise

Ineffective Praise	Effective Praise (Encouragement)
Is given indiscriminately and tends to be discounted by children—every child is given a "good job" star at the end of the day regardless of her behavior that day	Is selective—directed to an individual child or small group contingent upon performance of desirable behavior
Is general—overuse of pat phrases, often delivered mechanically "Good job." "Great." "You're such a nice boy, Joshua."	Is descriptive and specific--provides explicit feedback about the behavior being encouraged or the rule reinforced and delivered with a natural but enthusiastic tone of voice "You put all the lids on the markers. Now they won't dry out." "Kaniesha, you remembered to raise your hand before talking. That way two people weren't talking at the same time and I could hear what you had to say." "Joshua, I noticed that you shared the trucks with Troy today."
Makes negative comparisons or encourages competition between children "Tommy, you are the best runner!" "You are the best helper in the class."	Avoids comparisons or competition; compares children's progress with their past performance rather than other children "Tommy, you run so fast now." "You helped Max clean up all the puzzles."
Uses evaluative words like "good" or "beautiful" or focuses on the end product "What a beautiful picture." "You are a good reader."	Focuses on improvement of process rather than evaluation of a finished product "You painted a long time using lots of blue paint." "You are learning to read lots of words!"
Relies on external rewards or approval of teacher "You took turns with the tricycle today. Here is a sticker." "I like the way you worked together."	Links children's behavior to their own enjoyment and satisfaction or to the effect on another person "You took turns with the tricycle today. You and Sammy had lots of fun playing together." "You must feel proud of how you worked together." "Look at Cindy's face. She looks happy that you shared some play dough."

Sources: Hitz & Driscoll, 1988; Katz, 1993; Kohn, 2001

Ignore Non-Disruptive Inappropriate Behavior

Children who behave inappropriately often receive the most attention from adults. Children who chronically misbehave are usually convinced that the only way they can get attention is through negative actions. While some behaviors cannot be ignored (unsafe or hurtful actions), some simply annoying ones can be safely overlooked. By ignoring these behaviors, the child will eventually see there is no gain in using that language or that behavior, and it may not be repeated.

- Limit attention to children who are used to negative responses from adults.
- "Catch the child being good" and then use effective praise when children are engaging in *desired* behaviors. Too often children get attention for inappropriate behaviors and are left alone when they are playing appropriately or when things are quiet and controlled in early childhood settings.

Offer Choices

Offering choices gives children some control over their own behavior, shows respect for them as individuals, and encourages independence. When children are given options to choose from, they are more likely to cooperate and meet classroom expectations.

"It's time to clean up the house area. Which will you put away, the dishes or the dolls?"

Redirect and Offer Acceptable Substitutes

- Give children acceptable alternatives rather than telling them what they cannot choose.
- Privately (quietly so just that child can hear) remind the child of the classroom rule and then redirect by offering an alternative or giving a choice.
  "Mohammed, it's not safe to pull the rolling pin away from Mariah. Mariah is using that rolling pin right now. Pick another toy until she is done."
  "Bobbie is sitting there, Susie. Remember, there is only one child on a carpet square. You need to find another seat. Tomorrow you can have a turn sitting next to me."
  "Blocks are for building. You can make a house or a barn or a road for the trucks."
- When necessary, remove the child from the problem area and redirect to another activity.
  "Julie, you're having trouble sharing the blocks. I can't let you hurt other people by pushing. It's not so crowded at the water table. I think you might have fun there. We have some new toys there. Let's go to the water table."

Facilitate Problem Solving with Children

Children can be taught a problem-solving process to resolve interpersonal conflicts. Chapter 7 will elaborate on ways teachers help children to work through five steps to problem solving:

- What is the problem?
- What can you do?
- What might happen if . . . ?
- Choose a solution and use it.
- Is it working?

Use Logical Consequences

Logical consequences make an obvious connection between children's behavior and the disciplinary action that follows. As logical consequences are being carried out, adults remind children of the rule and why the consequence is necessary. They do so matter-of-factly, without humiliating or threatening children. Logical consequences are reasonable, respectful, and related to the behavior.

Logical consequences typically take one of three forms:

1. Rehearsal of a desired behavior

   "Ruben, I can see you didn't wash your hands before you sat down for lunch. You need to keep yourself safe and wash away germs before you eat. Please go wash your hands now and then come back to the table."

2. Restitution—making amends for misbehavior

   "Jeffrey, I cannot let you draw in the book. We need to take care of books and keep them safe. You need to get an eraser and erase the pencil marks. Would you like some help?"

3. Temporary loss of privilege

   "Alex, I reminded you that it wasn't safe to splash your friends at the water table. You will have to find another place to play today. Tomorrow you can play again at the water table if you remember the Safety Rule."

When a new consequence is being applied or a situation is new for a given child, give one clear reminder or warning before applying the consequence.

"Remember, the ball must stay in the play yard. If you throw the ball over the fence again, you will have to play with something else."

Once a rule and its consequence are well-known to the children, the consequence should be stated and applied in a matter-of-fact way immediately following an infraction, without blame, criticism, or extended discussion. Primary grade children can be involved in determining the consequences for behavior. One first-grade group developed the following consequences (Letts, 1997).

Problem	Consequences
Noisy during assemblies	Practice walking, sitting in auditorium
	Stay back from the assembly
Hitting or bullying others	Private "tutoring" after school to learn and practice alternative skills
	Social contract with student, parents and principal

EXTREME BEHAVIOR INTERVENTION METHODS

In the opinion of the authors, time-out and holding or restraining a child are considered to be crisis intervention methods for responding to extreme behavior; thus they are not included in the description of positive guidance techniques suggested for frequent use.

Many programs have banned the use of time-out, because it tends to be misused and over-used. Opposition to the use of time-out is evident in the following quotes. "Opponents argue that time-out damages self-esteem by punishing, embarrassing and humiliating the child in front of his peers. In effect it says, 'I don't want you here.' Techniques that preserve self-esteem are much more effective in the long run" (Kaiser & Rasminsky, 1999). "When used as a discipline, the time-out is one of a group of techniques—including name-on-the-board, an assigned yellow or red "light," and the disciplinary referral slip-that still rely on blame and shame to bring a child's behavior 'back into line.' This is the modern equivalent of the dunce stool" (Gartrell, 2001, p. 9).

Time Out from Reinforcement

Time-out means time away from rewarding events, including attention from adults and peers or use of materials. Time-out removes the child from the setting t hat has reinforced the child's negative behavior and provides out-of-control children with a cooling-off period during which they can regain their composure away from the group. Following an inappropriate behavior that is not safe or hurtful to people or things, the child is removed from the social reinforcers that come from being with others. **Time-out should be used *only* when a child has lost control, cannot respond to adult directions or efforts to comfort, is unable to reason or choose a more appropriate action, or continues to repeat very negative behaviors such as hurting another person or destructive behaviors.**

There are several distinct disadvantages to using time-out as the primary discipline strategy in the classroom. Time-out may teach a child what "not to do," but it does not teach more adaptive strategies to use in the future. Opportunities for learning through social interactions are lost during the period of isolation (Schreiber, 1999; Stephens, 1992). Time-out may actually worsen the problem if during the process the child "forces the caregiver to spend several minutes getting her into time-out, she gets the spotlight-which may be exactly what she wants" (Kaiser & Rasminsky, 1999).

Time-out should not be used for every infraction of classroom rules, as a threat ("One more face like that and you go to time-out, young lady."), or simply to provide relief to the adult (Kostelnik, Whiren, Soderman, Stein, & Gregory, 2002). Time-out is *only* effective as part of a behavior guidance plan that includes the simultaneous use of strategies to teach and encourage desirable behavior (as described in subsequent chapters of this book).

- Designate a non-frightening time-out area away from activity but within view of the teacher. It needs to be a quiet, out-of-the-way area where children will feel safe. Note: This must *not* be the Cozy Corner. (Some teachers have the child sit on the floor where the misbehavior occurred rather than designating a particular place.)
- Adults should apply time-out as a consequence in a matter-of-fact way, without reprimands or anger.
- When a child misbehaves, calmly insist that the child take a time-out while making clear the reason for removing the child.
  "You have a time-out for hitting. I'll tell you when you can get up from the chair."
  "You need to sit over here for a little while to calm down. You hurt Dominic when you threw that block. You are very angry. When you are quiet, we will talk."
- The adult remains nearby but does not speak to the child.
- If the child resists going to the time-out area, gently guide her by the hand, guide from under the arms, or pick her up. If necessary, have the child sit down on the floor right where she is.
- Keep the time-out short. A good rule of thumb is one minute of time-out per year of age of the child: a 3-year-old for 3 minutes, a 5-year old for 5 minutes. Using a timer to signal the end of a time-out period helps preschoolers recognize that the time-out

will have a definite end (Ucci, 1998). Time-out is not appropriately used as a means for indefinitely removing a "problem child." Time-out is a time for cooling off and ends when the child calms down or after the short designated time. However, the child may not leave time-out at the end of the 3–4 minute period if she is still out of control.

- Praise the child who participates in a time-out as planned. Give the child the option of discussing the incident leading to the time-out.
- "You are calm and quiet now. When you are ready you may return to the group. Do you want to talk about why you were so angry and threw the block?"
- After the child leaves time-out, allow the child to return to the group without lecturing or attempting to obtain promises to "be good" in the future. Assist the child to become engaged in another activity and watch for appropriate, positive behavior to notice and reinforce.

Holding an Out-of-Control Child (Restraint)

Occasionally a child may lose control so completely that she has to be physically restrained and removed from the scene to prevent her from hurting herself or others. Physical restraint and removal from the scene should not be viewed as punishment, but as a means of saying, "You can't do that." An adult should hold the child with just sufficient strength to protect the child or other children and help restore calm. With the child facing away from you, wrap one arm around the child's arms and your legs around the child's legs to prevent the child from hurting you or herself. Cup one hand behind the child's head to protect yourself from a possible head butt to your chest or chin. Before you begin this action, try to notify another adult (in the room or in the office) that you will be forcibly holding this child. This second adult can provide back-up protection to you and the other children as well as provide a witness to your action being carried out appropriately.

- Adults provide the control in a calm, non-punitive manner, using a soothing voice.
- "Carey, I'm going to hold you close so you won't hurt yourself or anyone else. I will let you go when you are calm and ready to talk."
- Record what you have done, including circumstances prior to the holding action, how you performed the action, and what followed.

SEQUENCE OF RESPONSE

To reduce or eliminate undesirable behavior and enhance children's development of self control, it is recommended that early childhood educators follow a specific sequence of actions (Kostelnik et. al., 2002):

1. Make a reflective statement in which the child's point of view is acknowledged. ("I know that you are having fun, but . . .")
2. Give children an explanation of the impact of their behavior on other children and the adult. ("You are scaring Jessica and I'm afraid someone will get hurt.")
3. State the rule that the child is expected to follow and describe an alternate behavior for the child to pursue. ("Chasing children with the dinosaurs is not allowed at school. You may play with the dinosaurs if you keep them in the sand table.")

4. Give a warning phrased as an either/or statement that repeats the rule and then tells the child what will happen if she does not follow it. ("Either keep the dinosaurs in the sand table, or you will have to leave the dinosaurs and go somewhere else to play.")
5. Follow through with appropriate negative consequences if the child does not comply. ("Remember I said that you would have to quit playing with dinosaurs if you couldn't keep them in the sand table.")

FAMILIES AND CHILD GUIDANCE

According to the National Association for the Education of Young Children Code of Ethical Conduct (1998), it is the responsibility of early childhood practitioners to bring about a collaboration between the home and early childhood settings in ways that enhance the child's development. Collaborating with families regarding guidance of children requires a "conscientious nurturing of relationships of mutual trust and the creating of bridges between families' cultures, values, and childrearing practices and our own" (Feeney & Freeman, 1999, p. 47–48).

Parents and educators may have different beliefs about what constitutes "good behavior" and how adults should respond to children's behavior. These differences stem from their respective personal perspectives based on family background, socio-economic status, other cultural factors, and community setting. According to Decker and Decker (1997), "professionals must develop understandings about the sources of these differences and show as much acceptance for the variety of parent views as they do for differences in children."

Although children can learn to accommodate different rules or standards between their child care or school setting and home, consistency in approaches reduces children's confusion about what is expected of them and how adults will respond. Therefore, frequent communication between families and care and education providers is necessary to enhance mutual understanding and develop a style of responding to children's behavior that is comfortable for all involved.

KEY TERMS AND CONCEPTS

Discipline: guidance and teaching; discouraging undesirable behavior and encouraging desirable behavior; also called positive guidance

Safety Rule: simple three-part guide for acceptable behavior in the classroom

Responsive language: teacher language that is respectful towards children, labels and validates children's feelings, and clarifies rules and responsibilities

Modeling: demonstrating a desired behavior in order to prompt an imitative response

Social reinforcers: behaviors coming from another person such as smiles, praise, pats on the back, winks, or the OK sign

Activity reinforcers: engaging in a special activity (such as extra time at the computer, feeding the gerbil, line leader for the day) as a reward for desired behavior

Tangible reinforcers: concrete rewards such as small toys, stickers, balloons, and happy face certificates

Effective praise: praise that is selective, specific, and positive

Time-out: time away from rewarding events, including attention from adults and peers or use of materials

LEARNING IN ACTION:
SMALL GROUP ACTIVITIES AND FIELD ASSIGNMENTS

1. In small groups, discuss ways in which a teacher could introduce the Safety Rule to staff (teaching assistant, lunch aide, bus driver) and children in: a) toddler setting; b) preschool setting; c) primary grade classroom.
2. Using poster board and pictures from catalogues or photographs, make your own Safety Rule chart.
3. Working in pairs, write a responsive/positive verbal guidance alternative for each of the teacher's statements below.
    "Stop that pushing right now young lady!"
    "No one is going anywhere until this room is clean."
    "I've told you a hundred times that running is not allowed inside."
    "Don't spill that paint on the carpet!"
    "Don't you talk to me that way!"
    "You'd better not forget your backpack again."
4. In pairs, write effective praise statements for the following classroom situations. Share with the large group and discuss.
    Andy cleans up after an art project.
    Libby walks quietly from the bathroom to the classroom.
    Manuel has been playing with blocks for a long time.
    Timmy raises his hand during group discussion.
    Tasha made you a picture at home and brought it to you.
    Marie helps Adam clean up spilled paint.
5. Investigate an early childhood center's policies on time-out and holding an out-of-control child. Compare to the suggestions in this chapter.
6. The following are typical scenarios observed in early childhood settings. All are examples of teacher behaviors which focus more on punishing, threatening, or delivering unrelated negative consequences rather than using positive guidance techniques. Work in groups of three or four. Discuss several positive guidance alternatives for each situation (or the scenario assigned to your group by the instructor). Because none of the children in these examples are totally out of control, do not consider time-out as an option.

Scenario 1
Two boys are recklessly driving trucks in the block area and knock down another child's building. Rushing over, their teacher says, "You know better than that. Do you always have to be so careless? Go sit in the corner until you can behave the way you should."

Scenario 2
Janet, a teacher in a preschool classroom, is leading a group of 15 four-year-olds in a structured art activity where they are gluing together circles to make a snowman and adding a hat, facial features, and buttons according to the model snowman posted on the wall. Several children are randomly gluing cut-out pieces on their paper. Several others are constantly getting out of their seats to wash their hands. Two boys are chasing each other around the table. Janet becomes frustrated and tells the children, "You are not following directions. Push the art materials out of the way and put your heads on the table for 10 minutes."

Scenario 3
During free play, two girls begin having a tug-of-war over a doll. The teacher takes the doll away saying, "If you can't play nicely, neither of you will get to use the doll."

Scenario 4
Megan is holding a plastic dinosaur and chasing other children around the room as she roars in a menacing voice. One child begins to cry. The teacher approaches and tells Megan, "See what you have done. Why do you always have to bother the other children? You cannot play with the dinosaurs for the rest of the week. Now go sit in the book corner quietly and read."

SUGGESTED READING AND RESOURCES

Adams, S. K., & Baronberg, J. (2001). *The CARES Model: Building social skills and reducing problem behaviors in early childhood classrooms.* Denver, CO: Western Media Products. (Instructional videotape depicting six class meetings in early childhood classrooms.)

Cherry, C. (1983). *Please don't sit on the kids: Alternatives to punitive discipline.* Carthage, IL: Fearon Teacher Aids.

Clarke, J. I. (1999). *Time-in: When time-out doesn't work.* Seattle, WA: Parenting Press, Inc.

Lynch, E. W., & Hanson, M. J. (1992). *Developing cross-cultural competence.* Baltimore, MD: Paul H. Brookes Publishing.

Miller, S. A. (2001). Tips for creating classroom rules. *Early Childhood Today, 15*(6), 8.

Sandall, S., & Ostrosky, M. (Eds.). (1999). *Practical ideas for addressing challenging behaviors.* Denver, CO: Division for Early Childhood of the Council for Exceptional Children.

REFERENCES

Artesani, A. J. (2001). *Understanding the purpose of challenging behavior.* Upper Saddle River, NJ: Prentice Hall.

Bredekamp, S., & Copple, C. (Eds.). (1997). *Developmentally appropriate practice in early childhood programs* (Revised ed.). Washington, DC: National Association for the Education of Young Children.

Decker, C. A., & Decker, J. R. (1997). *Planning and administering early childhood programs* (6th ed.). Upper Saddle River, NJ: Merrill/Prentice Hall.

Feeney, S., & Freeman, N. K. (1999). *Ethics and the early childhood educator: Using the NAEYC code*. Washington, DC: National Association for the Education of Young Children.

Gartrell, D. J. (1998). *A guidance approach for the encouraging classroom*. Albany, NY: Delmar/Thompson.

Gartrell, D. (2001). Replacing time-out: Using guidance to build an encouraging classroom. *Young Children, 56*(6), 8–16.

Hitz, R., & Driscoll, A. (1988). Praise or encouragement? New insights into praise: Implications for early childhood teachers. *Young Children, 43*(5), 6–13.

Kaiser, S., & Rasminsky, J. S. (1999). *Meeting the challenge: Effective strategies for challenging behaviors in early childhood environments*. Washington, DC: National Association for the Education of Young Children.

Katz, L. G. (1993). *Distinctions between self-esteem and narcissism: Implications for practice.* Perspectives from ERIC/EECE. A monograph Series, no. 5, ERIC Document 363–452. Urbana,IL: Eric Clearinghouse on Elementary and Early Childhood Education.

Kohn, A. (1993). *Punished by rewards*. Boston: Houghton-Mifflin.

Kohn, A. (2001). Five reasons to stop saying "Good job!" *Young Children, 56*(5), 24–28.

Kostelnik, M. J., Soderman, A. K., & Whiren, A. P. (1999). *Developmentally appropriate programs in early childhood education*. Upper Saddle River, NJ: Merrill/Prentice Hall.

Kostelnik, M. J., Whiren, A. P., Soderman, A. K., Stein, L., & Gregory, K. (2002). *Guiding children's social development*. Albany, NY: Delmar.

Letts, N. (1997). *Creating a caring classroom*. New York: Scholastic.

Levin, D. (1994). *Teaching young children in violent times*. Cambridge, MA: Educators for Social Responsibility.

Maslow, A. H. (1970). *Motivation and personality* (2nd ed.). New York: Harper & Row.

National Association for the Education of Young Children. (1998). *Code of ethical conduct: Guidelines for responsible behavior in early childhood education*. Washington, DC: Author.

Schreiber, M. E. (1999). Time-outs for toddlers: Is our goal punishment or education? *Young Children, 54*(4), 22–25.

Stephens, K. (September, 1992). What's so positive about positive discipline and other mysteries of child guidance. *Child Care Information Exchange*, 30–33.

Stone, J. (May, 1993). Caregiver and teacher language: Responsive or restrictive? *Young Children, 48*(4), 12–18.

Ucci, M. (1998). "Time outs" and how to use them. *Child Health Alert, 1,* 2–3.

Chapter 5

IDENTIFYING AND EXPRESSING EMOTIONS

> Evan walked into the preschool classroom yawning. He pulled away when his teacher, Mrs. Washington, tried to greet him and pat his shoulder. Mrs. Washington watched Evan as he headed for a basket of Legos™. He built quietly for a while until another little boy, Mario, attempted to use some of the many Legos™ left in the basket, at which time Evan pulled the basket closer to himself and pushed Mario away. When Mario tried to defend his right to use some Legos™, Evan swept the entire basket off the table and onto the floor. Mrs. Washington quickly moved to the area to handle yet another emotional outburst by Evan.

This classroom event represents the all-too-common plight of many young children today. They are unable to identify their feelings, understand the source of their feelings, or to express their emotions appropriately. They are lacking in what some have called **emotional intelligence** or **emotional literacy**.

The model of emotional intelligence was first proposed by Yale psychologist Peter Salovey and the University of New Hampshire's John Mayer to describe qualities such as understanding one's own feelings, managing emotions so they are appropriate, demonstrating empathy for the feelings of others, and responding to the emotions of others (Salovey & Mayer, 1990). Daniel Goleman (1995) shortened the term to EQ in his book *Emotional Intelligence*.

Goleman (1995) contends that addressing emotional intelligence should be an urgent priority for schools. School-based prevention programs which teach a core of emotional and social competencies such as empathy, impulse control, managing anger, and conflict resolution have been found to be far more effective than those prevention or intervention programs for older children targeting specific problems such as teen smoking, drug abuse, pregnancy, dropping out, and school violence. According to Goleman (1995, p. 284)

> In a time when too many children lack the capacity to handle their upsets, to listen or focus, to rein in impulse, to feel responsible for their work or care about learning, anything that will buttress these skills will help in their education. In this sense, emotional literacy enhances schools' ability to teach.

EMOTIONAL LITERACY IN THE EARLY CHILDHOOD SETTING

Many young children lack the words to express their feelings. A significant task in working with young children is to help them enhance their awareness of their emotional life and develop an emotional vocabulary. We begin by helping them increase their understanding of their feelings and those of others—recognizing them, naming them, and trying to identify the causal reason behind their feelings.

According to Kindlon and Thompson (1999), there are three parts to emotional literacy:
1. the ability to identify and name our emotions
2. the ability to recognize the emotions of others
3. understanding the situations or reactions that produce emotional states

To this list, Salovey and Mayer (1990) add:
4. managing emotions so they are appropriate
5. handling relationships

Emotional literacy is a prerequisite for emotional regulation, successful interpersonal interactions, and social problem solving. As such, emotional literacy is one of the most important skills for a child to acquire in early childhood (Webster-Stratton, 1999).

ABILITY TO IDENTIFY AND NAME EMOTIONS

Emotional self-awareness (recognizing feelings and building a vocabulary for them) is an essential foundation for emotional literacy. Children with a sufficient feelings vocabulary can communicate with others about their emotions and express their needs. Children who accurately identify and label emotions tend to be less aggressive, are more accepted by peers, and are generally more socially competent (Arsenio, Cooperman, & Lover, 2000; Denham, McKinley, Couchoud, & Holt, 1990; Izard, Fine, Schultz, Mostow, & Ackerman, 2001). All children need support in building a feelings vocabulary. Children with disabilities have a more limited vocabulary of feeling words than their typically developing peers (Feldman, McGee, Mann, & Strain, 1993), as do children from low-income families compared to their middle income peers (Hart & Risley, 1995; Lewis & Michalson, 1993).

Children learn to develop an awareness of feelings when adults serve as role models by expressing their own feelings in words and teaching a **feelings vocabulary** to children in class meetings, during conversation and play with children, and through games and activities. Through repeated examples, children learn to identify their own emotions and the feelings of others. They learn that their emotions are normal and an accurate reflection of their experience. They learn that feelings can change and that people may have different feelings about the same thing (Committee for Children, 2002).

Helping Children Identify and Label Emotions

- Provide an environment in which children feel safe to share their feelings. Remember that you might be offering the only emotionally safe haven for children experiencing abuse, neglect, violence, or other trauma in their lives. Expect that it will take some time for children to trust and feel safe to communicate openly with you.
- Pair a photograph or sketch of a "feeling face" with the corresponding emotion word. Introduce a variety of feeling words, beginning with the primary emotions (happy, sad, mad, afraid, surprised, and disgusted) and gradually add words to expand children's feelings vocabulary (disappointed, frustrated, excited, embarrassed, worried, etc.). See Figure 5.1.

FIGURE 5.1

Feeling Words for Young Children to Build an Emotional Vocabulary

Affectionate	Embarrassed	Overwhelmed
Afraid	Excited	Peaceful
Angry	Fantastic	Pleasant
Annoyed	Fearful	Proud
Awful	Friendly	Relaxed
Bored	Frustrated	Relieved
Brave	Furious	Sad
Calm	Gentle	Safe
Caring	Generous	Scared
Cheerful	Gloomy	Serious
Clumsy	Guilty	Shy
Confused	Happy	Stressed
Comfortable	Ignored	Stubborn
Creative	Impatient	Surprised
Cruel	Interested	Tense
Curious	Jealous	Thoughtful
Delighted	Joyful	Thrilled
Depressed	Lonely	Uncomfortable
Disappointed	Loving	Weary
Disgusted	Mad	Worried
Elated	Nervous	

- Teach feeling words by naming and describing emotions as children experience them. Observe children's facial expressions, tone of voice, and body language to assess their feelings. "Julian, you look sad." "Matthew, you are really having trouble with that puzzle. You seem frustrated." "Hector, you are shouting and your face is all red. You look really angry." These **affective reflections** (nonjudgmental statements that describe the emotion of the child) help children identify their own affective state and feel understood and accepted (Kostelnik, Whiren, Soderman, Stein, & Gregory, 2002).

- Because children are not always sure what they are feeling or why, make observational statements describing the probable emotions of a child rather than asking that child "How are you feeling right now?" or "Why are you so sad?" As children become more skilled at identifying emotions and the situations that create them, they may be able to answer questions such as, "You look angry. What happened?"

- Act as a role model by including emotions in your everyday conversations with children. "I was so worried when my child was sick yesterday." "I am so frustrated! This stapler keeps jamming and I am trying to display your artwork for your parents to see on this bulletin board." "Once my puppy got hurt and I was very sad and scared."

- Plan emotion-related class meetings, games, and activities. Create and use materials that encourage discussion of feelings. (See Figure 5.2.)

FIGURE 5.2

Class Meetings and Activities to Promote Emotional Literacy

Feelings Faces Class Meeting

Purpose: To help children identify the range of emotions possible in a given situation and appreciate that not everyone feels the same way at the same time.

Materials: Draw the following facial expressions on a large circle or paper plate: happy, sad, scared, angry, surprised, disgusted. Laminate the faces and staple each to a flat stick such as a tongue depressor or a stick from a hardware store for mixing paint. Make enough so that each child in a small group is able to hold at least two faces.

Procedure: With the help of the children, identify each feeling face. Pass out the feeling face sticks so that each child is able to hold at least two. Make up short scenarios that are typical of young children's experiences. At the end of each, ask the children to show how that person might be feeling by holding up one of their feeling faces. Some sample scenarios could be:

- "Donnell's mother tells him that they are having ice cream for dessert. How do you think Donnell feels?"
- "Jimmy took the tricycle away from Shakissha. How do you think Shakissha feels?"
- "Maria was not expecting to see her cousins today. When she got home from school, her cousins greeted her at the door. How do you think Maria feels?"
- "Lucy asks Gary to try putting catsup on his ice cream. How do you think Gary feels about that idea?"

Help the children notice that not everyone has the same opinion as to how the children in these stories will feel. For example, some might think that Shakissha will be angry, others think that she will feel sad if Jimmy takes her tricycle away.

Extensions: Parents and children can make feeling faces sticks at home. They can take turns describing a situation while the other chooses a response.

Feelings Beanbag Toss

Purpose: To promote children's ability to identify and name emotions based on facial expressions and to speculate on situations that produce each emotional state.

Materials: Beanbag. Floor poster with pictures of four basic emotions: happy, sad, angry, and afraid. Pictures on the poster can be photographs of faces cut from magazines or line drawings, each showing children or adults experiencing one of the emotions listed above. Glue one picture to each quadrant of posterboard. laminate.

Procedure: Show the poster to a small group of children who are sitting in a semicircle on the floor. Place the poster in front of the children. Identify each photographed emotion. The teacher begins the game by tossing the beanbag on one of the faces. She names the emotion, then states a reason or event that might make her feel that way. "I get sad when my child is sick." Children take a turn tossing the beanbag onto an emotion picture, naming it and saying what makes them feel that way.

Extensions: As children become adept at identifying these four basic emotions, add other emotion pictures (surprised, disgusted, excited, and jealous) and play the beanbag toss again.

Mood Wheel

Purpose: To promote children's ability to identify and take ownership of their feelings.

Materials: Mood wheels for each child in a small group (five to six children). Create a mood wheel by cutting a piece of tagboard into a circle. Draw lines to divide the circle into fourths. On each section of the circle, draw a face that reflects one emotion (happy, sad, angry, afraid). Write the emotion word next to the picture. Laminate or cover with clear contact paper. Affix an arrow to the center of the wheel with a fastener, so that the arrow can be moved to point to any emotion on the wheel.

Procedure: Show one mood wheel to a small group of children who are sitting in a semicircle on the floor. Identify each emotion drawing. The teacher begins the activity by moving her arrow to point to a feeling face. She names the emotion, then states a reason or event that might make her feel that way. "I feel angry when I can't find my car keys." Describe situations familiar to young children. Pass out a mood wheel to each child. One at a time, give the children a chance to indicate how they are feeling by turning their arrow to a certain feeling face. Ask the children to explain why they are feeling that way.

Extensions: Allow the children to keep their mood wheel in their classroom cubbie. Children may use the mood wheel at any time during the day to indicate how they are feeling. Children can bring their mood wheel to circle time and have a chance to show their friends how they feel. The wheel can be used during a classroom incident to help children communicate their feeling at the moment. This might be especially helpful for children who have a hard time using words.

Name That Emotion Chart

Purpose: To identify emotions and use feeling words.

Materials: Chart with each child's name and a piece of Velcro next to their name. Laminated feeling face pictures with Velcro on the back.

Procedure: As children arrive each morning they select a feeling face picture that best depicts their emotional state and put it next to their name. Adults greeting children can discuss each child's choice. "I see that you chose a happy face. What made you happy today?"

Extensions: Encourage children to change their feeling face picture throughout the day as their feelings change.

Feelings Song

After you have introduced many feeling words to the children, add new verses to "If you're happy and you know it" song. Teach the children the words and some exaggerated gestures to make for each verse.

> If you're happy and you know it, give a smile.
> If you're sad and you know it, make a frown.
> If you're mad and you know it, use your words "I'm mad!"
> If you're scared and you know it, say "Yikes!"
> If you're silly and you know it, make a face.
> If you're tired and you know it, go to sleep.
> If you're proud and you know it, pat your back.

- Read and discuss emotion-related picture books. This exposure helps to create awareness that they are not the only children that get scared, feel sad, or are occasionally overcome by anger. Keep books about feelings in the book area.
- Display photos and posters of people with various emotional expressions throughout the room.
- Use sign language, if you know it, to teach children the signs for basic emotions. *Signs for Me* presents illustrations for 24 feelings (see Suggested Readings and Resources).
- Respect cultural variations in emotional expression and communication. (See Suggested Reading and Resources.) Teachers should learn several basic emotion words in the languages spoken by children in their classroom.

In addition, teachers need to provide opportunities for children to express their emotions nonverbally by providing materials that encourage self–expression and invite the expression of feelings and empathic behaviors through play. This might be particularly important for children with limited verbal abilities. Such materials include dolls of all sorts with appropriate clothes, combs, diapers, washcloths, blankets, and bottles; dollhouses with small figures and furniture; dress-up clothes; people and animal puppets; play telephones; mirrors; and caregiving prop boxes such as "veterinary office," "doctor's office," or "taking care of babies."

Art is particularly important as a means of self-expression. Sometimes art can open the way for children to talk about an emotionally laden event that they would not speak of otherwise. On a daily basis, children need to have access to many kinds of open-ended art materials such as an easel with paints and large brushes; fingerpaint; markers, crayons, and other drawing materials; play dough and clay; or collage materials.

ABILITY TO RECOGNIZE THE EMOTIONS OF OTHERS

In addition to an awareness of their own emotions, children need the ability to recognize the emotional content of voice, facial expression, and body language reflecting the emotions of others.

Empathy can be defined as understanding, being aware of, being sensitive to, and vicariously experiencing the feelings or thoughts of another person. Empathy leads to caring, altruism, and compassion. Until recently, it was widely believed that young children were too egocentric to be empathetic, but recent research documents that empathy skills begin to take form as early as infancy and toddlerhood. One-year-olds often imitate the distress behaviors of someone else, crying or approaching their mothers for comfort as if they had been hurt. Toddlers and preschoolers may attempt to comfort another person in distress by offering a toy or patting them (Zahn-Waxler, Radke-Yarrow, Wagner, & Chapman, 1992).

The moment Hope, just 9 months old, saw another baby fall, tears welled up in her own eyes and she crawled off to be comforted by her mother, as though it were she who had been hurt. And 15-month-old Michael went to get his own teddy bear for his crying friend Paul; when Paul kept crying, Michael retrieved Paul's security blanket for him (Goleman, 1995, p. 98).

Four-year-olds are generally able to take the role of another person in pretend play (Vygotsky, 1966), can recognize others' expression of basic feelings (such as happiness, sadness, fear, surprise, and anger), understand causes of emotions in common situations (Kuebli, 1994; Levine, 1995), recognize that different people can feel differently about the same event (Gnepp, Klayman, & Trabasso, 1982), and are able to distinguish intended actions from accidents but tend to believe that most actions are intentional unless an explanation is given (Shultz & Wells, 1985).

Helping Children Identify Emotions of Others and Practice Empathy

- Help children distinguish cues that suggest how another person is feeling. Point out facial expressions, body language, tone of voice, and situational cues. "Kaniesha is sad. She has tears in her eyes and her mouth is down in a frown. She fell and hurt her knee." "Seth is angry. His lips are pressed together and his eyebrows are squeezed down. He is angry because his blocks fell down."
- Conduct class meetings to help children recognize emotions by listening to the tone of a person's voice. Have puppets act out simple scenes and make statements using different tones of voice. When the puppet shouts, "You knocked down my blocks!" the children guess that the puppet is feeling angry.
- Use photos, books about feelings, and emotion posters to point out facial expressions and body language associated with a variety of feelings.
- After children have developed a feelings vocabulary and have begun to distinguish emotional expression, ask the questions, "Look at Marco's face. How is he feeling?" "How can you tell he is feeling scared?" "How does his face and body show he is feeling scared?"
- While reading stories to children, stop occasionally and ask children to identify the characters' feelings in the context of the story. Discuss how the characters' observable behaviors reveal their feelings.
- Do simple role-plays by asking children, "Show me how your body and face would look if:
    1. You got a birthday present.
    2. A big dog barked at you.
    3. A friend put a worm in your hand.
    4. You found a snake on the playground.
    5. You fell down and tore your new pants.
    6. A friend knocked down your blocks.
- Help children recognize that people may have different feelings about the same thing; people have different likes and dislikes. "Jason is excited when there is a thunderstorm, but Juanita gets scared." "Timmy likes to climb high on the jungle gym, but Sam doesn't."
- Help children recognize that their feelings about a situation may change. "Alejandra, you are feeling sad now and want to sit by yourself, but later you may feel differently and may want to join the group at circle."
- Create concrete ways for children to demonstrate empathy such as a "helping basket" with tissues, Band-Aids, and other items children can use to help another child feel better.

- Explain the process used to understand another person's feelings and model empathic responses (Slaby, Roedell, Arezzo, & Hendrix, 1995).
    1. Identify the distress of another person. ("Irina is crying—she looks sad.")
    2. Try to figure out what is happening. ("Let's ask Irina why she is sad.")
    3. Figure out what others might feel in the same situation. ("Irina is sad because she tripped on the playground. She hurt her knee. I cry, too, when I hurt myself.")
    4. Assess what the other person needs. ("What would make you feel better, Irina? Do you want a cold cloth on your knee?")
    5. Try to comfort or meet the needs of the distressed person. ("Let's go get a cold cloth and a drink of water for Irina.")
    6. Demonstrate pleasure at the other person's relief or comfort. ("Irina stopped crying. Are you feeling better, Irina? I'm glad you feel better now.")
- Use puppets or dolls to role-play situations depicting different feelings. For example, act out a situation about a boy who is sad after breaking his favorite truck. Ask the children what the boy might need in order to feel better (e.g., to fix the truck with glue).

UNDERSTANDING THE SITUATIONS OR REACTIONS THAT PRODUCE EMOTIONAL STATES

It is important to help children to understand that there is a connection between a situation and the emotion it engenders (realizing what is behind a feeling) and to connect feelings with behavior. Teachers can help children become consciously aware of the link between loss and sadness, between frustration and anger, between fatigue and "grouchiness," or between threats to their safety and fear.

Teachers can draw children's attention to the context of a situation that triggered an emotion ("Miraya's painting got torn. That made her sad. She wanted to show her picture to her mommy."), offer explanations for events as children experience them (affective reflections), and help children anticipate situations that may evoke strong feelings ("At the fire station today, the firefighters will turn on the siren on the truck. It will be very noisy, and that might be a little scary.").

MANAGING EMOTIONS (EMOTIONAL REGULATION)

Emotional regulation includes the ability to express a range of emotions and react in appropriate ways in emotional situations. Children exhibiting emotional regulation skills usually adjust well to new people and situations, show a high tolerance for frustration, control their negative emotions, and consider the needs and preferences of others.

Young children who have difficulties with emotional regulation may portray few emotions, show signs of depression, cry excessively, have difficulty coping, worry excessively, or engage in inappropriate behaviors in response to intense emotions (Wittmer, Doll, & Strain, 1996). Internalizing behavior problems are characterized by social withdrawal, isolation, fearfulness, depression, dependence, and anxiety, whereas externalizing behavior problems are characterized by outbursts of emotional expression including anger, aggression, selfishness, and oppositional behaviors (Fox, 1994).

Identifying and expressing emotions verbally is the first step in learning to regulate emotions. Children may fail to express emotions verbally because they mistakenly think that others obviously know what they are feeling, they lack the words to use, or they are too emotional to use them (Kostelnik, Whiren, Soderman, Stein, & Gregory, 2002). Teachers help children learn to express emotions in acceptable ways by reminding them to use words to explain what they need ("Matthew, tell David, 'I'm not done with the fire truck yet,'" or "Holly, tell Angelica, 'I don't like it when you are bossy.'") and suggesting phrases to use in emotional situations:

"I want a turn, too."

"I want to do it my way this time."

"You can have it when I'm finished."

"Let's make a list for turns."

Sometimes, teachers need to acknowledge a child's feelings while insisting that hurtful actions are not tolerated, then suggesting the use of words to express feelings.

"Jacob, when Toby took your toy that really made you angry. But I can't let you hit Toby. Hitting hurts. You need to *tell* him what you feel. Say, 'I don't like it when you grab my toy.'"

Managing emotions also includes the ability to inhibit inappropriate impulsive behavior when experiencing strong emotions and calming down enough to use problem-solving strategies. Problem solving, calming down steps, and stress reduction will be covered in chapters 7, 8, and 9, respectively.

HANDLING RELATIONSHIPS

Emotional intelligence in handling relationships involves the ability to recognize another's feelings and to act in a way that is in tune with those feelings. These are the social competencies that make for effectiveness in dealings with others (Goleman, 1995). For young children, these skills include the ability to solve problems in relationships (see Chapter 7), being appropriately assertive rather than angry or passive (see Chapter 8), communication skills such as listening and asking questions, engaging in prosocial behaviors (sharing, cooperation, helpfulness, etc.), and being appropriately involved with peers (see Chapter 6)

KEY TERMS AND CONCEPTS

Emotional intelligence or **emotional literacy**: the ability to recognize, label, and understand feelings in one's self and others

Affective reflections: nonjudgmental statements that describe the emotion of the child and help children feel understood and accepted

Empathy: understanding, being aware of, being sensitive to, and vicariously experiencing the feelings or thoughts of another person.

Emotional regulation: the ability to express a range of emotions and react in appropriate ways in emotional situations

Feelings vocabulary: a bank of emotion words to express a variety of feelings

LEARNING IN ACTION: SMALL GROUP ACTIVITIES AND FIELD ASSIGNMENTS

1. Working in pairs, brainstorm two activities designed to help children identify primary emotions (happy, sad, angry, afraid, or surprised). Design one activity that is mostly language-based and one activity that uses concrete props and actions. How will these activities be presented to children (small group, large group, or individually)?
2. Read one of the children's books about feelings listed in this chapter to a small group of children. Record the comments they make. Decide on a follow-up activity to the book.
3. For each of the following scenarios, describe:
    - What emotions the children involved might be feeling
    - How you would use the strategies presented in this chapter to help the children recognize and label their own feelings and acknowledge and respond to the feelings of others

Scenario 1
Aysha was walking toward the sink carrying a pitcher of water when she accidentally bumped into Kimberly and spilled water all over her. Kimberly looked down at her brand new dress covered with water and began to cry. (Both of these children are 4 years old.)

Scenario 2
Sam and Abdul were playing together in the block area, building an airport for their toy planes. Sam pretended to land one of the planes and mistakenly knocked over the airport "tower." Abdul yelled at him, "You dummy. You knocked over the tower!" (Both of these children are 4 years old.)

Scenario 3
Evan sat by himself playing with Legos™. When Mario attempted to use some of the many Legos™ left in the basket, Evan pulled the basket closer to himself and pushed Mario away. When Mario attempted to defend his right to use some Legos™, Evan swept the entire basket off onto the floor, where the Legos™ scattered across the room. (Both of these children are 5 years old.)

RELATED CHILDREN'S BOOKS

Aaron, J.(1998). *When I'm angry*. New York: Golden.
Aliki.(1984). *Feelings*. New York: A Mulberry Paperback Book.
Anholt, C., & Anholt, L.(1994). *What makes me happy?* Cambridge, MA: Candlewick Press.

Argueta, B. (1998). *Baby faces.* New York: Playschool Books.

Avery, C. (1992). *Everybody has feelings/Todos tenemos sentimientos.* Beltsville, MD: Gryphon House, Inc.

Aylesworth, J. (1997). *Teddy bear tears.* New York: Aladdin Paperbacks.

Berry, J. (1995). *Let's talk about feeling afraid.* New York: Scholastic, Inc. This book is part of a series: Feeling Angry, Saying No, Feeling Sad, Being Helpful, and Needing Attention.

Carle, E. (1977). *The grouchy ladybug.* New York: Scholastic, Inc.

Conlin, S., & Friedman, S. L. (1991). *All my feelings at preschool: Nathan's day.* Seattle, WA: Parenting Press.

Crary, E. (1992). *I'm frustrated.* Seattle, WA: Parenting Press. Other titles are: *I'm Mad, I'm Proud, I'm Furious, I'm Scared,* and *I'm Excited.*

Crary, E., & Steelsmith, S. (1996). *When you're mad and you know it.* Seattle, WA: Parenting Press. Series: mad, happy, shy, and silly.

Eisenberg, P. (1986). *You're my Nikki.* New York: Dial Books for Young Readers.

Everitt, B. (1992). *Mean soup.* San Diego: Harcourt Brace.

Fernandes, E. (1987). *A difficult day.* Toronto, Canada: Little Kids Press Ltd.

Henkes, K. (2000). *Wemberly worried.* Hong Kong: Greenwillow Books.

Hubbard, W. (1990). *C is for curious: An ABC of feelings.* San Francisco, CA: Chronicle Books.

Labrosse, D. (1998). *The grumpy morning.* New York: Hyperion Books for Children.

Leonard, M. (1997). *How I feel: Angry.* San Diego, CA: Smart Kids Publishing, Inc. Part of a series: Angry, Happy, Scared, Silly.

Mayer, M. (1983). *I was so mad.* Racine, WI: Western Publishing Company Inc.

Mayer, M. (1990). *There's a nightmare in my closet.* New York: Dial Books for Young Readers.

Mayer, M., & Mayer, G. (1995). *Just a bad day.* New York: Golden Books.

Miranda, A. (1997). *Glad monster, sad monster: A book about feelings.* Boston, MA: Little, Brown & Company.

Modesitt, J. (1992). *Sometimes I feel like a mouse.* New York: Scholastic, Inc.

Murphy, J. (1985). *Feelings.* Ontario, Canada: Black Moss.

Prestine, J. (1993). *Sometimes I feel awful.* Torrance, CA: Fearon Teacher Aids.

Simon, N. (1989). *I am not a crybaby.* New York: Puffin Books.

SUGGESTED READING AND RESOURCES

Acredolo, L., & Goodwyn, S. (1996). *Baby signs: How to talk with your baby before your baby can talk.* Chicago: Contemporary Books.

Bahan, B., & Dannis, J. (1990). *Signs for me: Basic sign vocabulary for children, parents, and teachers.* Dawn Sign Press.

Committee for Children. (2002). *Second Step: A violence prevention curriculum for preschoolers and kindergartners.* (3rd ed.). Seattle, WA: Committee for Children.

Garcia, J. (1999). *Sign with your baby: How to communicate with infants before they can speak.* Seattle, WA: Northlight Communications/Stratton-Kehl Publications, Inc.

Hewitt, D., & Heidemann, S. (1998). *The optimistic classroom.* St. Paul, MN: Redleaf Press.

Hyson, M. (1994). *The emotional development of young children.* New York: Teachers College Press.

Kusche, C. A., & Greenberg, M. T. (1994). *The PATHS Curriculum*. Seattle, WA: Developmental Research and Programs.

Locke, D. C. (1992). *Increasing multicultural understanding*. Newbury Park, CA: Sage Publications.

Lynch, E. W., & Hanson, M. C. (1992). *Developing cross-cultural competence: A guide for working with young children and their families*. Baltimore, MD: Paul H. Brookes Publishing Co., Inc.

Rice, J. A. (1995). *The kindness curriculum*. St. Paul, MN: Redleaf Press.

Smith, C. A. (1993). *The peaceful classroom*. Mt. Rainier, MD: Gryphon House, Inc.

Webster-Stratton, C. (1990). *The teachers and children videotape series: Dina dinosaur school*. Seattle, WA: The Incredible Years.

REFERENCES

Arsenio, W. F., Cooperman, S., & Lover, A. (2000). Affective predictors of preshoolers' aggression and peer acceptance. *Developmental Psychology, 36*, 438–448.

Committee for Children. (2002). *Second Step: A violence prevention curriculum for preschoolers and kindergartners*. (3rd ed.). Seattle, WA: Committee for Children.

Denham, S. A., McKinley, M., Couchoud, E., & Holt, R. (1990). Emotional and behavioral predictors of preschool peer ratings. *Child Development, 61*, 1145–1152.

Feldman, R. S., McGee, G., Mann, L., & Strain, P. S. (1993). Nonverbal affective decoding ability in children with autism and in typical preschoolers. *Journal of Early Intervention, 17*(4), 341–350.

Fox, N. (1994). The development of emotion regulation: Biological and behavioral considerations. Monographs of the Society for Research in *Child Development, 59*(2–3, Serial No. 240).

Gnepp, J., Klayman, J., & Trabasso, S. (1982). A hierarchy of information sources for inferring emotional reactions. *Journal of Experimental Psychology, 33*, 111–123.

Goleman, D. (1995). Emotional intelligence. New York: Bantam Books.

Hart, B., & Risley, T. (1995). *Meaningful differences in the everyday experience of young American children*. Baltimore: Paul H. Brooks.

Izard, C., Fine, S., Schultz, D., Mostow, A., & Ackerman, B. (2001). Emotional knowledge and social behavior. *Psychological Science, 12*, 18–23.

Kindlon, D., & Thompson, M. (1999). *Raising Cain: Protecting the emotional life of boys*. New York: Ballantine Publishing Group.

Kostelnik, M. J., Whiren, A. P., Soderman, A. K., Stein, L., & Gregory, K. (2002). *Guiding children's social development*. Albany, NY: Delmar.

Kuebli, J. (1994). Young children's understanding of everyday emotions. *Young Children, 49*(3), 36–47.

Levine, L.J. (1995). Young children's understanding of the causes of anger and sadness. *Child Development, 66*, 697–709.

Lewis, M., & Michalson, L. (1993). *Children's emotions and moods: developmental theory and measurement*. New York: Plenum Press.

Salovey, P., & Mayer, J. D. (1990). Emotional intelligence. Imagination, Cognition, and *Personality, 9*, 185–211.

Shultz, T. R., & Wells, D. (1985). Judging the intentionality of action-outcomes. *Developmental Psychology, 21,* 83–89.

Slaby, R., Roedell, W., Arezzo, D., & Hendrix, K. (1995). *Early violence prevention: Tools for teachers of young children.* Washington, DC: National Association for the Education of Young Children.

Vygotsky, L. S. (1966). Play and its role in the mental development of the child. *Soviet Psychology, 12,* 62–76.

Webster-Stratton, C. (1999). *How to promote children's social and emotional competence.* London: Paul Chapman Publishing.

Wittmer, D., Doll, B., & Strain, P. (1996). Social and emotional development in early childhood: The identification of competence and disabilities. *Journal of Early Intervention, 20*(4), 299–318.

Zahn-Waxler, M., Radke-Yarrow, M., Wagner, E., & Chapman, M. (1992). Development of concern for others. *Developmental Psychology, 28,* 126–136.

Chapter 6

ENHANCING PROSOCIAL SKILLS

Four-year-old Joseph chooses the block-building center. He builds next to two other boys for a few minutes, then he turns around and knocks their bridge down. The boys build their bridge up again. A few minutes later Joseph knocks it down. The boys go to the teacher to complain. The teacher returns with them to the block area and discusses the problem with all three children. She talks about how to be a friend and how to cooperate. Joseph listens and then walks away sulkily. Similar situations develop when he plays in the housekeeping area and the puzzles. The teacher continues to talk with Joseph and the children involved about how to join in to play and how to take care of each other.

Compare this scene with one several weeks later. Joseph approaches the block center. He stands and watches two other children building. Soon one 3-year-old grabs two large blocks from the builders. Joseph turns to the children whose blocks have been taken and says, "He's just little. We have to help him learn."

Over time, Joseph's teacher helped him recognize prosocial actions—concern for others, taking care of and defending others, joining a group, and being a friend. Through modeling, focused discussions, gentle direction, and patience, Joseph's teacher enabled him to develop and apply new prosocial skills.

Socially skilled young children are well-integrated within their peer groups and demonstrate behaviors such as being friendly toward another child, helping, sharing, taking turns, working together, negotiating, cooperating, comforting, defending, showing concern, and demonstrating empathy. Socially skilled children are generally cooperative with adults, appropriately compliant, welcome teacher participation in their activities, and accept adult suggestions for compromises in a conflict situation.

WHY ARE PROSOCIAL SKILLS IMPORTANT?

Prosocial behaviors are positive social actions performed to benefit others. These socially desirable behaviors allow a group, community, or society to work for the common good. Children who engage in prosocial patterns of interaction with others enjoy their relationships with children and adults and receive more positive feedback in their encounters. Social competence is critical to the well-being of the individual and to the smooth functioning of the group. Katz & McClellan (1997) conclude that "most of the experiences people count as meaningful and significant include or even depend on relations with others." In recent years, research has shown that social competence forms the foundation of academic learning and is a strong predictor of academic success, with lasting effects into adulthood (Bandura, Barbaranelli, Caprara, & Pastorelli, 1996; Peth-Pierce, 2001).

Peer relationships in childhood are shown to be the single best predictor of adult adaptation and success (McClellan and Katz, 1993). Prosocial children are rated as more likeable by their peers and are sought out as playmates, whereas children who are not able to engage in prosocial actions are at risk of being disliked and developing negative peer reputations (Denham, McKinley, Couchoud, & Holt, 1990).

Children lacking social skills tend to be overly dependent on adults, interrupt their interactions with peers to request adult help when it is unnecessary, and cling to the teacher

(Katz & McClellan, 1997). They may be oppositional, resist adult authority, defy instructions, and reject adult suggestions for negotiating conflict (Kuczynski & Kochanska, 1990).

Young children with poor social skills are seriously at risk for lifelong problems extending from school to family to the work place and the community (Katz & McClellan, 1997).

WHY ARE SOME CHILDREN NOT DEVELOPING PROSOCIAL SKILLS?

Children are not born knowing prosocial skills, nor do they grow up learning them in all environments. Positive social behaviors are most likely to be developed by children who have had a close bonding experience with a loving caregiver and have participated in a relationship of trust and attachment to a reliable adult. However, even children who have had this positive period in their youngest years can be impacted negatively by other environmental factors as they grow. The ever-increasing quantity of violence shown on television and in videos and video games has a significant negative impact on young children (Levin, 1998). Exposure to antisocial behaviors by real-life models (such as politicians, professional athletes, movie stars, and wrestlers) and fantasy figures (such as superheroes) has a powerful influence on young children.

Children model their actions and words directly upon the actions and words they see and hear in their own lives. If adults have neither practiced nor taught positive social skills to them, children will have had little opportunity to see or learn these. Too many children today have not experienced prosocial behaviors directed towards them or others in their environments while simultaneously, they are exposed to negative lessons as they witness or participate in negative social behaviors.

Even under the best of circumstances, children need time and practice to become good at prosocial behaviors. Opportunity to interact with peers and to see the consequences of their behaviors is a powerful learning experience for all children.

Thus it is incumbent upon early childhood educators to make a concerted, programmed effort to teach and role-model prosocial skills and provide young children with experiences designed to improve their social skills. Such a program can have tremendous positive effects on children's development and on replacing negative, aggressive behaviors with positive, constructive, and cooperative behaviors. Strategies to promote prosocial skills are appropriate for all children, no matter their extent of risk, their age or social-cultural background, or their developmental level.

TEACHING PROSOCIAL SKILLS

The preschool years are an optimal time to start teaching social skills. Even young children can learn social skills given terms they can understand and plenty of concrete examples and chances to practice (Mize & Ladd, 1990). Following are several social skills strategies successful with young children.

Show We Value Prosocial Behavior

Educators can consciously re-balance the time and energy given to negative behaviors by increasing their reinforcement of children's positive behaviors. This simple change in adult behavior will make an immediate difference in children's behavior as they instinctively move to do what the adult shows she likes. Prosocial behaviors are increased when "adults implement curriculum that promotes interpersonal consideration and cooperation in children" (Wittmer & Honig, 1994, p.4). Thus, instead of initially responding to the child who is disrupting group time, the teacher will say "Thank you for listening" to the children who are indeed listening.

Frequent acknowledgement of prosocial behavior facilitates perspective-taking and empathy skills in young children.

> I kneeled on the floor to join two boys using turkey basters at the water table. One not so accurate aim resulted in me being squirted on my sweater. I said, "I'm all wet." To which one boy said, "You should be wearing a paint shirt. They're over there." He proceeded to go across the room, get a vinyl paint shirt, and hand it to me. "Now you won't get wet."

Be Very Specific When Encouraging Prosocial Behavior

"You really helped Darian. You carried that toy with him." "You were being a friend to Wei when you made sure she got some markers." "Thank you for sharing the play dough with Shandra." "You were very kind, Adak, when you found a Band-Aid for Christina." "You four children did such a terrific job cooperating to put the blocks away." Toddlers, who are naturally just beginning to be aware of others, may be surprised at first to hear these comments but will soon become quite accustomed to them.

Help Children Use Specific Prosocial Skills Throughout the Day

Maintain age appropriate expectation while helping children use prosocial skills during their regular day. For example, teach children the difference between sharing and taking turns. **Sharing** means two people using the same thing at the same time. Children can share a large chunk of play dough (and should be helped to practice doing so), but they cannot share a single magic marker. **Taking turns** means one person uses the object while the other one waits (or does something else), then the second person uses the object. Thus, children can take turns using a single magic marker. Kindergarten and older children can easily learn the difference between sharing and taking turns and even start to learn how to trade while preschoolers need time to adjust to these new concepts.

> Four children were playing in the rocking boat and there was no more room in the boat. One little girl was looking on, wanting to get in and almost ready to cry. Heather got out of the boat and said, "Marlene, you get in. We're taking turns."

Preschoolers can be expected to share some of the time but not all of the time. Provide duplicates of some popular materials (especially for infants and toddlers) so the need for sharing is reduced. Miller (2000) suggests that teachers "show children where to safely place personal items brought from home that they aren't willing to share" (p. 33).

Facilitate Friendship Skills

The inability to make a new friend, to maintain a friendship, or to join in with a group of other children is often the cause of anger, frustration, or aggression. For some children, these are occasional problems while for others, they are an ongoing source of difficulty and disappointment. Children of different ages have different problems with friendship skills. Toddlers are just beginning to feel comfortable playing alongside another child and participating in minimal interaction; they benefit from having an adult as part of the group. Older children see the advantages of friendship but need help with how to be a friend. (See Appendix A for lesson plans on Friendship.)

One teacher in a preschool classroom recognized that successful friendships for young children depend upon an array of prosocial skills. This teacher described her work on friendship:

> I work on friendship skills the whole year, but one month I actually label "Friendship Month" and write up my lesson plans all around activities dealing with friendship. We read books about friendship such as *Just My Friend and Me* and *I'm Not Your Friend*. Even when a book isn't directly about friends, I relate it to friendship. The children help me make a colorful poster about friendship. This time the theme was "Ask a friend for help." The culmination of our month is a family event we called Friendship Celebration.

Teach Group Entry Skills and Play Partner Behaviors

Entering groups is a vital skill for play success. The following is a sequence of behaviors that results in the most positive peer response (Kaiser & Rasminsky, 2003):
1. Waiting and observing on the outskirts of the group to get a sense of the group's activities.
2. Mimicking the actions of the children in the group.
3. Saying something positive that relates to the group's activity and expressing interest. Adults can help children by giving them specific words to use ("I'd like to play trucks with you." "Are you building a bridge?") or actions to take such as bringing a relevant prop to add to the play.

To organize and extend children's play, adults can model play partner behaviors such as statements to suggest a new play idea ("Let's build a road."), suggest roles ("You be the dumptruck driver."), or suggest specific activities to achieve a goal ("You bring the long blocks over here."). Eventually, children incorporate these behaviors into their play without adult facilitation.

Some children need help finding a playmate. Adults can bring children together who have common interests ("Dakota likes to build with blocks just like you do.") or plan paired activities such as errands or painting side by side at the easel.

Integrate Concrete Props When Teaching Prosocial Skills

- Use puppets to do puppet role-plays of typical classroom experiences in which children have to share or take turns or use other prosocial skills.
- During a class meeting discussion, make charts that reinforce prosocial skills, such as a chart of "Who was a friend to you today?" or "Did anyone ask you for help today?" An interesting variation on the regular job chart is one that identifies which children

can help others with various classroom tasks (Levin, 2003). This chart can be titled "Who to Ask for Help" or "I Can Help You." Using a large, white poster board, the teacher makes boxes with each having a classroom task (such as feeding the fish, washing tables, building with blocks, tying shoes, writing letters, or zipping coats), an illustration of the task, and two pieces of Velcro that can hold children's names. At a class meeting, she asks the children which task each can help others with. If a child cannot identify a task or wants to add a new one, the teacher can provide assistance. Each child then puts her name on the Velcro in the appropriate box. The chart is read often at class meetings and referred to during the regular school day when help is needed by anyone. "Remember, Kim can spell your name." Older children can add or change their names on their own but should be reminded to check before removing anyone's name.

- Use large pictures or posters to show children in situations where taking turns or being a friend or defending someone occur. The *Second Step* program (Committee for Children, 2002) is an example of an excellent curriculum that helps teachers plan lessons such as these. Teaching materials include large photographs of children in typical school situations to encourage discussion and suggestions for questions and role-plays.

- Create writing projects that focus on prosocial skills. One preschool teacher found that every few weeks, at least one child left the school or was away for an extended period of time. She brought this up at a class meeting, and together she and the class recognized that they missed the children who were not there. They made a bulletin board labeled "People Who We Miss." Everyone was encouraged to dictate stories and draw pictures about the people whom they missed. This became an ongoing project throughout the year.

- Change the dramatic play area to encourage prosocial themes. Using prop boxes of related materials, the children can act out behaviors related to a hospital, a veterinarian office, a rescue squad, a zoo nursery, or a plant shop. Teachers can provide toddlers with infant diapers, bottles, pacifiers, blankets, and baby beds so they can practice good caregiving skills.

Select Books with Prosocial Themes

Read books that help children understand prosocial behaviors and see admirable characters engaging in these behaviors. (See list of children's books at the end of this chapter.) Highlight the prosocial behaviors by asking questions about them. Kindergarten and older children can rewrite endings or develop sequels.

Plan Fun Activities that Highlight Prosocial Skills

When one teacher was working on the prosocial skill of cooperation, she planned a special snack time involving taking turns, thinking of others, and cooperation. Each child had a partner. Their job was to make ice cream sundaes for their partner. First, one child would ask the other which flavor she wanted, which syrup she wanted, and which topping. Then, she would make the sundae and give it to her partner. The partner would then ask the first child which flavor, syrup, and toppings she wanted and make her sundae for her.

Another teacher used a multi-pieced caterpillar puzzle for taking attendance each day. Each piece of the puzzle had one child's name written on the back, and all the children learned to recognize which piece was for each of the classmates. When Ann took attendance, she would raise a puzzle piece, and the appropriate child would say "I'm here." If a child were absent, Ann would say, "This is Joseph's piece. He's not coming to school today because he is sick. How does our puzzle look?" The children would say "It doesn't look good now" or "Something is missing" or "We are missing Joseph."

Adrienne, a first grade teacher, developed a long unit on friendship based on Patricia Polacco's book *Mrs. Katz and Tush*. After reading the book several times with the children, she held a class meeting to gather ideas for how to apply the book's theme in their own class. One of the first ideas on their list was to find an older woman whom they could befriend, based on the intergenerational theme of the book. One of the children said that he had a "grandma at home who doesn't have any friends." The children wrote her notes asking her to visit their class. During subsequent class meetings, the class talked about how to prepare for Grandma's visit. They voted on what food to cook and what games to have ready. They decided to ask her questions about her background, as the child does in the book. Several of the children made pictures for Grandma to take back home with her, and others began work on building picture frames. Adrienne talked with the children about older people and their needs and brought in related library books. One boy suggested they borrow a rocking chair from another classroom when Grandma came. After Grandma's visit, which was very successful, Adrienne reviewed with the children what made their time together so nice—how all had shown friendship skills. She helped the children write notes to Grandma, and then introduced another theme from the book—that of intercultural understanding and friendships between people of different backgrounds.

Promote Acceptance and Respect for Diversity

Help children respect both similarities and differences among them—in learning style, dress, skin color, ethnicity, family composition, cultural customs, religion, language, gender, abilities, and ideas. Children can learn that it is okay to be different, that they all do not have to like the same things, look the same way, or be able to do the same things. Young children can identify personal preferences (such as what they prefer for snack or their favorite television show) and see that some others may feel the same way and still others may feel very differently. "Comments such as, 'Hey, my grandma lives at our house too!' or 'Our family likes to play a game like bocce, but we call it bowling,' are indicators that children are building bridges between each other" (McCracken, 1993, p. 16).

Young children can learn to appreciate differences through many types of activities. Preschool children enjoy cooking projects, art, and singing songs. Primary grade children can explore diversity by researching different home styles, designing blueprints for them, and building houses with blocks and cartons.

Educators can help children redefine stereotypes by expanding ideas. Derman-Sparks (1992, p. 5) cites an example of a teacher who notices a group of children playing in the sandbox.

> The girls cook and the boys dig tunnels. One boy calls out to the girls, "We're finished working now. Get us our supper." At group time their teacher decides to read one book about the different kinds of work women do and another book about men doing household work. The next day she helps each child make a book about what kinds of work, at home and out of the home, their own family members do, pointing out the diversity of roles.

Early care providers can also help children talk about differences they notice. Crary (1992) offers guidelines for dealing with children's questions about physical, ethnic, or racial differences.

Replace Competitive Games and Activities with Cooperative Activities

One teacher described how she adapted the traditionally competitive musical chairs game with her group of 3-year-olds:

> First we played musical chairs in the traditional way, taking away one chair each time the music ended. Then we had a discussion about how it felt to be left out. "Not so good" most of the children said. We brainstormed ways we could make things better. The children came up with many ideas: squeeze together, use laps, don't take away any chairs, or just play.
>
> They all loved the new musical chairs and asked to play it often. It turned out to be a great help for other situations in our classroom too—like letting others join in games or block building.

Create activities and tasks that need more than one child to accomplish. Cooking and gardening projects depend on cooperation as does carrying a heavy pail or taping large pieces of paper on the wall. *The Peaceful Classroom* (Smith, 1993) has many suggestions for cooperative games and activities.

Develop a Sense of Group Association and Belonging

Sing songs that help children identify the names of their peers and that recognize the class as a group. Recognize and celebrate children's accomplishments together: "Jenny learned to button her coat today." Develop a sense of the group as an identifiable unit by having a class book with children's photos as they grow and change and do things together during the year, have a class name or logo, or make class t-shirts. Older children can practice complimenting each other and identifying actions that would make their classroom a better place.

Invite Community People to Speak to Children

Young children respond particularly well to teenagers. Older children may listen to sports figures or local news anchors. Follow up these visits with projects to help the community, such as visits to a nursing home to sing songs or help with local gardening projects.

SUPPORTING PEER INTERACTION SKILLS FOR CHILDREN WITH SPECIAL NEEDS

When they enter early childhood care and education settings, children with disabilities generally display fewer socially competent behaviors, including peer interactions, than their typically developing peers (Kopp, Baker, & Brown, 1992; Merrell & Holland, 1997). Fortunately, in classrooms where teachers consistently implement the strategies for teaching prosocial skills presented in the previous section, children with special needs can learn and use positive friendship and play skills (Adams, 2002). To further assist in their beginning attempts to practice friendship skills, the use of a "buddy system" has been particularly helpful (Joseph & Strain, 2002).

In a buddy system, children are assigned a partner or small group before a free-play period. They begin freeplay in some planned play activity with their partner or group for the first 10 minutes of free choice time. Joseph and Strain (2002) suggest several guidelines to enhance the success of using buddies:

- Assign two or more buddies for each child with special needs to keep the play interesting for the socially competent children and maximize modeling of positive play behaviors.
- Rotate buddies so that children have the opportunity to engage in friendship skills with a wide variety of playmates and children do not resent being "assigned" to play with the same individual or group.
- Pair the most popular children with those that need the most help—this increases the social acceptance of peers helping peers.
- At the end of the free-play period, praise children for being buddies, mentioning specific ways children interacted positively with their assigned buddies.

Another less formal way to encourage children to interact with peers is to set up a "buddy" table. Set out high-preference toys or materials at the table. Before the free-play period, announce that children must find a friend to play with in order to come to the buddy table.

INCLUDING FAMILIES IN TEACHING PROSOCIAL SKILLS

Involve parents and other family members with your work on prosocial skills. Communicate in person, by phone calls, and newsletters what you are trying to accomplish and why. Since children in early childhood settings come from so many different backgrounds and cultures, providers often need to learn more about the various backgrounds represented in their group. Cultural background influences interpretations of social behaviors, such as eye contact, use of praise, sharing feelings, and nonverbal behaviors such as gestures (Gopaul-McNicol & Thomas-Presswood, 1998). Parents can be very helpful in promoting cross-cultural understanding, explaining customs and individual preferences.

Send home books with prosocial themes. Give parents suggestions of age-appropriate videos and television shows that reinforce prosocial behaviors. Ask parents for ideas for prosocial resources.

Invite parents, grandparents, and siblings to the early childhood setting to talk about their own prosocial activities at work or in the community.

Offer parents specific prosocial activities they can do at home (see Figure 6.1 for sample family newsletter).

FIGURE 6.1

CARES for FAMILIES

Activities in your child's class this month are focusing on sharing, cooperating, being a friend, developing empathy (understanding another person's feelings), showing kindness, and caring for others. Sometimes we call these *prosocial skills.*

Research shows that the single best childhood predictor of adult success is not IQ, nor even school grades, but the adequacy with which the child gets along with others. Children with prosocial skills are less aggressive and better problem solvers. So it is in the best interests of all our children, our communities, and our society to place importance on learning and expanding prosocial skills.

One way of helping children become aware of others is to make taking care of someone else fun. You and your child might enjoy this teddy bear pretend game together.

- Have your child choose a Teddy bear or other stuffed animal for a special "kindness day."

- Make up things to do for the Teddy bear, such as offering him his favorite food or playing a special game with him.

- Pretend with your child that Teddy gets sick sometime during the day. Together with your child put Teddy to bed, cool her forehead with a wet wash cloth, put a blanket over her, sing her a song, read her a story.

- Compliment your child for being kind, gentle, and caring.

KEY TERMS AND CONCEPTS

Prosocial behavior: positive social actions performed to benefit others

Sharing: more than one child using materials at the same time

Taking turns: one person using an object at a time, while another person waits for a turn with that object

LEARNING IN ACTION:
SMALL GROUP ACTIVITIES AND FIELD ASSIGNMENTS

1. Observe in an early childhood setting. Note each prosocial behavior one child exhibits, her age, and the teacher's response.
2. In a small group, develop several children's activities that promote the prosocial skills of caretaking and gentleness. Reference some of the ideas in this chapter. Record the objective of each of your activities, the age group, the materials needed, and the roles of teacher and other adults in the room.
3. The following activity is for the adult class and can be done in groups of 10-16. One blown-up balloon and one leader is needed for each circle.

    Each group stands and makes a circle. Pairs of people become partners, with each holding one hand behind her back and clasping the partner's hand with her other hand. The leader tosses the balloon into the air. The group's task is to keep the balloon afloat. Each pair can use only their clasped hands to keep the balloon afloat.

    After the circle has accomplished their task (it may take several tries), they return to their seats and discuss the activity. What prosocial skills were involved? How did they work as a team?

RELATED CHILDREN'S BOOKS

Allan-Meyer, K. (1995). *I have a new friend: A true story of two friends from different worlds.* Hauppauge, NY: Barron's Educational Series.
Berenstain, S., & Berenstain, J. (1994). *No se permiten ninas.* New York: Random House.
Bourgeois, P. (1994). *Franklin is bossy.* New York: Scholastic Paperbacks.
Brown, M. (1998). *Arthur's boo-boo book.* New York: Random House.
Canizares, S., & Chessen, B. (1999). *Two can do it!* New York: Scholastic Inc.
Carlson, N. (1992). *Arnie and the new kid.* New York: Puffin Books.
Cheltenham Elementary School Kindergartners. (1991). *We are all alike . . .we are all different.* New York: Scholastic.
Cosby, B. (1997). *The best way to play.* New York: Cartwheel Scholastic.
Cosby, B. (1999). *Hooray for the dandelion warriors.* New York: Cartwheel Scholastic.
Dwight, L. (1997). *We can do it!* New York: Star Bright Books.
Hallinan, P. K. (1994). *A rainbow of friends.* Nashville, TN: Ideal Children's Books.
Henkes, K. (1988). *Chester's way.* New York: Mulberry Books.

Hoffman, E. (1999). *Play lady/la senora juguetona*. Beltsville, MD: Redleaf Press.

Hutchins, P. (1986). *The doorbell rang*. Littleton, MA: Sundance Publishers and Distributors.

Lobel, A. (1979). *Frog and toad are friends*. New York: HarperCollins.

Martin, A. (1993). *Rachel Parker, kindergarten show-off*. New York: Scholastic.

Minarik, E. (1988). *Little bear's friend*. New York: Harper Trophy.

Petty, K., & Firmin, C. (1991). *Feeling left out*. Hauppauge, NY: Barron's Educational Series.

Petty, K., & Firmin, C. (1991). *Making friends*. Hauppauge, NY: Barron's Educational Series.

Pfister, M. (2001). *Where is my friend?* New York: North South Books.

Polacco, P. (1992). *Mrs. Katz and Tush*. New York: Dell Publishing.

Silverstein, S. (2002). *The giving tree*. New York: HarperCollins.

Simon, C. (1999). *Wash day*. Brookfield, CT: Millbrook Press, Inc.

Stimson, J., & Rutherford, M. (1998). *Oscar needs a friend*. Hauppauge, NY: Barron's Educational Series, Inc.

Thomas, P. (2001). *My friends and me: A first look at friendship*. New York: Mulberry Books.

Tidd, L. (1999). *Let me help!* Brookfield, CT: Millbrook Press, Inc.

Welch, W. (2000). Playing right field. New York: Scholastic, Inc.

Williams, R. (1997). *Nosotros podemos compartir en la escuela*. Cypress, CA: Creative Teaching Press.

Zolotow, C. (1997). *My friend John*. New York: Dragonfly Books.

SUGGESTED READING AND RESOURCES

Acredolo, L., & Goodwyn, S. (1996). *Baby signs: How to talk with your baby before your baby can talk*. Chicago: Contemporary Books.

Bahan, B., & Dannis, J. (1990). *Signs for me: Basic sign vocabulary for children, parents, and teachers*. Dawn Sign Press.

Beaty, J. J. (1999). *Prosocial guidance for the preschool child*. Upper Saddle River, NJ: Merrill/Prentice Hall.

Bleiker, C. (1999). Toddler friendship: The case of Hiro and John. *Young Children, 54*(6), 18–23.

Copple, C. (2003). *A world of difference: Readings on teaching young children in a diverse society*. Washington, DC: National Association for the Education of Young Children.

Derman-Sparks, L., & the A.B.C. Task Force. (1989). *Anti-bias curriculum: Tools for empowering young children*. Washington, DC: National Association for the Education of Young Children.

Duke, M., Martin, E., & Nowicki Jr., S. (1996). *Teaching your child the language of social success*. Atlanta, GA: Peachtree Publisher.

Kirchner, G. (2000). *Children's games from around the world*. San Francisco, CA: Benjamin Cummings.

Levin, D. E. (2003). *Teaching young children in violent times: Building a peaceable classroom*. (2nd ed.) Cambridge, MA: Educators for Social Responsibility.

Lumour, S., & Lumour, J. (1990). *Everyone wins*. British Columbia, CAN: New Society Publishers.

McGinnis, E., & Goldstein, A. (1990). *Skillstreaming in early childhood: Teaching prosocial skills to the preschool and kindergarten child*. Champaign, IL: Research Press.

Orlick, T. (1982). *The second cooperative sports and games book*. New York: Random House.

Poole, C., Miller, S., & Church, E.B. (1998). Share with me! *Scholastic Early Childhood Today, 18*(3), 18–21.

Rice, J. A. (1995). *The kindness curriculum.* St. Paul, MN: Redleaf Press.

Scharmann, M. (1998). We are friends when we have memories together. *Young Children, 53*(2), 27–29.

Stone, J. (2001). *Building classroom community: The early childhood teacher's role.* Washington, DC: National Association for the Education of Young Children.

Trawick-Smith, J. (1997). *Early childhood development in multicultural perspectives.* Upper Saddle River, NJ: Merrill/Prentice Hall.

Webster-Stratton, C. (2000). *How to promote children's social and emotional competence.* London: Paul Chapman.

York, S. (1991). *Roots and wings: Affirming culture in early childhood programs.* St Paul, MN: Redleaf Press.

REFERENCES

Adams, S. K. (2002). *ECE-CARES Training and Mentoring Project*: Safe Schools Health Students Initiative Report for Denver Public Schools. Denver, CO: University of Colorado at Denver.

Bandura, A., Barbaranelli, C., Caprara, G. & Pastorelli, C. (1996). Multifaceted impact of self-efficacy beliefs on academic functioning. *Child Development, 67,* 1206–1222.

Committee for Children. (2002). *Second Step: A violence prevention curriculum for preschoolers and kindergartners.* (3rd ed.) Seattle, WA.: Committee for Children.

Crary, E. (1992). Talking about differences children notice. In B. Neugebauer (Ed.). *Alike and different: Exploring our humanity with young children* (pp. 11–16). Washington, DC: National Association for the Education of Young Children.

Denham, S. A., McKinley, M., Couchoud, E. E., & Holt, R. (1990). Emotional and behavioral predictors of preschool peer ratings. *Child Development, 61,* 1145–1152.

Derman-Sparks, L. D. (1992). "It isn't fair!" Antibias curriculum for young children. In B. Neugebauer (Ed.). *Alike and different: Exploring our humanity with young children* (pp. 2–10). Washington, DC: National Association for the Education of Young Children.

Gopaul-McNicol, S., & Thomas-Presswood, T. (1998). *Working with linguistically and culturally different children: Innovative clinical and educational approaches.* Boston: Allyn & Bacon.

Joseph, G. E., & Strain, P. S. (2002). *You've got to have friends.* Champaign, IL: Center on the Social and Emotional Foundations for Early Learning.

Kaiser, B., & Rasminsky, J. S. (2003). *Challenging behavior in young children.* Boston, MA: Allyn & Bacon.

Katz, L., & McClellan, D. (1997). *Fostering children's social competence: The teacher's role.* Washington, DC: National Association for the Education of Young Children.

Kopp, C. B., Baker, B. L., & Brown, K. W. (1992). Social skills and their correlates: Preschoolers with developmental delays. *American Journal of Mental Retardation, 96,* 357–366.

Kuczynski, L., & Kochanska, G. (1990). Development of children's noncompliance strategies from toddlerhood to age 5. *Developmental Psychology, 26,* 398–408.

Levin, D. (1998). *Remote control childhood? Combating the hazards of media culture.* Washington, DC: National Association for the Education of Young Children.

Levin, D. (2003). *Teaching young children in violent times.* (2nd ed.) British Columbia, CAN: New Society Publishers.

McClellan, D., & Katz, L. (1993). *Young Children's Social Development.* Urbana, IL: ERIC Clearinghouse on Elementary and Early Childhood Education. See also: http:www.ed.gov/databases/ERIC_Digests/ed356100.html

McCracken, J. B. (1993). *Valuing diversity: The primary years.* Washington, DC: National Association for the Education of Young Children.

Merrell, K., & Holland, M. (1997). Social-emotional behavior of preschool-age children with and without developmental delays. *Research in Developmental Disabilities, 18*(6), 393–405.

Miller, S. (2000). Sharing. *Scholastic Early Childhood Today, 15*(2), 32–33.

Mize, J., & Ladd, G. W. (1990). Toward the development of successful social skills training for preschool children. In S. R. Asher & J. D. Coie (Eds.). *Peer rejection in childhood* (pp. 338–361). New York: Cambridge University Press.

Peth-Pierce, R. (2001). *A good beginning: Sending America's children to school with the social and emotional competence they need to succeed.* Monograph from the Children's Mental Health Foundations and Agencies Network (FAN). Bethesda, MD: National Institute of Mental Health.

Smith, C. A. (1993). *The peaceful classroom.* Mt. Rainier, MD: Gryphon House.

Wittmer, D., & Honig, A. (1994). Encouraging positive social development in young children. *Young Children, 49*(5), 4–12.

Chapter 7

PEACEFUL PROBLEM SOLVING

A teacher in a preschool classroom of 3- and 4-year-olds is frustrated by the number of children who use Tinker Toys™, Legos™, and bristle blocks to create some form of weapon and run around the room imitating television characters. The teacher presents this concern to the children in a class meeting by saying, "I've noticed that many children are using toys such as Tinker Toys™ and Legos™ as guns. I am worried that someone will get hurt by these toys." Several children acknowledge that they have seen this happening. After some creative brainstorming, the children decide that toys from the table toy area should be "sit-down toys." From now on, the children will sit on the floor or at a table to build instead of running around with their creations. This simple rule makes a noticeable difference. The children's creations are more creative and less likely to be used as weapons.

This classroom anecdote demonstrates that very young children can use a problem-solving process to resolve interpersonal conflicts. These accomplishments are particularly striking, given that early childhood teachers report an increase over the last 5 to 10 years in the number of children coming to school angry, aggressive, or lacking the social skills to get along in school (Adams, 1998).

Teachers of young children recognize the benefit of helping children learn social problem solving strategies that can be generalized across situations and settings. As the children become more independent at solving problems peacefully, the teachers will need to spend less valuable time arbitrating disputes. The classroom climate improves as incidences of aggression and victimization are reduced and positive social skills are promoted. Children who exhibit aggressive behavior discover acceptable ways to have their needs met without infringing on the rights of others. Children who practice simple problem-solving steps learn what to *do* when faced with conflict, rather than simply what *not* to do (as when they are punished and sent to time-out for inappropriate ways of responding to conflict). Children who tend to withdraw can become empowered to express their feelings and assert themselves appropriately, reducing the chances that more powerful children will victimize them. A systematic approach to teaching a problem-solving process can yield such positive outcomes (Carlsson-Paige & Levin, 1992; DeVries & Zan, 1994; Levin, 2003).

KINDS OF CONFLICT IN EARLY CHILDHOOD CLASSROOMS

There are several kinds of interpersonal conflicts typically observed in early childhood classrooms (Figure 7.1).

FIGURE 7.1

Types of Interpersonal Conflicts in Early Childhood Classrooms

Type of Conflict	Description
Possession disputes	Young children in a preschool setting may be enchanted with the child-sized environment filled with all kinds of toys and activities. Since their egocentric nature does not easily recognize the needs and desires of other children, power struggles over toys and materials account for the most frequent disputes in early childhood classrooms.
Space	Children may have conflicts because they want to use the same space at the same time.
Privileges	Conflicts occur over a privilege such as being the line leader, doing a favorite task (feeding the bunny), or helping to pass out the snack.
Attention Getting	Children who crave attention often try to get it in negative ways such as hitting or shoving other children, disrupting play activities, or destroying materials. If these behaviors gain them the attention they desire (even if it is in the form of reprimands and punishment), then they continue using these attention-getting ploys.
Power struggle	Some children assert themselves to be in control of everything that happens around them. They want to have their choice of materials, be first to take a turn, delegate roles in dramatic play, choose their seat at the snack table, and decide how to build the block structure. If other children do not comply, a power struggle results.
Group-entry or exclusion	This type of conflict occurs when an individual tries to enter a group of children already at play and is rejected. Group entry strategies most often rejected by other children include: asking the question "Can I play?" making a claim ("I was here first!") or an aggressive statement, or disrupting the play physically by taking or disturbing the play materials or pushing a child aside.
Name-calling or putdowns	Name-calling may be the result of friendly teasing, an angry response to another child's actions or words, or an attempt to gain attention in inappropriate ways.
Teasing	Remarks or actions intended to annoy or embarrass a child may be enacted by a single child or a group of children.
Blaming	Disputes often occur when children deny responsibility for their actions and try to shift the blame onto another child.

Sources: Beaty, 1995; Evans, 2002; Kriedler, 1984; Shantz, 1987

In these common classroom confrontations, many children resort to yelling, biting, or other aggressive behaviors. Others retreat, physically or verbally. Teachers may be tempted to simply remove the disputed object, separate the quarrelling children, or impose a solution. Although these teacher responses stop the immediate dispute, they do not teach children better ways to handle conflict in the future. Consider a typical teacher reaction to conflict where the teacher comforts the "victim" and shames and punishes the "perpetrator." While being punished in time-out, the perpetrator learns no positive alternative behavior. The next time a similar situation arises, the child has no other alternative but to do what he already knows—to engage in hurtful behavior to express his needs. Or instead of being punished, the aggressor may be forced to apologize to the victim. Unfortunately, all that may be learned in this case is that a simple "I'm sorry" absolves the aggressor from any responsibility. In addition, the child may *not* feel sorry; in fact, he may still be angry and wants to push his friend again!

The victim also suffers in this scenario, receiving comforting by the authority figure and the occasional forced apology, but failing to learn more appropriate responses to use in future conflict situations. Thus, this traditional discipline approach to conflict, combined with failure to teach appropriately assertive behaviors and conflict resolution skills, tends to perpetuate bully-victim relationships in the classroom (Gartrell, 2002).

A more effective strategy is to teach young children a nonviolent problem-solving process and help them to practice the steps to resolve interpersonal conflicts as they arise in the classroom.

A PEACEFUL PROBLEM-SOLVING MODEL

Early childhood settings can offer children opportunities to learn and practice fundamental problem-solving skills. Various writers recommend differing versions of a social information-processing model (Carlsson-Paige & Levin, 1998; Crick & Dodge, 1994; Dinwiddie, 1994; Gartrell, 2002; Hewitt & Heidemann, 1998; Kreidler, 1996; Levin, 2003; Shure, 1992) but typically include the basic steps of: 1) "reading" a social situation to identify feelings and define the problem; 2) generating alternative solutions; 3) evaluating proposed solutions; 4) agreeing on a solution and carrying it out; and 5) evaluating the outcome of the solution to determine if it is successful.

Many teachers have success with a problem-solving approach that presents five steps to problem solving, which includes the children asking themselves questions and seeking answers in order to arrive at a solution to the problem at hand (Committee for Children, 1992). The goal is to determine a **win-win solution**—one that takes into account each child's point of view, is more or less agreeable to all, and restores a sense of safety, as opposed to a "win-lose" solution (where one child's position prevails) or "lose-lose" solutions (where neither child's needs are met) (Levin, 2003). The five steps to problem solving presented below are the ones presented in *Second Step*, a violence prevention curriculum for preschoolers and kindergartners (Committee for Children, 1992) and successfully used by the authors in early childhood settings. First, each step will be explained, along with the role of the adult in that step. (For simplicity, we use the term "teacher" to stand for all adults—teachers, caregivers, and parents.) Then detailed suggestions for teaching the steps to young children will be presented.

1. What Is the Problem? Identifying the problem includes a discussion of each child's point of view-that is, the feelings and needs of the victim and the aggressor (Dinwiddie, 1994). This helps to define the problem or conflict as a shared one, where there are two competing points of view. Children usually phrase the problem from their own point of view based on concrete actions such as "Alexi took my truck" or "Kayla won't give me the fire truck" rather than "We both want the truck." It is up to the teacher to show how both children have legitimate, albeit incompatible points of view, and to clarify the feelings of each party in the dispute: "Kayla, you looked angry when Alexi grabbed the truck." and "Alexi, look at Kayla's face. How do you think she is feeling?" (Obviously, teaching young children an emotional vocabulary is an essential prerequisite skill for effective problem solving.)

The role of the teacher at this step is to help children tune in to each other's needs and feelings and redefine the problem as a shared one. "So the problem is, Kayla was using the truck and Alexi wants the truck, too. You *both* want to play with the truck."

2. What Can I Do? In **brainstorming** sessions, children think of many ideas in a short amount of time. At this point, teachers encourage ideas without evaluating or placing judgments on the suggested solutions. It is useful to have children, even 4-year-olds, suggest whatever ideas come to mind, good or bad, so that they have a chance to evaluate consequences of impulsive and aggressive behavior (in step 3). If a child suggests a less-than-ideal option, the teacher should include it in the list the children are creating with a comment such as, "Yes, you are right. Sometimes children do grab toys. Let's write that down."

3. What Might Happen If. . . ? In this step, the class evaluates ideas by generating consequences for each solution. "What might happen if Kayla decides to push Alexi away? Is that safe? How would Alexi feel?" At this point, any potential solutions that are unsafe or hurt another child's feelings are eliminated. For other ideas, the children need to answer the questions "Is it fair? Will it work?" Now is the time to respond to any of the children's inappropriate suggestions from the brainstorming session. For younger children, the teacher may need to show puppets acting out some of the solutions, so that the children can judge the appropriateness of ideas.

4. Choose a Solution and Use It. Once children decide on a best solution, they need to figure out how to implement their plan successfully. Often young children verbalize such solutions as "take turns with the truck." Given the natural egocentricity of young children, however, they each tend to assume they can go first. To deal with this dilemma, some teachers have developed methods that children use to decide who actually goes first. (One creative teacher had several Popsicle sticks in a covered can. Only the tips of the Popsicle sticks were visible. The bottom of one stick was colored with green marker. "Green means go." The child drawing that Popsicle stick takes the first turn. After the children in her class became accustomed to this idea, they trusted that they would always get their turn eventually, even if they weren't "first." Soon the children were racing to find the "turn can" on their own.) Once it is decided who will be first, the teacher helps the children determine the length of the turn and may need to watch the clock, or set up a timer, to ensure fair turn-taking.

The teacher's role in this step is to rephrase the chosen solution, "So you've decided to take turns with the truck" and clarify how the solution will be implemented. Teachers need to remain nearby as children enact the solution and monitor progress to make sure the agreement is going according to plan.

5. Is It Working? If Not, What Can I Do Now? During this final, evaluative step of problem solving, children have an opportunity to reflect on how well their plan worked and on their feelings about the outcome. Teachers support the children's successful solutions with an affirming statement. "You thought of a good solution. You worked together to solve the problem!"

If any child is not satisfied with the outcome, he or she may decide to try another solution instead. They would then need to retrace the five steps to problem solving.

(Note: In the 2002 revision of the Second Step curriculum, the problem-solving steps are presented to preschoolers using a poster depicting only 3 steps:

1. How do I feel?
2. What is the problem?
3. What can I do?

It is the opinion of the authors that the simplified poster could be a useful reminder for young children, but it has been our experience that preschool-age children can follow the five-step format and benefit from a discussion of the potential outcomes for various solutions.

For primary grade children, the five-step process was retained, with slight variation in the wording on the poster to read:

1. What is the problem?
2. What are some solutions?
3. For each solution, ask yourself: Is it safe? How might people feel about it? Is it fair? Will it work?
4. Choose a solution and use it.
5. Is it working? If not, what can I do now?

TEACHING THE PROBLEM-SOLVING STEPS TO YOUNG CHILDREN

Upon hearing about a five-step process for solving problems with young children, teachers often feel overwhelmed. ("I just can't see that working with my group of 3- and 4-year-olds.") Fortunately, there are several methods to teach problem solving that are successful with young children, those lacking solid verbal skills, and children with disabilities. Teachers can foster the development of problem-solving skills by directly teaching them to children, demonstrating and modeling their use in a variety of ways, and guiding children to use the problem-solving process in their ongoing interactions with peers.

Facilitating Regular Class Meetings

The problem-solving process is introduced and taught during regular class meetings. In these meetings, small or large groups of children meet with a teacher to solve specific problems. The first goal of class meetings is to generate open discussion among the children. To do this, teachers must be accepting and validate each child's contribution to the discussion. The second goal is to develop the children's ability to solve problems using the social problem solving approach described above. In a class meeting it is vital that children, not the teacher, propose and choose the solutions they think will work.

Problem-solving class meetings should be regularly scheduled at a specific time each day, or several days per week. The teacher also can spontaneously call for a class meeting in response to a more immediate problem, such as a playground incident. Many of the following techniques are used as teaching strategies during class meetings.

Using Puppet Role-Plays

Puppets provide a captivating means of holding children's attention. The authors have observed young children talking to and identifying with puppets, almost as if they were fellow classmates. Puppets can be used to role-play problems based on common classroom situations (such as name-calling, lack of sharing, or difficulty taking turns), or in response to actual conflicts (such as two children arguing over who gets to use the watering can to water the plants). Playing out the scenario with puppets protects the identity and feelings of the children involved in the specific conflict. Puppet role-plays also allow the teacher to raise his concerns ("I've noticed that during cleanup time, some children continue to play and don't help others clean up. What can we do about this problem?"), or to introduce or reinforce specific skills such as turn-taking, asking the teacher for help, listening in a group, or asking another child to play.

Kreidler (1984) suggests that the teacher identify some puppets as "problem puppets." The teacher operates the puppets, enacting the problem situation up to the point of conflict (i.e., the point where someone is going to hit, yell, cry, or call the teacher). The puppets "freeze" at the point of conflict, and the teacher then involves the children in the problem-solving steps. Once the children choose the solution they like best, the puppets role-play its conclusion.

> The children in my class became so attached to our class puppets that they wanted to name them (Mandy the monkey and Leo the leopard). They made a "home" for them, using a small box. After using the puppets in a class meeting, children took turns carefully putting Mandy and Leo in their box and covering them up with a blanket.

Using Children's Literature

Children love to listen to stories and often identify strongly with the characters. Books can introduce or extend a conflict resolution skill, provide a non-threatening way to talk about conflict, and show characters learning how to solve problems nonviolently.

Kreidler (1994) makes the following suggestions for reading books about conflict:

- Read the book up to the point of conflict.
- Ask the children how they think the characters are feeling. "How is Koala Bear feeling now?"
- Have the children identify the conflict. "Children, what's the problem here?"
- Brainstorm ways that the characters could solve the conflict. Discuss which one the children think the characters in the story will use.
- Read the rest of the story. Discuss the characters' solution to their conflict. "Was that a good solution? Why? How do the characters feel now?" For primary grade children, extend these questions to include, "Was it an effective, win-win solution? What would you have done differently?" If the solution presented is a poor model of conflict resolution, have the children write new endings (Kriedler, 1984).

The book *Teaching Conflict Resolution through Children's Literature* (Kriedler, 1994) has an abundance of ideas for extensions appropriate for primary grade children, including the "conflict escalator," creating a conflict resolution chart, the ABCD Problem Solving Method, and "Thumbs up/Thumbs Down" chart.

Using Pictures and Posters as a Stimulus

Large photographs or posters can provide a stimulus to discussions of conflict scenarios. Teachers create a story, based on the picture (as they would with puppets and books), leading up to a conflict. Then, they talk the children through the steps to problem solving. For example, using a large photograph depicting a crying young girl, the teacher says, "This is Sarah. Look at her face. Let me tell you what happened to Sarah. One day at preschool, Sarah asked two friends if she could play with them in the playhouse. Her friends said, 'No, we're busy!' How do you think that made Sarah feel? What is the problem? What do you think Sarah could do?" In one classroom presented with this scenario, the children brainstormed the following solutions: Sarah could bring something for the girls to play with as she tried to join them, find someone else to play with, or ask the teacher for help.

Creating a "Solution List"

After children become familiar with the problem-solving process, they can be engaged in creating a master list of positive solutions to problems. Teachers can create a solutions poster with simple words and illustrations. Children may then refer to the poster during actual conflicts to give them ideas for potential solutions to a problem. The poster can also be used during teaching situations. See Figure 7.2 for a sample solution list poster.

Acting-Out Make-Believe Role-Plays

Role-playing is a good technique for practicing solutions to conflict and promoting children's ability to see a situation from another person's perspective. Usually a teacher-directed, small-group activity, teachers describe a conflict situation, define the roles, and have the children act out different ways to resolve the conflict.

One teacher asked the children to set the snack table with four place settings, and then chose five children to role-play how they would handle attempting to sit down for snack. Another teacher had two children simulate an argument over who could ride the tricycle: one child sat on the seat as another child held on to the handlebars, blocking her way. The rest of the children identified the problem, and the two girls acted out scenarios to complete the problem-solving process.

For primary-grade children, instead of setting up the conflict situation for them, have children brainstorm situations they want to role-play. Check with the group to make sure that they have determined a reasonable resolution that gets to "win-win," then let the role-play begin. Kreidler (1984, p. 73) suggests several questions to ask the class (second- to third-grade level) after the role play:

- What was the conflict?
- How was it resolved?
- Was it a win-win resolution?
- Could other solutions have worked?
- How could the situation have been prevented?
- How did the players feel in their roles?
- How did these feelings affect their actions?

FIGURE 7.2

Solution List Poster in a Preschool Classroom

When we have a problem we can....

☆ Share....
☆ Take turns....
☆ Trade toys....
☆ Ask another friend....
☆ Ask teacher for help...
☆ Find another toy....
☆ Walk away...
☆ Apologize....
☆ Go to Cozy Corner...

Telling Stories

Because many preschoolers like to create their own stories, teachers can encourage a problem-related story theme. The teacher may initiate this activity by saying, "Tell me a story about a little girl who wanted the toy someone else had and what she did to try and get the toy." For younger children, who may need more structure, the teacher can provide the beginning of a fairy-tale type story and then ask a child to finish it. "Once upon a time there was a boy named Kevin (do not use the name of a child in the class) who didn't get along with anyone at school because he couldn't share. One day, a little girl started to play with a blue car, and Kevin grabbed the car so fast it scared her and made her cry." Young children can dictate stories to the teacher and illustrate them later. (Children who enjoy make-believe and imaginary play can later act out their problem-solving stories as a role-play.)

For primary grade children, storytelling can be a creative writing assignment. Have children write stories of conflicts with win-win resolutions in a picture-book format, using a few sentences per page and their own illustrations.

Creating Problem Cards (Primary Grades)

Give a small group of children a problem written on a card and a giant sheet of paper with the problem solving steps written on it. Their task is to write and draw pictures for each step to solve the problem assigned to them. Each group then shares their ideas with the class—through discussion or role-play.

Developing a Class Meeting Agenda

In the primary grades, the children can be involved in creating the class meeting agenda. Sometimes teachers post a class meeting agenda on a clipboard. Anytime during the day, children may sign up to present an issue. During a day in February in one second-grade classroom, the agenda looked like this:

Class Meeting Agenda
1. Ariel—yelling
2. Fernando—saying mean things
3. Ayesha—taking stuff
4. Gabriela—food at school

EXAMPLES OF CONFLICT FAMILIAR TO CHILDREN IN SCHOOL

Use the following examples to create your own puppet shows, skits, role-playing, and class meeting discussions. (Adapted from *The Friendly Classroom for a Small Planet*, 1988.)

Possession: Two children are fighting over a quarter. Chantelle accuses Timmy of stealing the quarter. Timmy says he brought the quarter to school and it fell out of his pocket.

Space: Shek-yee and Rashida want to sit next to the teacher during storytime and begin to push each other.

Privilege: Hakeem and Mitchell are arguing over who gets to water the plants.

Attention: Akia likes to tell her own stories and often interrupts other children during circle time.

Exclusion: Miguel and Santiago are playing catch with a ball. Jeffrey comes along and asks to play. Miguel and Santiago say "no."

Aggression: While waiting in line to go outside, Jeremy keeps intentionally bumping into the child in front of him in line.

Name-calling: Paul is pushing a truck in the block area. He pushes too hard, and the truck knocks over Ryan's block building. Ryan shouts, "I hate you, you stinky!"

Teasing: Outside on the playground, Derek grabs the hat off of Daniel's head. Derek and two other boys throw the hat back and forth, playing "keep away" from Daniel.

INTRODUCING PROBLEM SOLVING IN YOUR EARLY CHILDHOOD SETTING

Introduce the problem-solving process gradually. Start by having children engage in the first two steps. Role-play a short problem with the puppets, then stop and ask the children, "What is the problem here?" Rephrase their answers to establish a shared problem, such as, "They both want to play with the computer." Have the children identify the probable feelings of the puppets. Then have them brainstorm some possible solutions, which you write on a large piece of paper.

Later in the day, remind the children of the problem and read the answers they gave earlier. Now do the next two steps with the children. Evaluate each possible solution asking, "Is it safe?" "Is it fair?" "Will it work?" "How will they feel?" Ask the children to choose one idea that "passes the question test," and use the puppets to act out the solution. Repeat this two-part process several times. Eventually the children can complete the first four steps during a class meeting. The puppets can role-play the chosen solution, and the children will decide if the selected idea worked (step 5).

PROBLEM SOLVING AT WORK

After the children have been *repeatedly* exposed to the problem-solving process through the strategies described above, teachers can facilitate their use in real-life classroom situations.

To initiate the mediation, the adult needs to approach calmly and stop any hurtful actions. Body language is critical to create a calm and neutral climate at the beginning of the mediation. Evans (2002) recommends several reassuring techniques:

1. Position yourself between the children at their level. "Neutralize" an object of contention by holding it in your hand while assuring the children you will listen to them. "When children are fighting over an object, it is usually very difficult for them to discuss possible solutions as long as one of the children is holding the object" (p. 76).

2. If necessary, stop any hurtful actions. Gently reach out to each child, "putting your arms around both children, placing a hand on each child's shoulder, or even holding one of each child's hands" (p. 56). You may need to encourage a child to calm down (see Chapter 8 for calming-down techniques).

3. Offer eye contact, but do not force it or physically turn the child's face to yours.
4. If the children's voices are loud, speak just above their level to begin. Use a calm voice as children become quieter. Assure the children that each will have a turn to tell his or her story.

After children become more independent with negotiating solutions themselves, teachers may choose to introduce the concept of a "peace table" or a "peace rug" as a site for conflict resolution. The solution list may be posted at this area. When a conflict erupts, the children involved go to the designated area to complete the problem-solving steps. Moving to an area away from the initial conflict helps to defuse the emotions and allow children to concentrate more on the process of solving the problem. (See Appendix B for detailed descriptions of problem solving in action.)

SITUATIONS IN WHICH THE PROBLEM-SOLVING PROCESS CAN BE USED

Negotiating Routine Interpersonal Conflicts

The most common use of the problem-solving process is to facilitate a peaceful resolution of conflict between two or more children

> One Head Start classroom had been working on the five steps to problem solving since October. The teacher, Julie, had been paying particular attention to two 3-year-olds girls whom she described as "feisty" because they are known to pull hair or pinch when frustrated by a conflict. One day in February, Julie brings in a set of new plastic dishes, a dishpan, a dish drying rack, a Handiwipe for washing dishes, and two dish towels. At free play time, both of these girls head straight for the dramatic play area and grab the Handiwipe. Julie gets prepared to intervene, when she hears one of the little girls say, "We have a problem here. We both want to wash dishes. What can we do?" The girls, on their own, decide to cut the Handiwipe in half. They proceed to share the dishpan happily, and wash the dishes together.

In one second-grade classroom, the teacher used a different kind of strategy for negotiating a conflict with peers wherein children are given the responsibility for creating a plan of action and then meeting with the teacher prior to implementing the plan. The teacher created a "hassle log," a form on which the student can describe a problem he is having with another child. The form includes the problem-solving steps to assist the child in formulating a plan to resolve the problem. The student then requests a conference with the teacher wherein the plan is reviewed and refined before the child proceeds.

Negotiating Responses to Behavior Problems with an Individual Child

In this case, the teacher typically initiates a conversation with a child.

> A teacher in an early childhood classroom approaches a little boy during a quiet time and invites him to sit and draw a picture with her. They proceed to draw a picture about the book that was read in class that morning. While they were drawing, the teacher says, "I've noticed that you have trouble sitting next to your friends during story time. Sometimes you get too close to other children or you get up on your knees and children can't see the book. What do you think we can do about this problem?" After thinking and drawing for a few minutes, the child decides that he should sit in a cube chair in the back row. (The other children typically sit on the floor in loosely defined rows facing the teacher.) He seems to know that the cube chair will help define his "space" and allow him to sit up high enough to see the book.

Sharing Power over Classrooms Decisions

Teachers who are willing to share their power over classroom decisions involve children in the process. Such decisions can relate to the schedule, a routine, or an activity that affects the class. In this case, either the teacher or a child may present the problem to the class.

> During a class meeting, a preschool teacher introduces a problem by saying, "Children, I need your help with a problem. Every day, several children want to feed the gerbil. If too many children feed the gerbil, he can't eat all the food and just plays with it instead. Lots of times, he knocks part of the food out of the cage and it makes a mess on the floor. How can we pick just one child to feed the gerbil every day?" The children decide to add "feed the gerbil" to the daily classroom chore chart.

PROBLEM SOLVING WITH TODDLERS

When negotiating a conflict situation with toddlers, the teacher needs to determine what the problem is, express it verbally for the children, and validate each of their feelings using responsive language. To do this, teachers provide a lot of the language involved in problem solving and ask simple questions to which the child can answer with "yes," "no," or a simple nod of the head (Evans, 2002). If Jamal and Micah were both toddlers, instead of asking "What is the problem?" the teacher Rhonda might say, "I see you both tugging on the truck. You look mad. Do you both want the truck?" If the boys respond "yes" through words or nods, then Rhonda can proceed with "It looks like you both want a turn with the truck. What can we do?" Toddlers in this situation often respond to the adult by looking at or getting another truck or handing the truck to the other child. Then the teacher can reinforce the children by saying "You decided to find another truck, Jamal. That was a good idea. Now both of you have a truck to play with." "Jamal, you decided to let Micah have a turn. That was being a good friend. Now, what would you like to play with?"

If the teacher asks, "What can we do?" and after sufficient wait time neither boy makes a response to indicate a preference for a solution, the teacher can volunteer an idea or a choice. "I have an idea. We could find another truck. Then you would both have a truck. Shall we go look for another truck?" After the teacher assists the boys to find another truck, she stays awhile to make sure they are both happily engaged in play and then reinforces them for solving the problem.

As toddlers become more verbal, teach them to use key vocabulary to express their needs in conflict situations, such as "mine," "I want it," "stop," and "I need a turn" (Reynolds, 1990).

MODIFICATIONS FOR CHILDREN WITH SPECIAL NEEDS

Social problem-solving skills can be learned by all children. This process is not exclusive to highly verbal, high-achieving, or socially competent children. The learning process may take longer for children with developmental delays or for children already demonstrating social problems. For many such children, it is helpful to practice problem solving with limited choices. The teacher approaches the conflict calmly and asks "What is the problem?" He helps children identify their feelings and restate the problem. Next, instead of asking the children to suggest solutions to the problem and evaluate their potential effectiveness, the teacher presents limited choices for solutions. "Your choices are to take turns with the computer using the timer or find another activity. Which will you do?" The teacher remains in the area to ensure that the selected solution is successful and compliments the children, using specific feedback. "You decided to take turns using the timer and it worked. You solved the problem!" (Incidentally, this limited-choice alternative is also a successful strategy to use with typically developing children when time is short, when everyone is tired at the end of the day, or when health or safety needs dictate a narrow range of acceptable solutions.)

When teaching problem-solving skills to children with language delays or auditory processing difficulties, teachers use many of the techniques described for toddlers. They also pair short phrases with pictures, or use sign language. For example, Katlyn, whose ability to speak is virtually nonexistent, learned to make the sign for "stop" when she did not like what another child was doing.

BENEFITS TO TEACHERS AND CLASSROOMS

As adults teach and facilitate a social problem-solving process, both they and the children reap the benefits. Children gain independence as they learn to solve difficult problems and express feelings in acceptable ways. When faced with conflict, they are better able to have their needs met without resorting to aggression. They learn to negotiate fair solutions and assert themselves appropriately to avoid becoming victims of other children's aggression. Children with effective problem-solving skills gain self-esteem as they learn to interact with others in more positive ways.

Teachers who make the initial investment of time, energy, and thoughtful planning to teach social problem solving to children reap time benefits later, as they spend less time disciplining children and intervening in their conflicts (Adams & Wittmer, 2001). These teachers then have more time to do more meaningful and productive things in the classroom. Teachers also have the satisfaction of knowing that they have promoted coping skills that enhance children's abilities to live peacefully.

INCLUDING PARENTS IN TEACHING PROBLEM SOLVING

Whenever teachers share their philosophy of discipline and classroom problem solving (Back to School Night, parent conferences, or everyday interactions with parents), they can introduce and reinforce the Five Steps to Problem Solving. Some teachers develop a workshop for parents around the theme of teaching problem solving to children and model many of the strategies discussed in this chapter. Others include problem solving as part of their monthly newsletters to families. (See Figure 7.3 for a sample workshop handout or family newsletter article.)

FIGURE 7.3

Sample Problem-Solving Workshop Handout or Family Newsletter Article

CARES for Families

Activities in your child's class are focusing on helping children learn the process of problem solving. We want children to learn to settle their own problems—in caring and nonviolent ways. We have been teaching the children a process for solving problems using the following steps:

1. What is the problem?
Help children to identify everyone's feelings based on facial expressions, body language, and the words people are using. Help children state the problem as a shared one. Children usually consider only their <u>own</u> wants and needs.
  "So the problem is you <u>both</u> want to play with the red truck."

2. What can I do? (What are some solutions?)
This step is "brainstorming." Help children think of a variety of possible solutions to the problem.
  "What could you do about the problem that you both want to play with the red truck? Let's talk about some ideas."

3. For each solution, ask yourself:
Help children evaluate each possible solution by thinking of the consequences.
Evaluate the ideas on the basis of safety, the effect on those involved, fairness, and workability.
  "What would happen if you decided to take turns with the truck?"
  "Is it safe?"
  "How will you and Johnny feel?"
  "Is it fair?"
  "Will it work?"

4. Choose a solution and use it.
Once children decide on a best solution, they need to come up with a plan for putting it into action. They will need your help in deciding <u>how</u> to share, take turns, ask for help, apologize, or any other non-aggressive idea for solving problems.
  "You've decided to take turns with the truck. How will you work out taking turns? Should I set the kitchen timer for three minutes? First John can play with the truck for three minutes and then Maria can play with the truck for three minutes. Does that sound like it will work?"

5. Is it working? If not, what can I do now?
Help the children evaluate the success of the solution to the problem. Reinforce children when it is working.
  "You both look happy now. It looks like taking turns with the truck is working."
  "I still hear some arguing here. Is taking turns with the truck not working? What else can you try?"

We have been teaching this process through discussions, stories, puppet role- plays, and games. Our goal is to get children to think of many different ways to solve each problem presented in these teaching situations. Then we practice using this problem-solving process in actual conflict situations as they arise in the classroom.

One of the things we do is make lists (sometimes just in our heads, sometimes written on a large sheet of paper) of what are possible solutions. For example, when two children both want the same toy, they could:

> ➢ Play with the toy together (share)
> ➢ Have one child use it first and then the other child use it next (take turns)
> ➢ Offer a different toy (trade)
> ➢ Stand still and both "cool off" for a minute
> ➢ Go away and play in a different area or with someone else
> ➢ Ask an adult for help

KEY TERMS AND CONCEPTS

Brainstorming: rapidly thinking of a variety of ideas for solving a problem without evaluating or placing judgments on the suggested solutions

Win-win solution: a solution that takes into account each child's point of view, is agreeable to all, and restores a sense of safety when implemented

LEARNING IN ACTION:
SMALL GROUP ACTIVITIES AND FIELD ASSIGNMENTS

1. Based on your experience with children, write an example of five types of conflict discussed in Figure 7.1: a possession dispute, a power struggle, a group-entry conflict, a space dispute, and name-calling.
2. Working in pairs, create a puppet role-play for each of the problem situations described above. Role-play the problem situation up to the point of conflict. Discuss how you would facilitate a small group of children to: a) define the problem; b) discuss the feelings involved; c) brainstorm possible solutions to the problem; and d) evaluate the potential consequences of each solution. Finish by using the puppets to role-play a desirable solution. Practicing a puppet role-play with a peer first will make you more comfortable when you introduce it to children.
3. In each of the following situations, describe how you would approach the conflict and initiate conflict mediation.
   - Situation A: Gathering for storytime, Alisa and Sandy both try to sit on the pink carpet square next to the teacher and begin pushing each other.
   - Situation B: Emily has been standing watching three other girls play in the housekeeping area. It seems as if she'd like to join in, yet she makes no move to do so.
   - Situation C: Lupe is watching Josh play a game on the computer. He asks Josh for a turn, who refuses. Lupe begins to push Josh off the chair and attempts to sit down in his place. Soon both are screaming.
4. Select a children's book that contains a conflict situation. Decide how you would present the book to children. Bring the book to class and be prepared to share your ideas with classmates.
5. In small groups, discuss whether you think the problem-solving model presented in this chapter consumes too much time for the busy classroom teacher to use, or whether the effort will pay off in the long run. Defend your position by your own observations or experience.
6. View the *CARES* Model video segment "Learning a Problem-Solving Process." (See Suggested Readings and Resources.) What activities would you plan to follow-up to a class meeting on problem solving?

RELATED CHILDREN'S BOOKS

Blaine, M. (1975). *The terrible thing that happened at my house*. New York: Scholastic.

Bottner, B. (1972). *Bootsie Barker bites*. New York: G.P. Putnam's Sons.

Carle, E. (1977). *The grouchy ladybug*. New York: Harper Collins.

Carlson-Paige, N. (1998). *Best day of the week*. St. Paul, MN: Redleaf Press.

Clifton, L. (1974). *Three wishes*. New York: Dell Yearling.

Clymer, E. (1968). *A big pile of dirt*. New York: Holt.

DePaola, T. (1980). *The knight and the dragon*. New York: G. B. Putnam's Sons.

Henkes, K. (1991). *Chrysanthemum*. New York: Greenwillow Books.

Jones, R. (1995). *Matthew and Tilly*. New York: Puffin Books.

Kellogg, S. (1973). *The island of the skog*. New York: Dial Books.

Lionni, L. (1985). *It's mine!* New York: Random House Inc.

Lionni, L. (1988). *Six crows*. New York: Alfred a. Knopf.

Naylor, P. R. (1994). *King of the playground*. New York: Aladdin Books.

Polland, B. K. (2000). *We can work it out: Conflict resolution for children*. Berkeley, CA: Tricycle Press.

Scieszka, J. (1989). *The true story of the three pigs by A. Wolf*. New York: Viking.

Seuss. (1961). *The Zax* included in the book The Sneetches. New York: Random House.

Seuss. (1984). *The butter battle*. New York: Random House.

Steig, W. (1988). *Spinky sulks*. New York: Farrar, Straus, and Giroux.

Surat, M. (1983). *Angel child, dragon child*. New York: Scholastic.

Udry, J. M. (1961). *Let's be enemies*. New York: Harper Collins.

Viorst, J. (1972). *Alexander and the terrible, horrible, no good, very bad day*. New York: Artheneum.

Wildsmith, B. (1971). *The owl and the woodpecker*. Oxford: Oxford University Press.

Zolotow, C. (1969). *The hating book*. New York: Harper Collins Children's Books.

SUGGESTED READINGS AND RESOURCES

Acredolo, L., & Goodwyn, S. (1996). *Baby signs: How to talk with your baby before your baby can talk*. Chicago: Contemporary Books.

Adams, S. K., & Baronberg, J. (2001). *The CARES Model: Building social skills and reducing problem behaviors in early childhood classrooms*. Denver, CO: Western Media Products. (Instructional videotape depicting six class meetings in early childhood classrooms. Available at www.media-products.com)

Bahan, B., & Dannis, J. (1990). *Signs for me: Basic sign vocabulary for children, parents, and teachers*. Dawn Sign Press.

Crary, E. (1984). *Kids can cooperate: A practical guide to teaching problem solving*. Seattle, WA: Parenting Press, Inc.

Sandy, S. V., & Boardman, S. K. (2000). The peaceful kids conflict resolution program. *The International Journal of Conflict Management, 11*(4), 337–357.

Sheanh, G. (1996). *Helping kids deal with conflict*. Winnipeg, CA: Peguis Publishers

Verbeek, R., & DeWaal, F. B. M. (2001). Peacemaking among preschool children. *Journal of Peace Psychology, 7*(1), 5–28.

REFERENCES

Adams, S. K. (1998). *ECE-CARES Rural Project: Safe and Drug-Free Schools and Communities Grant Program Report*. Denver: University of Colorado at Denver.

Adams, S. K., & Wittmer, D. S. (2001). "I had it first": Teaching young children to solve problems peacefully. *Childhood Education, 78*(1), 10–16.

Beaty, J. J. (2004). *Skills for preschool teachers*. Upper Saddle River, NJ: Merrill/Prentice Hall.

Carlsson-Paige, N., & Levin, D. E. (1992). Making peace in violent times: A constructivist approach to conflict resolution. *Young Children, 48*(1), 4–13.

Carlsson-Paige, N., & Levin, D. E. (1998). *Before push comes to shove*. St. Paul, MN: Redleaf Press.

Committee for Children. (1992). *Second Step: A violence prevention curriculum for preschoolers and kindergartners*. (1st ed.). Seattle, WA: Committee for Children.

Committee for Children. (2002). *Second Step: A violence prevention curriculum for preschoolers and kindergartners*. (3rd ed.). Seattle, WA: Committee for Children.

Crick, N. R., & Dodge, K. A. (1994). A review and reformulation of social information-processing mechanisms in children's social adjustment. *Psychological Bulletin, 115*, 74–101.

DeVries, R., & Zan, B. (1994). *Moral classrooms, moral children: Creating a constructivist atmosphere in early education*. New York: Teachers College.

Dinwiddie, S. A. (l994). The saga of Sally, Sammy, and the red pen: Facilitating children's social problem solving. *Young Children, 49*(5), 13–19.

Evans, B. (2002). *You can't come to my birthday party: Conflict resolution with young children*. Ypsilanti, MI: High Scope Press.

Gartrell, D. (2002). Replacing time-out: Using guidance to maintain an encouraging classroom. *Young Children, 57*(2), 36–43.

Hewitt, D., & Heidemann, S. (1998). *The optimistic classroom: Creative ways to give children hope*. St. Paul, MN: Redleaf Press.

Kreidler, W. J. (1984). *Creative conflict resolution: More than 200 activities for keeping peace in the classroom*. Glencoe, IL: Scott Foresman Company.

Kreidler, W. J. (1994). *Teaching conflict resolution through children's literature*. New York: Scholastic Professional Books.

Kreidler, W. J. (1996). *Adventures in peacemaking: A conflict resolution guide for early childhood providers*. Boston, MA: Educators for Social Responsibility.

Levin, D. E. (2003). *Teaching young children in violent times*. (2nd ed.). Cambridge, MA: Educators for Social Responsibility.

Prutzman, P., Stern, L., Burger, M. L., & Bodenhamer, G. (1998). *The friendly classroom for a small planet*. Philadelphia, PA: New Society Publishers.

Reynolds, E. (1990). *Guiding young children: A child-centered approach*. Mountain View, CA: Mayfield Publishing Company.

Shantz, C. U. (1987). Conflicts between children. *Child Development, 58*, 283–305.

Shure, M. B. (1992). *I can problem solve: An interpersonal cognitive problem-solving program*. Champaign, IL: Research Press.

Chapter 8

ANGER MANAGEMENT AND CALMING DOWN

I'd been teaching the children about calming down for about a month when I did a little puppet role play. Our two puppets are Benjie and Stella. Benjie was building a house with blocks. Stella comes over and wants to build with Benjie, but he tells her to go away. Stella makes a very angry face, growls, and goes over and gets a truck and crashes it into Benjie's house. Benjie begins to cry. At this point, I stopped and asked the children, "Why is Benjie crying?" Many of the children answered "Because he's sad." Or "His building is broken." Two of the children dashed up, petted Benjie, and told him not to cry, that they would help him rebuild his house.

I thanked the two children and asked them to sit down in their places. Then I asked one of the older children how she would feel if someone knocked down her building or ripped her art project. "Really mad!" she exclaimed with her hands on her hips. So I redid the puppet play again, this time with both Benjie and Stella being angry. Then I asked the children for ideas about what the puppets could do to make things better. One of our most rambunctious and impulsive four-year-olds said: "Stella, stop, take a deep breath, and calm down."

I was so pleased I was grinning from ear to ear. But I went on. I asked the children if they had any more ideas for Benjie or Stella. One little girl said, "Benjie, you have to tell Stella that you don't like it when she is rough." So I continued the puppet role-play, using the children's words and ideas. When I stopped, I asked if the children could understand why Stella was so upset. At first they didn't say anything but then they started talking about how it can make you really angry when someone doesn't want to play with you.

During the course of any day in an early childhood setting, young children have many reasons to be angry. They may not get what they want from their teachers, from the other children, or even from themselves. They may not know how to play with others and suffer rejection from peers. They may be frightened by the new environment or frustrated by inappropriate expectations. Sometimes children bring angry feelings along with them from another place and into the classroom or home care setting. Some children respond more angrily to situations than others, and some seem to be angry most of the time.

Many early childhood educators are uncomfortable with children's angry feelings. Miller (1996) contends that often "we want to stop its expression, sometimes at all costs" (p. 357). We do not like the thought that little children can be angry, or that they might have good cause to be. We feel like more responsible adults when we solve their problems, make the angry feelings go away, and enable everyone to be happy. Unfortunately, angry feelings do not go away, and unresolved or repressed, they can lead to aggressive behaviors, withdrawal, depression, physical problems (such as stomach aches, headaches, or muscle aches), and distraction from learning.

WHAT IS ANGER?

Anger is an intense emotional state often characterized by loss of self-control. Anger can be seen in the body through facial expression, body posture, muscle tension, and heightened levels of blood pressure and temperature. These physiological changes are brought on by a specific set of biochemicals called neurotransmitters that act as emotional messengers telling the body and brain to react with anger.

Anger is an arousal state experienced by children when they are thwarted in reaching a goal, their self-esteem is threatened (when insulted, rejected, or treated unfairly), or their needs are not met (Goleman, 1995; Marion, 1997). Once aroused, anger is easily escalated. This is why venting anger verbally (shouting "I am so mad!") or hitting a pillow doesn't calm a child down but may actually increase anger and aggression (Bandura, 1973; Berkowitz, 1993; Slaby, Roedell, Arezzo, & Hendrix, 1995).

Anger is often a **secondary emotion**. Although anger may be the identified feeling, it generally is not the initial emotion but rather the "umbrella" covering up other emotions such as fear, frustration, disappointment, hurt feelings, jealousy or envy (Reynolds, 1990).

Anger can be the response to a single event or to an ongoing situation, it can be short-lived, or it can remain unexpressed but fester and grow. Anger can be an appropriate response, leading to constructive action, or it can be an inappropriate response, leading to destructive consequences. Given guidance, young children can learn to cope with anger directly in ways that minimize further conflict and damage to social relationships (Fabes & Eisenberg, 1992). There are many potential causes for children's anger. Figure 8.1 presents several factors that may result in angry feelings.

STRATEGIES TO REDUCE CHILDREN'S ANGER

- Limit exposure to violent media.
- Identify and provide for children's needs for rest, sleep, and healthy food.
- Identify and provide for children's needs for space, quiet, and moderate temperature.
- Provide adequate supervision with age-appropriate expectations, especially for sitting, waiting, and sharing.
- Offer teacher assistance with frustrating situations.
- Provide opportunities for active play and large-muscle activities such as pounding clay or play dough with a wooden mallet, hammering golf tees into blocks of Styrofoam, using fluid materials such as shaving cream or finger paints, or jumping rope or running.
- Provide soothing activities, such as water play or sand in the sensory table or play dough or clay in a quiet area.
- Offer time in the Cozy Corner.
- Reinforce children's positive actions dealing with anger. (I'm glad you could tell me how you were feeling." "You were very powerful when you figured out a way to handle what was upsetting you."
- Acknowledge and accept anger but not aggressive behaviors.
- Practice stress reduction activities (see Chapter 9).
- Teach assertiveness skills.

FIGURE 8.1

Factors Related to Anger in Children

Environmental factors
- Crowding in school, home, and/or community
- Chaotic conditions in school, home, and/or community
- Unexpected conditions in school, home, and/or community
- Traumatic event in school, home, and/or community
- Stress caused by temperature, chemicals, lighting, or noise in the environment
- Scarcity of age-appropriate materials
- Lack of opportunity for physical exercise

Relationship and role model influences
- Role models in the media that promote violence, immediate gratification, and/or harsh language
- Community and society real-life violence
- Domestic violence, child abuse, or neglect in home
- Critical family change such as marital separation, divorce, or new adult in household
- Stressful changes such as moving, new baby, or death of a grandparent
- Inappropriate demands made on child—"You're too big to cry." "You should be able to sit still and be quiet."
- Personality differences between child and caregivers
- Control battles between child and caregivers
- Authoritarian parenting with harsh punishments
- Early care provider experiencing physical or emotional problems

Individual child factors
- Sensitive to environmental stimuli
- Easily aroused
- Low frustration level
- Lack of sleep or food
- Illness
- Reactions to medication
- Food allergies or sensitivity
- Inability to express emotions verbally
- Limited language skills
- Limited prosocial skills
- Lack of impulse control
- Prolonged problems separating from parent
- Auditory, visual, or physical limitations resulting in frustration or unhappiness

Peer influences
- Disputes over possessions, space, privileges, or need for attention
- Teasing or bullying
- Rejection by peers

Assertiveness Skills as an Anger Prevention Tool

Many children become angry because they do not know how to get their needs met. Their automatic response is to either be aggressive toward the person blocking their way or to withdraw from the situation. Victimized children reinforce their attackers by acquiescing to their demands, crying and assuming defensive postures, and failing to stand up for themselves (Termine, 1997).

The alternative both to being aggressive and to being passive is to be assertive. Being **assertive** means expressing one's own needs and feelings and defending one's own rights while at the same time respecting the rights and feelings of others. The assertive child uses nonviolent ways to get her needs met without trampling on the needs of anyone else. An assertive response can protect a child from being victimized and cause an aggressive child to back down.

Adults can help children develop assertiveness by directly teaching and supporting children in using assertive behaviors. Assertive behaviors include:

- Speaking and responding directly to peers
- Using a clear, firm voice to ask for what you want
- Telling an aggressor to stop ("Stop pushing me.")
- Resisting giving up objects one is still using ("I'm still using this truck.")
- Making requests for a toy or a turn or a favor in a respectful way ("I'd like to play with blocks, too.")
- Standing up for one's own rights ("You forgot my turn." "I want to do it my way this time.")
- Expressing feelings without using put-downs ("That makes me mad." "I don't like it when you..." "Cut it out." "Leave me alone.")

At first, adults may need to be right by the side of the child who is learning to be assertive. If Kenji comes to tell the teacher that Tobias is hitting him, the teacher may need to go and stand next to Kenji while he tells Tobias, "I don't like it when you hit me. Stop doing that."

It is helpful to ask the nonassertive child about her feelings, "How did you feel when James rode by so fast on his bike?" and to help her take some action, "We can tell James how that made you feel." As children become more comfortable with these procedures, the adult can also ask the hurt child to tell the perpetrator what she needs to do to make her and the situation better.

Older children can be helped to learn assertiveness by playing games or acting out role-plays. MacNeill (2003) suggests playing the "what if" game in which children act out scenarios based on common situations, such as "What if Johnny or Jane came up to you in the playground and started calling you names?"

Besides these direct approaches to teaching appropriate assertiveness, teachers can also help in indirect ways by giving children practice in making choices and acknowledging their power to make good choices; reinforcing them for being nonviolent, strong, and clear about their needs; and teaching them to sometimes ignore the annoying behaviors of others. Adults also have to recognize that some situations are simply too dangerous for children to handle themselves. Children have a right to seek adult help and to expect adult support to stop the aggression or extricate them from the scene.

When teaching assertiveness skills, adults need to be sensitive to language and cultural differences. For non-English-speaking children or children with limited language, teach one- to two-word assertive responses, such as "Stop" "Please stop" or "Later." Sensitivity to child-rearing styles and child expectations in different cultures comes from knowledge; educators can learn by consulting with family members and reading related books. In cultures in which humility and group harmony are central values, assertiveness, direct eye contact, and disagreeing with authority figures may be discouraged. Native American children, for example, are often taught at home to "stay back, be quiet, listen, and figure out what's going on. Only speak when you have something to say. As a show of respect, children are taught not to challenge their elders by looking them directly in the eyes or speaking out and questioning what is being taught" (GossMan, 1992, p. 150). Depending on the degree of assimilation or acculturation into mainstream American society, families may approach these issues differently.

CALMING-DOWN STEPS

Children who are in a very agitated state are not able to listen to direction, ask for help, or solve problems. Before progress on alleviating the root cause of their anger can be made, they first need to calm down. Calming oneself is a part of self-regulation. **Self-regulation** refers to controlling impulses, tolerating frustration, and postponing immediate gratification (Marion, 2003).

Children exhibit a wide range of ability to self-regulate depending on their age, the role models in their lives, and the particular incident. Ideally, children will have had experience with self-regulation through the use of the Cozy Corner and practice identifying and expressing emotions and may be familiar with slow breathing techniques taught to them as a stress-reduction strategy. This preparation will help them to learn the following **Calming- Down Steps** (adapted from the Second Step Curriculum, Committee for Children, 1992, 2002).

1. How do I feel?
   Adult helps child to identify how she feels and how she looks (red face, tight eyes, scowling mouth, tensed muscles).
2. Take three deep breaths.
   Slow breathing gives the child something concrete to concentrate on and removes their attention from the incident causing their anger. Slow breathing also reduces the oxygen level in the blood which, in turn, decreases stimulation of the muscles and nerves.
3. Count slowly to five.
   Counting slowly provides a cognitive distraction and helps reduce the arousal level. This step can be modified to meet the child's skills by making it easier (count to three) or harder (count to ten or count backwards from five).
4. Say "calm down" to yourself.
   Self-talk helps children remember how to change their behavior. Children with limited language may prefer to practice the word "stop."
5. Talk to a grown-up about it.
   Now that the child has calmed down, she can talk about what has made her angry and what could be done.

The Calming-Down Steps can be introduced to children in many ways. A simple, clear poster with the steps and illustrations should be prepared in advance. A small book illustrating the steps can also be made and placed in the Cozy Corner for children to "read" individually. Simple puppet role-plays work very well even with toddlers and can be presented in a more complex form for older children. Young children or older children with developmental delays or language problems can be helped to adapt the Calming-Down Steps by using fewer words ("stop" can be put in the place of "calm down" or "count to two" in the place of "count to five"). Many teachers introduce all of the five steps at one class meeting and then review and practice them one at a time at subsequent class meetings. One child care provider did it this way:

> I made a full plan in advance. First, I made my poster and showed it to parents when they brought their child in the morning or picked her up in the evening. Several of them liked it so much that they asked for copies. So, I spent the next week making copies of the Calming-Down Steps in the form of little booklets held together with rings. That was all before I even introduced them to the children. Then, I did a puppet show for the children, with one puppet getting very upset and the other puppet telling her how to calm down. Then, I had the children practice the steps. The next day I enacted a similar role-play and asked the children to teach the puppet how to calm down. They were delighted to be the teacher!

DEALING WITH ANGER IN THE EARLY CHILDHOOD SETTING

- Listen to children's anger. Help them use the words to express anger and talk about its causes. Be sensitive to what may be behind the anger. One kindergarten teacher described her experiences this way:

  > I had never talked directly with the children about feeling angry. I tried opening a class meeting by asking "Is it okay to feel angry?" They all responded "no." That made me think that I had created a climate in my classroom in which they didn't feel it was safe or acceptable to feel angry and maybe that was also the way some of them felt in their homes. I went on to ask them, "Who has ever felt angry?" First one boy raised his hand, then a girl and soon everyone had their hands up. We talked about how all of us feel angry sometimes, and that is okay.

- Be prepared for many demonstrations of anger. The most common immediate triggers of children's anger are conflicts over property or space, responses to physical or verbal attacks, unfulfilled desire for attention, or outright rejection by peers or adults. Help yourself and the child understand the real problem. "It seems to me that you are angry that you can't do that puzzle." "It looks like you want to join in on the hide-and-seek game." "I wonder if you are feeling angry today that the baby got to stay home with Mommy while you came to school." "Some children feel angry when their daddy is away a lot."

- Note individual children's pattern of dealing with angry feelings. Typical patterns include crying, sulking, talking about it, hitting, kicking, biting, teasing or taunting, excluding another child, going away, withdrawing emotionally or physically, or asking an adult for help or support. Prepare a plan of prevention such as altering the physical environment, changing the amount of materials, suggesting the Cozy Corner, redirecting to another activity center, or assisting with a frustrating project. Respond to the anger based on each child's needs (bringing child to Safety Rule poster, helping child share or trade, giving child a place to rest or something to eat, or reading a related book).

- Offer open-ended activities to allow children to express anger-in nonverbal ways such as painting with large paintbrushes, large paper, and thick brushes at the easel; dictating stories to an adult or into a tape recorder; or acting out scenarios using dollhouse figures.
- When incidents of aggression occur, deal with both the perpetrator and the victim. Use the Safety Rule for both. Stop the perpetrator from physical or verbal aggression. "Biting hurts. I can't let you bite Sally. That is not keeping Sally safe." Attend to the victim's physical and emotional needs immediately. When possible, have the perpetrator help correct the situation. "What can you do to make Sally feel better?" "Sally, what would help you feel better?" Once the situation is corrected, compliment both children on their being able to work things out.
- Teach children anger management skills during quieter times of the day (in class meetings or while interacting with children during regular routines and play periods).
- Teach sign language for the word "angry" to toddlers and preschool children without verbal speech. Reinforce use of the sign throughout the day by saying the words "angry" and "mad" and making the sign (Schneider, 2001).
- Create a calming-down poster and talk with the children about it often. Make a small book of the Calming-Down Steps. Place the poster or book in the Cozy Corner.
- Read books about anger to individual children and small groups. (See suggested books at the end of this chapter.)
- Use visual cues

A teacher in a toddler child care center reported:

> I made big cards with angry faces on them and told the children that when they felt themselves getting angry, they should come get one of the big cards and hold it up. It took about two weeks for the process to really catch on, but then most all the children did it. Just this one thing changed the climate of our room entirely.

A second-grade teacher had the children help make stoplights to visualize calming down and problem solving.

> I always find that having visuals works best with my children. We cut out large colored circles from red, yellow, and green construction paper. We wrote words in each circle using the same color magic marker as the paper. In the red circles, we wrote: "Stop, calm down, take three deep breaths." In the yellow circles, we wrote: "How am I feeling? Think about the problem. Think about some solutions. What would happen if I did . . .?" In the green circles, we wrote: "Go ahead and talk to someone about it. Try one of the solutions."

INCLUDING FAMILIES IN TEACHING ANGER MANAGEMENT

Communicate with families about your work on anger management with children. Ask them what makes their child angry at home. Ask for suggestions of what they think would be helpful to their child in school.

Offer concrete materials (homemade calming-down books or children's picture books about anger). One parent told a third-grade teacher that her child had a calming-down poster in her bedroom, one in the bathroom (where she would sit when she was mad), and one on the refrigerator. Several fathers in one preschool class told the teacher that the Calming-Down Steps were helping them even more than their sons.

Send home a newsletter (See Figure 8.2 for an example) that helps parents teach and reinforce the calming down steps at home.

FIGURE 8.2

Sample Newsletter for Families

CARES for Families

Activities in your child's class this month are focusing on the Calming-Down Steps. These steps are helpful when a child is too upset or angry to be able to handle a situation or problem. They help the child to calm down enough so he or she can talk about the problem and help work it out (or sometimes just to feel relaxed enough to go on to something else).

Some parents have asked the teacher for a Calming-Down poster or booklet so they can use it at home. You might also ask your child to tell you about the Calming-Down Steps. Here they are:

- ❑ How do I feel?

- ❑ Take three deep breaths.

- ❑ Count slowly to five.

- ❑ Say "calm down" to yourself.

- ❑ Talk to a grown-up about it.

Using the Calming-Down Steps yourself will show your child that they are important and effective for everyone. Help your child think of different home situations in which the Calming-Down Steps might help the whole family.

KEY TERMS AND CONCEPTS

Anger: an intense emotional state often characterized by loss of self-control

Secondary emotion: the emotion displayed in response to an initial feeling—anger acts like an umbrella, covering up other emotions such as fear, frustration, disappointment, hurt feelings, jealousy, or envy

Assertiveness: expressing one's own needs and feelings and defending one's own rights while at the same time respecting the rights and feelings of others

Self-regulation: controlling impulses, tolerating frustration, and postponing immediate gratification

Calming-Down Steps: a sequence of actions to help a child calm down from a state of anger

LEARNING IN ACTION:
SMALL GROUP ACTIVITIES AND FIELD ASSIGNMENTS

1. Partner chats: Two people discuss the following questions about anger.
    How do I look when I am angry?
    How was I taught as a child to deal with my anger?
    What helps me when I feel angry?
    First, one person speaks while the other simply listens; then the second person speaks while the first person listens. The goals of this activity are to practice good listening skills and to understand one's own personal attitudes towards anger.
2. In small groups, create a puppet role-play for a class meeting on the Calming-Down Steps. Depict a typical classroom situation that causes either or both of the puppets to be angry. After deciding the theme of the puppet role-play, one adult in the group manipulates the puppets, acting out the classroom scenario ("freezing" the puppets before any aggression occurs) and asking the "children" to teach the puppets the Calming-Down Steps (the other adults in the group act out the role of a group of children).
3. Make a Calming-Down poster. Use large, white poster board. Refer back to text for the five calming down steps. Add simple, clear illustrations for each step.
4. Consider the case study described below.
    Robbie is a 4 ½-year-old who has joined your class in the middle of the year. He seems to have a very "short fuse." When things don't go exactly as he wants them to, he flies into a rage. Sometimes he tears up his own or another child's picture, sometimes he hits and kicks, sometimes he yells.
    In groups of three or four, create a plan of action for Robbie. How will you determine what is underlying his bouts of anger? What are your short-term goals, over the next two weeks, for Robbie? What are your long-term goals, during the course of the year, for Robbie? What strategies will you try immediately with Robbie?

RELATED CHILDREN'S BOOKS

Aaron, J. (1998). *When I'm angry.* New York: Golden.

Berry, J. (1995). *Let's talk about feeling angry.* New York: Scholastic Inc.

Berry, J. (1996). *Let's talk about needing attention.* New York: Scholastic Inc.

Berry J., (1996). *Let's talk about saying no.* New York: Scholastic Inc.

Bourgeois, P., & Clark, B. (1997). *Franklin's bad day.* New York: Scholastic Inc.

Crary, E. (1992) *I'm mad.* Seattle, WA: Parenting Press, Inc.

Crary, E., & Silversmith, S. (1996). *When you're mad and you know it.* Seattle, WA: Parenting Press, Inc.

Jenell, L. (2002). *When mommy was mad.* New York: Putnam Publishing Group.

Katz, K. (2002). *No biting.* New York: Grosset & Dunlap.

Lachner, D. (1995). *Andrew's angry words.* New York: North South Books.

Leonard, M. (1997). *How I feel: Angry.* San Diego, CA: Smart Kids Publishing, Inc.

Leonard, M. (1999). *No new pants!* Brookfield, CT: Millbrook Press.

Mayer, M. (1983). *I was so mad.* Racine, WI: Western Publishing Inc.

Oram, H. (1994). *Fernando furioso/Angry Arthur.* Venezuela: Ekare, Ediciones Banco del Libro.

Simon, N. (1991). *I was so mad.* Morton Grove, IL: Albert Whitman & Co.

SUGGESTED READING AND RESOURCES

Acredolo, L., Goodwyn, S., & Abrams, D. (2002). *Baby signs: How to talk with your baby before your baby can talk.* New York: Harper Festival.

Axelrod, A., Holtje, J., & Holtje, J. (1997). *210 ways to say no effectively and gracefully.* New York: McGraw Hill.

Chess, S., & Thomas, A. (1987). *Know your child: An authoritative guide for today's parents.* New York: Basic Books.

Dinwiddie, S. *Help! It's another tantrum.* Retrieved September 15, 2003 from http://kidsource.com/better. world.press/tantrums.html

Fensterheim, H., & Baer, J. (1975). *Don't say yes when you want to say no.* New York: Dell.

Fetsch, R. J., & Jacobson, B. (2002). *Children's anger and tantrums.* Retrieved September 15, 2003 from http:// www.ext.colostate.edu/pubs/consumer/10248.html

Garcia, J. (2002). *Sign with your baby: How to communicate with infants before they can speak.* Seattle, WA: Northlight Communications.

Johnson, E. H. (1998). *Brothers on the mend: Understanding and healing anger for African-American men and women.* New York: Pocket Books.

Kurchinka, M. S. (1992). *Raising your spirited child: A guide for parents whose child is more intense, sensitive, perceptive, persistent, energetic.* New York: Harper Perennial.

Marion, M. (2003). *Guidance of young children* (6th ed.). Upper Saddle River, NJ: Merrill/Prentice Hall.

Paul, H. A. (1995). *When kids are mad, not bad.* New York: Berkley Books.

Provence, S. (1985). *Helping young children channel their aggressive energies.* Retrieved September 15, 2003 from http://www.zerotothree.org/help.html

Shapiro, L. E. (1997). *25 ways to help children control their anger.* Secaucus, NJ: Childswork/Childsplay.

Smith, M. J. (1975). *When I say no, I feel guilty*. New York: Bantam Books.

Whitehouse, E., & Pudney, W. (1996). *A volcano in my tummy: Helping children to handle anger: A resource book for parents, caregivers and teachers*. British Columbia, CAN: New Society Publishers.

REFERENCES

Bandura, A. (1973). *Aggression: A social learning analysis*. Upper Saddle River, NJ: Prentice Hall.

Berkowitz, L. (1993). *Aggression: Its causes, consequences, and control*. New York: McGraw-Hill.

Committee for Children (2002). *Second Step: A violence prevention curriculum for preschoolers and kindergartners*. (3rd ed.). Seattle, WA: Committee for Children.

Fabes, R. A., & Eisenberg, N. (1992). Young children's coping with interpersonal anger. *Child Development, 63*, 116–128.

Goleman, D. (1995). *Emotional intelligence*. New York: Bantam Books.

GossMan, H. (1992). Meeting the needs of all children-An Indian perspective. In B. Neugebauer (Ed.) *Alike and different: Exploring our humanity with young children* (pp. 146–151). Washington, DC: National Association for the Education of Young Children.

MacNeill, E. (2003). *Assertiveness for children*. Retrieved September 15, 2003 from http://www.kidscape.org.uk

Marion, M. (1997). Guiding young children's understanding and management of anger. *Young Children, 52*(7), 62–65.

Miller, K. (1996). *The crisis manual for early childhood teachers: How to handle the really difficult problems*. Beltsville, MD: Gryphon House.

Reynolds, E. (1990). *Guiding young children: a child-centered approach*. Mountain View, CA: Mayfield Publishing Company.

Schneider, E. E. (2001). *American sign language series III Lesson 2: Emotions and feelings*. Retrieved September 15, 2003 from http://www.lessontutor,com/eesASLemotions.html

Slaby, R. G., Roedell, W. C., Arezzo, D., & Hendrix, K. (1995). *Early violence prevention: Tools for teachers of young children*. Washington, DC: National Association for the Education of Young Children.

Termine, L. J. (1997). *Integrating prosocial skills in preschool and kindergarten education*. Retrieved September 20, 2003 from http://www.termine.com/ProsocialSkills.html

Chapter 9

STRESS REDUCTION

Tony is a 7-year-old who is dropped off at Mrs. Mendoza's child care home about 7:30 every weekday morning. He stays with Mrs. Mendoza until the school bus picks him up later in the morning and then again each afternoon when the school bus drops him off after the end of the school day. Lucia, his mother, picks Tony up about 6:00 in the evening.

Tony had been coming to this child care home for almost 2 years when his behavior suddenly changed dramatically. He was no longer generally cooperative or relaxed with Mrs. Mendoza, and he got into frequent confrontations with the other children. When Mrs. Mendoza brought this up with Tony's mother, she was told that Tony's father had moved out of their house and threatened never to see her or Tony again. Lucia then told Mrs. Mendoza that she didn't want this discussed with Tony or anyone else.

Mrs. Mendoza was at a loss as to how to proceed. She wanted to help Tony, while at the same time honoring Lucia's insistence on not talking with him about his father's absence. She finally decided that teaching Tony some stress reduction techniques could help relax Tony while still respecting his mother's request.

Mrs. Mendoza taught Tony how to slow down his breathing and consciously relax his tense muscles. She offered to give Tony gentle back rubs and at other times suggested that he sit by himself and listen to quiet music. Soon Tony was requesting these "relaxation sessions" almost every afternoon. Mrs. Mendoza was pleased with how much this seemed to be helping Tony, but she was also worried about the time it took away from her attention to the other children. She decided to ask Tony to teach the younger children these techniques. Soon Tony had them stretching and then doing group back rubs. Mrs. Mendoza noted a significant reduction in stress behaviors in Tony and increased calmness in the total group of children in her care. A few of the mothers, including Lucia, even asked for her "miracle prescription."

Stress (as discussed in Chapter 1) is a stark reality of children's lives today. Common stresses include: two parents working long hours, single-parent households, divorce, stepparents and blended families, frequent moves, the negative influence of the media, and the hectic pace of modern life. All children today hear about terrorism and war. Some children are exposed to additional stress related to poverty, substance abuse in their family, or exposure to violence in their homes and communities. These stressful situations take a toll on children's physical and emotional health. Witkin (1999, p. 3) reports:

> Doctors throughout the country are seeing more and more children as young as three years old with stress-related ailments like ulcerative colitis. Studies show that at least one in twenty children under age ten suffers from depression, a typical stress-related condition. . .and that as many as 90 percent of office visits to primary care physicians {may be} connected to stress.

Early childhood care and education providers typically cannot diminish the stresses that children face in their lives outside of school or child care. However, educators can play an important part in teaching even young children how to relax themselves.

WHAT IS STRESS?

Stress is a natural phenomenon that can either work to our advantage or to our detriment. **Stress** is the body's response to any demand that exceeds the individual's ability to cope and a mental state that occurs in response to unusual or everyday strains. Stress comes from the instinctive **fight or flight response** that all humans possess. In response to a threatening situation, the brain's hypothalamic-pituitary-adrenal (HPA) system activates to release the primary stress hormone cortisol. Cortisol organizes all the body's systems to respond quickly to deal with the stress. The HPA system also releases chemical messengers (we know some of these commonly as adrenaline) which trigger an emotional response. These chemical messengers also "suppress activity in areas at the front of the brain concerned with short-term memory, concentration, inhibition, and rational thought. This sequence of mental events allows a person to react quickly to a stressful situation while it also hinders the ability to handle complex social or intellectual tasks and behaviors" (UC Davis Health System, 2001).

This heightened state of preparedness may lead to a quick and constructive solution to the taxing situation. Or it may not. If this heightened state is prolonged, as happens with children exposed to chronic stress, physical and emotional problems are likely to occur. Sustained high levels of stress reduce the body's ability to fight disease and illness, impede the digestive system, and may contribute to depression. Learning how to manage and reduce stress is thus essential to physical and emotional well-being.

SIGNS OF STRESS IN CHILDREN

Childhood stress involves any unusual adaptation that forces children to draw on energy reserves exceeding what they would normally require for dealing with ordinary events in their lives (Hart, Burts, Durland, Charlesworth, DeWolf, & Fleege, 1998). Witkin (1999, p. 63) describes children's response to stress:

> Unlike adults, who may have learned how to channel that energy
> productively or at least have developed various coping strategies, children
> "act up" as we say. They are like small pumps about to explode. With more
> energy than they know what to do with, they resort to their own strategies in
> an effort to burn off that energy.

Children's behavioral reactions to stress may include poor concentration and distractibility, aggression, irritability, outbursts of anger, temper tantrums, restlessness, whining, or crying. Some children exhibit excessive dependence, clinging, unwillingness to separate from parents or participate in school activities, stuttering or dysfluent speech, or regression to behaviors typical of an earlier developmental stage. Physical reactions to stress may include somatic complaints such as headaches or stomachaches, excessive fatigue, sleep disturbances, changes in eating habits, lapses in toileting, or susceptibility to colds, flu, or other infections (Brenner, 1997).

Stress can affect the way children think, act, and feel (Zeitlin & Williamson, 1994). Early childhood providers may suspect that a child is particularly stressed if the child has experienced a life-changing event (such as a new baby in the house, marital separation or divorce, or moving to a new home or school), acts in a way not previously seen, presents consistent behavioral problems, or lives daily with the challenges of special needs. All children in contemporary society, no matter their developmental stage or individual circumstances, have some amount of stress.

CAN STRESS BE REDUCED?

It would be unrealistic to think that educators could eliminate stress from children's lives. It is possible, however, to help children manage stress and begin to learn how to make their bodies and minds less tense.

Recent research suggests that a relaxation response can be taught. The **relaxation response** can interrupt or reverse the fight or flight response and result in an actual lowering of metabolism, heart and breathing rates, and blood pressure (Benson & Kipper, 1990). Researchers and practitioners have used the pioneering work on the relaxation response to develop and test different methods of stress reduction, including muscle relaxation, meditation, and yoga. If done regularly, these can all have positive effects in counteracting the harmful influences of stress. Early childhood educators can adapt these methods and add their own based upon the practices of developmentally appropriate education.

PRACTICES THAT REDUCE STRESS IN THE EARLY CHILDHOOD SETTING

- Reinforce the Safety Rule and assure children that here everyone will be kept safe.
- Keep the physical environment uncluttered and not over-stimulating.
- Encourage children to use the Cozy Corner.
- Offer an "Alone Table" to children who want to play quietly away from the general group hubbub.
- Establish routines and keep to them. When routines must be changed, alert children in advance.
- Use good listening skills and reflective language to acknowledge children's concerns and worries.
- Try to keep snack time or mealtimes unhurried and pleasant. Facilitate pleasant conversations about the children's activities at school or their interests outside school. Consider offering food when children are hungry rather than always at pre-set times.
- Help children slow down and transition into nap or rest times. Peaceful music, quiet games, or reassuring stories before they are expected to rest or sleep are helpful. The following anecdotes demonstrate the effectiveness of this technique, reported by a child care center director.

> I started collecting cassettes of relaxing music when we first learned about doing stress reduction with our children at our child care center. I keep them in my office, and the teachers check them out. This year the favorite seems to be a collection of Native American pieces using wind instruments and gentle drumming. Other popular ones are tapes of rain, the ocean, and classical music.
>
> A bilingual teacher uses cassette stories with simple, repetitive themes for stress reduction at transition times. "One of the children's

enduring favorites is *Seven Little Rabbits*. It's a very relaxing counting rhyme, and all the children, including my Spanish speakers, understand it before long. It's the story of seven little rabbits who get tired out on their walk and one by one, they are tucked into bed and fall asleep."

- Provide extra physical activity and large motor experiences for those children with a naturally high energy level. Steer those children who fatigue easily to quieting activities.
- Use smiles and a sense of humor as often as possible throughout the day. Make up silly stories, have the children join in using gibberish language. Read funny poetry or limericks.
- Keep the sensory table available every day. Relaxing materials for the sensory table include warm water, coarse salt, autumn leaves.
- Plan times with children just to look out the window and observe the weather, the changing seasons, or people walking by.
- Be a good role model on how to deal with stress. Admit to children that you are sometimes stressed, tell them when you are, and describe what you are doing to deal with and reduce your stress.

TEACHING STRESS REDUCTION STRATEGIES

Difference Between Feeling *Tense* and Feeling *Relaxed*

Show children examples of *tense* bodies, using a doll with rigid limbs or toy robot to show stiff, tight muscles. Have the children squeeze their own muscles tightly, making their hands tense, their arms tense, and their legs tense. Then show them examples of relaxed bodies, such as a Raggedy Ann or Andy doll or a floppy stuffed animal. Let them hold the dolls to see how they feel. Have the children relax their muscles to make their neck, hands, and arms relaxed and floppy. Then alternate tense and relaxed. Practice the tense/relaxed exercises frequently in class meetings. During the course of the day, point out when you see their bodies—or your own—looking tense or relaxed.

For toddlers, begin by introducing these new vocabulary words throughout the day: "Keri, you are looking *tense* and *tight* while you're doing that puzzle." "Tomas, you seem so relaxed while you are drawing."

Teach Children How to Visualize

Young children have a natural capacity for pretending. Build on this by helping them learn how to "make pictures behind their eyes." One teacher of 3-year-olds uses the children's favorite books as a basis for **visualizations**.

I love the *Runaway Bunny* especially and so do the children. They lie down on their mats and close their eyes while I read the story in summary form. For each page, I describe what is happening in very simple terms and ask them to see that with their eyes closed, "to make a picture behind their eyes." They love doing this so much I get requests throughout the day for our "lie down and make a picture time."

A kindergarten teacher introduced visualization to her children by showing them pictures of clouds. Then they lay down on the floor and pretended they were putting their heads on a cloud. They rested that way for a few minutes and then she asked them to sit up and talk about how it felt. After several children described how soft and "floating" it felt, she had them try it again.

> After a few days of doing this, I added "pulling the cloud down to wipe our faces." Afterwards, we talked about how relaxed this made our faces feel. The next week, we pulled the cloud further down over our bodies. The children now talk about "our clouds" all the time and use the process to relax at other times too.

Practice Slow Breathing

For preschool-age children, start with teaching the difference between inhaling and exhaling. Inhaling is taking a breath in, while exhaling is blowing the breath out. Blow the breath out onto your fingers so you can feel it. Put up five fingers and pretend they are birthday candles. Slowly inhale and then blow out each candle.

After children understand how to inhale and exhale, teach them to slow down their breathing. Slowly count to three out loud while they inhale through their noses, then count to three while they exhale through their mouths. Have them practice this many times until they can really slow down.

Toddlers can learn to take deep breaths by blowing cotton balls. Adults can demonstrate how to take a slow, deep breath, and the children can practice this by *slowly* blowing the cotton balls across a table or on the floor.

Preschoolers and primary-grade children can practice **abdominal breathing**. By forcing air slowly into the base of the lungs, the diaphragm is stretched, and the nerves attached to the diaphragm trigger the body's natural relaxation response (Manassis, 1996). Remind children to breathe very slowly, pushing out their abdomen each time they inhale. A visual aid, such as putting a pillow on top of the stomach or a hand on one's belt, helps children see when their stomach is rising and falling.

Introduce Children to Simple Massage and Back Rubs

Teach children the following sequence for a self-massage:
1. Place the right hand on the back of the left shoulder. Squeeze gently, then rub the fingers in a circular motion. Do the same with the left hand on the right shoulder.
2. Place the fingers of both hands on the forehead and gently massage in a circular motion.
3. Place the fingers of both hands on the back of the neck. Press down and count to three. Then massage in a circular motion.

Once children lose their self-consciousness about relaxing, they are even able to give each other back rubs. Ask each child if he would like a back rub. (Children who choose not to have one should be respected but can be encouraged to watch. You will be surprised how many of these more cautious children will decide to join in later.) Assign partners, with first one child rubbing the other's back and then the second child rubbing the first one's back. Stop frequently and remind them to ask the child who they are massaging if it is too strong. Circulate among the children and help them be gentle and safe with each other.

One teacher of 4-year-olds reported how she never expected this activity to be so successful.

> I know I love back rubs, and sometimes I even had asked a child to give me one or if he wanted me to give him one. But I was amazed how quickly and easily the children moved into giving each other back rubs. One day they suggested we make a train, and have a "trainful of back rubs." Now we do our train almost every day.

A popular back rub activity is the "weather report." Children form a circle or a straight line with each child sitting so that they can touch the back of the child in front of them. The adult asks the children to "follow my directions for rubbing the back of the child sitting in front of you." "Today we're going on a long pretend trip. We will go through lots of different kinds of weather. First it's very sunny, and the warm air feels good." {Instruct the children to place both hands on the back of the child in front and firmly but gently press his open palms along the top of the back and shoulders.) "Now it begins to rain, a soft, gentle rain." (Tell the children to use the tips of their fingers to tap up and down the back of the child in front of them.) "Then it begins to thunder." (*Gently* pound with fists up and down the back.) "We travel onto a mountain side, and there is a lot of mud that makes a mudslide." (With flat hands, slide from top to bottom of back.) "We move near the ocean where it is very windy." (Tell the children to make circular motions with the whole palm over the shoulders and back.) "Finally, we are back to the sunny place where we started. Feel the warm sun." (Press open palms along the top of the back and shoulders.)

Teach Yoga Stretches and Yoga Exercises

Although young children will not do a full program of yoga, they can still enjoy and benefit from age-appropriate adaptations. "Studies have found that when large muscle groups repeatedly contract and relax, as in yoga-type activities, the brain is signaled to release specific neurotransmitters that prompt feelings of relaxation and mental acuity" (Bodger, 1999, p.130). Books that illustrate yoga postures in terms of animals are very appealing to young children who love trying to look like a lion or a whale.

Design Movement Activities and Dramatics

Even toddlers love obstacle courses and can help build them from materials such as tables, cardboard boxes, and pillows. Create a path of going over, under, through, around. For preschoolers, add a balance board or ask them to move through the course very slowly, or sometimes backwards!

Children can imagine they are different animals and physically act like them. "Imagine you are a cat walking on a fence. Balance yourself so you won't fall off. Walk very slowly, one careful step at a time."

Practice "Feather Painting"

Purchase large, natural feathers. Teach the children how to "paint" their skin by stroking their neck, arms, or legs with the feather. Later, they can ask a friend if he wants to be "painted." Pairing children to gently stoke each other with feathers promotes gentleness and caring.

Use Stress Reduction Techniques Throughout the Day

Teachers find that many different times are good times for stress reduction, including transitions from outside to indoors and from active periods to quieter times (such as eating or resting).

> After teaching stress reduction strategies for several months, a preschool teacher held a class meeting during which she asked the children what they did to relax. The children came up with the following list: lie down, do neck rolls, do shoulder rolls, ask for a back rub, sleep, draw a picture. Then she asked them *when* they liked to do these things. They answered: "When we're tense." She felt so energized by this proof that the stress reduction techniques had really made an impact on the children that she decided to share all this information with their parents. Her next class meeting was to brainstorm with the children how they could "teach" their parents stress reduction, too.

INCLUDING FAMILIES IN STRESS MANAGEMENT

Early child care educators report that they enjoy the stress reduction techniques as much as the children. Many parents will as well. Communicating with families about child-friendly stress management techniques appropriate for young children will give them another avenue for interacting with their children while at the same time, possibly reducing their own stress.

Invite parents to observe a class meeting during which you practice a stress reduction exercise. Ask parents about the signs of stress in their own children and what they like to do at home to try to alleviate stress. Share some relevant ideas you are using in your setting. Mention the benefits to both children and adults.

> One teacher assistant noted that dismissal time was always very harried. Children seemed to be very active after their outdoor play time, and parents felt pressured by the children's high energy levels and insistent demands when they picked them up. "So we started doing different stress reduction exercises just before dismissal. It really helped slow the children down, and now when they greet their parents, they are so much more relaxed and pleasant. The parents have really noticed the difference and keep thanking us. They say that it even makes the rest of their day go better."

Positive experiences of this type help to open the door for conversations with parents about the benefits of stress reduction and the causes of stress. One theme to work on with parents can be that of the stressful effects of media violence. Child care providers can help parents understand that exposure to violent, sexually disturbing, and age-inappropriate television and videos can create stress and fears for their children. Once parents see these connections, they may be open to providers' suggestions to reduce media watching for their young children, substitute prosocial, age-appropriate programs for less appropriate ones, and introduce alternative fun and stress-reducing activities at home.

KEY TERMS AND CONCEPTS

Stress: the body's response to any demand that exceeds the individual's ability to cope; a mental state that occurs in response to unusual or everyday strains

Fight or flight response: the instinctive response that programs humans to prepare to either fight or flee in a threatening situation

Relaxation response: A six-step process of relaxing developed by Dr. Herbert Benson to reduce the activity of the autonomic nervous system

Visualization: the formation of mental, visual images

Abdominal breathing: breathing involving the area beneath the rib cage instead of high in the chest; allows increased oxygen to the brain and musculature and promotes a state of calmness

LEARNING IN ACTION: SMALL GROUP ACTIVITIES AND FIELD ASSIGNMENTS

1. Choose two stress reduction activities mentioned in this chapter and practice them with a partner. Then, create a class meeting in which you introduce them to children. Discuss the size of the group of children and the space needed to make the class meeting most successful.
2. Observe in an early childhood setting for at least a half-day session. Note times of day and situations in which you would add stress reduction activities based upon suggestions in this chapter.
3. Write a "case study" in which you describe a child, giving gender, age, and specific stresses he is facing. Design a program of stress reduction strategies and activities for that child, noting when and how often you will use them.
4. Investigate music CDs that would help create a relaxing mood for children. Check your college or public library. Listen carefully to the music and define why you think it would be appropriate for stress reduction.

RELATED CHILDREN'S BOOKS

Becker, J. L. (1994). *Seven little rabbits*. New York: Walker & Co.

Berenstain, S., & Berenstain, J. (1992). *The Berenstain Bears and too much pressure*. New York: Random House.

Carlson, N. (1991). *Take time to relax!* New York: Viking.

Lite, L. (1996). *A boy and a bear: The children's relaxation book*. Plantation, FL: Specialty Press.

Mainland, P. (1998). *A yoga parade of animals: A first book of yoga for children*. New York: Harper Collins.

Moser, A. (1988). *Don't pop your cork on Mondays: The children's anti-stress book*. Kansas City, MO: Landmark Editions.

Slap-Shelton, L., & Shapiro, L. (2001). *Every time I blow my top I lose my head.* Plainview, NY: Childswork/Childsplay.

SUGGESTED READING AND RESOURCES

Allen, J., & Klein, R. (1997). *Ready, set, relax: A research-based program of relaxation, learning and self-esteem for children.* Watertown, WI: Inner Coaching.

Brenner, A. (1997). *Helping children cope with stress.* San Francisco, CA: Jossey-Bass.

Garmezy, N., & Rutter, M., (Eds.) (1983). *Stress, coping, & development in children.* New York: McGraw Hill.

Gruenberg, A. (1998). Creative stress management: "Put your own oxygen mask on first." *Young Children, 53*(1), 38–42.

Honig, A. (1986). Stress and coping in children. *Young Children, 41*(5), 47–59.

Humphrey, J. H. (1998). *Helping children manage stress: A guide for adults.* Annapolis Junction, MD: Child Welfare League of America, Inc.

Jewett, J. (1997). Childhood stress. *Childhood Education, 73*(3), 172–173.

Kersey, K. (1995). *Helping your child handle stress.* New York: Berkley Publishing Group.

Kielar, J. (1999). An antidote to the noisy nineties. *Young Children 54*(5), 28–29.

Lewis, S., & Lewis, S. (1996). *Stress-proofing your child.* New York: Bantam Books.

Make way for baby: postnatal stimulation baby massage (n.d.).Retrieved August 14, 2003 from http://www.makewayforbaby.com/massages.htm

Oehlberg, B. (1996). *Making it better: Activities for children in a stressful world.* Beltsville, MD: Redleaf Press.

Piper, F. (1998). *Stress management techniques for young children.* ERIC Document No. ED299052. [Electronic version]. Retrieved August 16. 2003 from http://ericir.syr.edu/plweb-cgi/fastweb?getdoc+ericdb-adv+ericdb+937126+0+wAAA+%28

Roe, D. (1996). Young children and stress: How can we help? *AECA Resource Book Series, 3*(4). ERIC Document No. ED409090. Retrieved August 16, 2003 from http://wricir.syr.edu/plweb-cgi/fastweb?getdoc+ericdb-adv+ericdb+91960+0+wAAA+%28E

Swartz, F., Ritchie, R., Sacks, L., & Phillips C. (1998). Music, stress reduction and medical cost savings in the neonatal intensive care unit. *International Society for Music in Medicine.* Retrieved October 10, 2003 from http://www.transitionsmusic.com/ ISMM_ARTICLE.html

REFERENCES

Benson, H., & Kipper, M. (1990). *The relaxation response.* New York: Avon Books.

Bodger, C. (1999). *Smart guide to relieving stress.* New York: Wiley.

Brenner, A. (1997). *Helping children cope with stress.* San Francisco: Jossey-Bass.

Gold, P. (2001, October). Encountering daily life: How our emotions affect us, the high costs of stress. *National Institute Mental Health Project on the Decade of the Brain: The Science of Emotion.* Retrieved October 12, 2003 from http://www.nimh.nih.gov/dob/gold.cfm

Hart, C., Burts, D., Durland, M., Charlesworth, R., DeWolf, M., & Fleege, P. (1998). Stress behaviors and activity type participation of preschoolers in more or less developmentally appropriate classrooms: SES and sex differences. *Journal of Research in Childhood Education,* 12(2), 176–196.

Manassis, K. (1996). *Keys to parenting your anxious child.* Hauppauge, NY: Barron's Educational Series, Inc.

UC Davis Health System. (2001). *What are the biological effects of acute stress?* Retrieved October 10, 2003 from http://www.ucdmc.ucdavis.edu/ucdhs/health/a-z/31Stress/doc31 biologicaleffects.html

Witkin, G. (1999). *KidStress: Effective strategies parents can teach their kids for schools, family, peers, the world-and everything.* New York: Viking.

Zeitlin, S., & Williamson, G. (1994). *Coping in young children.* Baltimore, MD: Paul H. Brookes.

Chapter 10

EMOTIONALLY-RESPONSIVE CURRICULUM PLANNING

Much to my dismay, our class was scheduled to move to a new building in December. I was worried about how this change would affect the children and their sense of safety and security that I had worked so hard to establish in our group. I decided to begin preparing the children for the move 6 weeks in advance. We created a book about moving. We took photographs of our current classroom and building and scheduled a field trip to the new building near completion to take pictures of the outside of the building and our new classroom. We read the book many times before the move. We had class meetings about "what would be the same" and "what would be different" after we moved. In the days just prior to the move, the children helped me pack and label boxes. They kept reminding me to pack our Safety Rule poster and pictorial schedule. The children painted pictures to decorate the walls of our new room.

To my surprise, the children adapted remarkably well to the move. They were delighted to see their pictures on the wall and the learning centers set up in a similar fashion as in their previous classroom. They asked to read "Our Moving Book" many times. We soon settled into our established routines and "moved on" with the school year.

WHAT IS AN EMOTIONALLY RESPONSIVE CURRICULUM?

An **emotionally responsive curriculum** is centered on the emotional needs of children. It is curriculum that reflects and responds to experiences and issues in children's lives. Classroom activities are thoughtfully planned to promote social and emotional competencies related to success in school. Although important for all children, such a focus is especially important when working with at-risk populations or children demonstrating problem social behaviors. According to Lesley Koplow (1996), acting-out behaviors can be seen as an indication that children need more help to tolerate their feelings, to understand emotional cause and effect, and to express their emotions clearly.

To select the content (or "themes") for an emotionally responsive curriculum, teachers carefully observe children and communicate with their families to gain insights into the children's lives and backgrounds.

Observe Themes Expressed in Children's Spontaneous Play

Careful attention to children's play themes allow teachers to determine what topics are on children's minds (Koplow, 1996). These may be developmentally common issues such as separation, autonomy, peer relationships, power, or fantasy versus reality. Play themes also center on real experiences in their lives and re-enactment of roles: saying good-bye to a person or place, mommy and baby at home, going to the grocery store, or pretending to be a construction worker or firefighter. More disturbingly, some of these re-enactments can reflect the stressful environmental realities of some children's lives: adults purchasing drugs, police arresting someone, family violence, or knowledge of sexually inappropriate information for their age.

Emotionally responsive teachers watch children as they play, to learn more about what they are struggling to understand or may be worried about. When young children observe scary events in their own lives or through the media, it is normal for them to act out what interests, confuses, or frightens them in their play. Spontaneous play becomes a vehicle for self-expression, to symbolically play out events in an attempt to understand and make sense out of their experiences. Classrooms need to be well-equipped to provide the materials for symbolic play, with toys, props, and dramatic play opportunities that can mirror children's real living environments. Plastic family figures, dolls, and housekeeping props, reflecting diverse cultures, are essential for role-playing family dynamics. Community helper figures and props encourage more complex play (Oehlberg, 1996).

Toddlers engage in early level symbolic play with baby dolls and housekeeping props. Repetitive block stacking and knocking down may represent the toddler's attempt to master separation fears as separate things become one thing, then separate again. They may work through body integrity issues through simple doctor/patient play with medical props.

The interests of 4- and 5-year-olds expand into the larger world beyond their home and family. Often they play out occupational roles (e.g., firefighter, police officer, astronaut, teacher) and fantasy roles (e.g., kings, queens, monsters, TV characters). Many are fascinated with nature, growth, and change.

It was early April and many children brought bouquets of spring flowers to their teacher Mara. After helping the children to put the flowers in water, Mara placed the vase on the classroom science table. In the coming days, Mara noticed how the children frequently gathered around the flowers, gently touching them, and making comments about the changes as buds blossomed. She decided to create a curriculum unit on planting and growing to give the children an opportunity to take care of plants and flowers. Since it was near the end of the school year, she also included books and class meetings about the way the children had grown and changed.

Children's play may reflect issues of power, dominance, and powerlessness, especially in children who have had frightening experiences. Children may work through these issues playing with toys of various sizes and "power levels" such as sets of dinosaurs and plastic animals of various sizes (Oehlberg, 1996).

Similarly, superhero play represents a developmentally appropriate power/fear fascination, especially for 4-year-old boys. Unfortunately, this often results in aggression or play which may frighten some other children. If children's play gets too scary or dangerous, teachers can gently intervene and redirect it, asking open-ended questions that encourage the child to role-play an alternative resolution of the situation they are re-enacting (Oehlberg, 1996). With superhero play, teachers can ask how the superheroes might help other people and offer toys such as rescue vehicles and medical equipment. Teachers can model gentler ways of play, saying for example, "Weapons hurt people, and I don't want any of my friends to get hurt or feel unsafe. How else could your superheroes solve their conflict without fighting?" (See Suggested Readings and Resources for more information about handling media-related play.)

Gain Knowledge of Children's Developmental Histories and Life Experiences

Ongoing communication with families allows teachers to understand each child's developmental history and life experiences. At an initial conference, care and education providers can ask parents about their child's birth history, developmental milestones, frightening or significant experiences particular to their child, and anything about the child that parents feel it is important for the teacher to know.

Frequent communication during the school year can keep teachers abreast of changes in children's lives such as an upcoming move, a new baby on the way, a parent's military deployment overseas, or the impending divorce between parents. Throughout these exchanges, care and education professionals must be respectful of families and recognize that some may consider questions related to family experiences to be an invasion of privacy. Others may feel it is a wonderful opportunity to enlist their child's care providers in supporting their mode of helping their child.

There are three types of change that children may experience. Each has a potentially different effect on children (Devall & Cahill, 1995).

Developmental change includes those typical experiences encountered by every child as a part of growing up—learning to use the toilet or coping with separation from parents while attending child care are two typical examples of developmental changes.

Even though developmental change may cause some stress at first, children learn from these experiences and become better prepared to handle future changes. Given the support of loving and responsive caregivers, most children successfully handle this type of change.

> A teacher in one toddler classroom made certain that the dollhouse was always available to the children. She noticed that a much of the toddlers' play involved the dollhouse bathroom and the little wooden potty. Many of the toddlers going through toilet training would manipulate the family figures to use the toilet over and over.

Another type of change is **critical change**. These are events that are fairly common, but do not occur to every child, and require some adaptation on the part of the child. Examples of critical change include a change in child care arrangements (transitioning from a home care provider to a center program with 50 children), the birth of a younger sibling, moving to a new home in a new community, or being in the hospital. Although these situations can cause temporary stress, children are usually able to adapt to these transitions also, given loving support from parents and other caregivers (Devall & Cahill, 1995).

> Maryann received the kind of phone call dreaded by every parent. "Your daughter has fallen on the playground. We suspect that she has a broken arm. We suggest that you pick her up and take her to the hospital for x-rays." Before she dashed to the car to pick up her 5-year-old daughter Kristin, Maryann gathered up Kristin's blanket that she slept with each night and a favorite teddy bear, knowing that Kristin would need the comfort of these familiar things. On the way to the hospital, Maryann explained to Kristin what would probably happen during the doctor's exam, getting x-rays taken, and maybe having a cast put on if the arm was really broken. She reassured Kristin that she would be right beside her and that everyone at the hospital would be careful and try to make her arm feel better.

The most stressful type of change is **catastrophic change**, which includes events that are sudden, unexpected, life-changing, and perhaps life-threatening such as accidents, natural disasters, witnessing a violent act, the death or serious illness of a loved one, homelessness, incarceration of a parent, or any form of abuse. (An in-depth discussion of these topics and their impact on young children is beyond the scope of this book. Please refer to Suggested Readings and Resources at the end of this chapter.)

Understandably, children are quite distraught when faced with this type of stress and may need counseling in addition to the support system teachers and caregivers provide (Devall &

Cahill, 1995). (Chapter 11 presents information about when to seek support from other professionals for a child about whom teachers have concerns.) Given background information, caregivers play an important, supportive role.

> Whenever the furnace turns on, the hot-water heating pipes in the preschool classroom begin to make a clanging noise. Diego stops what he is doing and frantically asks the teacher, "Did you hear that? What was that? Was that the bad man?" From a conversation with Diego's parents, his teacher Rita knows that recently Diego's home was broken into in the middle of the night. The robbers forced open a door which made considerable noise. When Diego's father went to investigate the noise, he was attacked with a knife. Fortunately he was not seriously injured. Ever since, Diego has become very anxious hearing noises. Rita takes Diego aside and says, "Mommy said that when the heating pipes make noise, it reminds you of something scary that happened at your house. So, if the pipes start making noise and you start feeling scared, come over and stay by me. I'll remind you that it is just the noisy heating system and that you are safe here at school."

PLANNING THEMES WITH A SOCIAL-EMOTIONAL FOCUS

Using the process of observing the spontaneous play of children, recognizing important life experiences, and noting children's unique interests and strengths, teachers can choose curriculum themes that will address issues important and relevant to the children. Caregivers then design theme-related activities to support these themes and provide for integrated, purposeful learning across all developmental domains (cognitive, language, physical, social, and emotional) and to accommodate a range of developmental levels so that all children will successfully be involved in the theme.

Sometimes, early childhood teachers engage children in a discussion of the theme before finalizing activity plans in order to gather more information about the children's prior experience, knowledge, and questions related to the theme. For example, one teacher structured a class meeting around the topic of friends, and asked these questions:

- How do friends act?
- What kinds of things do friends do together?
- Where can you make friends?

She made a "friends" concept web to visually depict the children's original ideas about friendship (Figure 10.1). During subsequent class meetings that week, she added children's new ideas as the theme progressed to expand and build on children's knowledge and understandings and interests. (Indicated on web with italics.)

Notice that after reading books about friends and engaging in several class meeting discussions, the children added a new topic "How friends look" which slowly grew to include a sense of acceptance and respect for diversity.

Activities related to an emotion-centered theme can be developed for each part of the daily routine (circle time, teacher-directed small groups, class meetings, outdoor activities, snack, and special activities such as field trips). During child-selected, independent activities, materials can be added to interest centers to stimulate peer interaction and social skills practice related to the theme.

127

FIGURE 10.1

Concept Web for "Friends" Theme

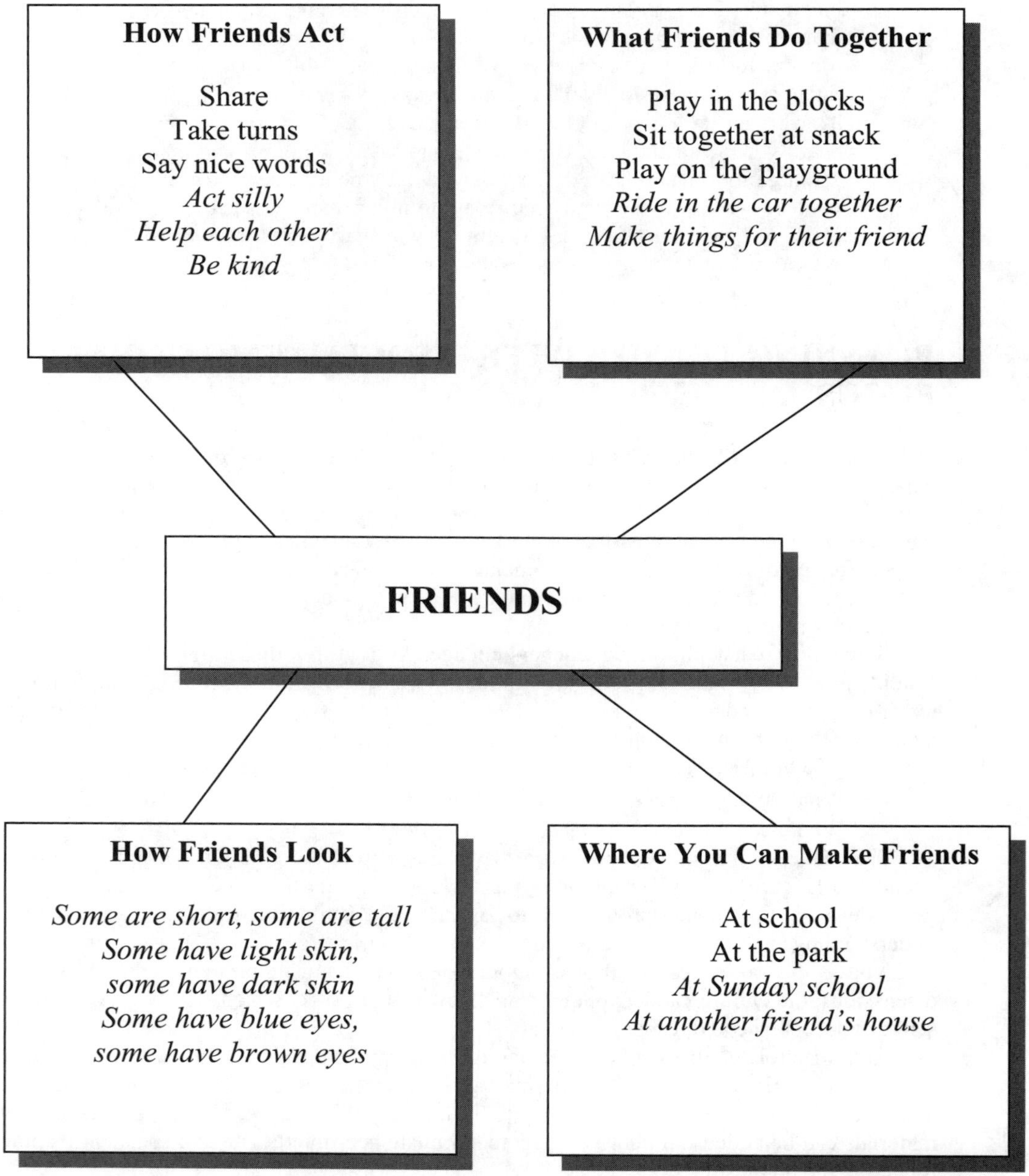

How Friends Act

Share
Take turns
Say nice words
Act silly
Help each other
Be kind

What Friends Do Together

Play in the blocks
Sit together at snack
Play on the playground
Ride in the car together
Make things for their friend

FRIENDS

How Friends Look

Some are short, some are tall
Some have light skin,
some have dark skin
Some have blue eyes,
some have brown eyes

Where You Can Make Friends

At school
At the park
At Sunday school
At another friend's house

Planning curriculum themes with a social-emotional focus does not mean ignoring the other developmental domains, program goals and objectives, or required school district student outcomes. With practice, teachers can become adept at achieving multiple objectives within one activity. In the lesson plan forms depicted in Figure 10.2, relevant school district objectives are shown in bolded italics. (See Appendix A, C, and D for more sample lesson plans.)

Planning curriculum themes based upon the needs and interests of young children while incorporating program goals and objectives is much more challenging than repeating the same, traditional themes every year (such as September—colors and shapes, October—autumn leaves and Halloween, November—numbers and Thanksgiving, etc.). However, the benefits of an emotionally responsive curriculum to children, adults, and the overall learning environment are many. Emotionally responsive curriculum meets the emotional needs of children and reflects their individual interests and strengths. Children feel more secure and valued. Because children's interests and "need to know" motivate learning, themes relevant to the lives of children encourage them to be more enthusiastic and engaged in learning activities. Compare this to an incident observed by the authors in a rural Colorado community where the preschool children were studying about the "rain forest."

> Throughout the morning, teachers pulled children away from the window, where they were watching sheep being unloaded from a truck into the field next to the school, so that the children could color in pictures of monkeys whose name they couldn't remember!

FIGURE 10.2 Lesson Plan Form for "A New Baby at Home" Theme

	Monday	Tuesday	Wednesday	Thursday	Friday
Group Time (songs, stories, etc.)	Read book: *That New Baby*	Read book: *When You Were a Baby* Ask children what they did when they were a baby. Have children show their baby picture.	Read book: *Betsy's Baby Brother* Ask open-ended questions about their experiences with new siblings as you read. *Responds to a read-aloud story with questions and comments.*	Read book: *La Silla de Pedro* Ask if child if they have a brother or sister. Make a list of their names.	Read book: *Nobody Asked Me if I Wanted a Baby Sister* Ask the children about the character's feelings as you read. *Verbalizes feelings and shows empathic concern for others.*
Small Groups (teacher-directed)	Make baby food by mashing soft foods or using blender. Eat this baby food as part of snack today.	Make baby beds from shoeboxes that children paint and decorate. Cut soft cloth to make baby blankets.	Create class book entitled *When I Was a Baby.* Have each child complete a page: draw a picture, add words, and "sign" their page *Labels drawings; Prints first and last name.*	Read class book. Let each child give details about their page.	Make a family collage by cutting out pictures of families from magazines and gluing them on construction paper
Class Meeting	Create a concept web about babies. Use *Baby Science* by Ann Douglas as a resource. Begin the conversation with questions: What do babies need? How do babies let you know what they need? What can babies do? What is hard for babies to do?	Teach some signs for simple words related to babies.	Ask children to recollect the book *Betsy's Baby Brother.* Make a list of emotion words that children may feel about having a baby in the family such as happy, jealous, worried, annoyed, angry, or frightened. *Repeats what happened in story previously read by another.*	Discuss reasons why it is hard sometimes to be a big brother or sister. Create a language experience chart entitled: *Sometimes It Is Hard To Have a Baby in the Family*	Follow-up to yesterday's class meeting. Focus on problem solving. What can you do about "problems" with having a new baby in the family? What can you do when you feel like the baby is getting all the attention from your mother? *Tells as many solutions as possible for a given problem situation.*

Outdoor Activities	Take baby dolls and baby carriages outside	Set out crawling tunnel and mats	Wash baby dolls in water table using baby soap, shampoo, washcloths, and towels	Take out props for a baby picnic	Wash baby clothes and hang on line
Family Involvement	Ask families to bring in baby pictures of children		Ask families with young babies to stay for a few minutes after arrival and let older siblings introduce the babies to their friends		Older children can compose a note to parents—What I want to tell my parents about how it is to have a new sibling

Environmental Changes and Objectives for Children

Center	Changes to the Environment	Objectives	Center	Changes to the Environment	Objectives
Dramatic Play	Diaper baby dolls using baby wipes, baby powder. Borrow a high chair if you don't have one and have children practice feeding and playing with the baby.	*Assumes simple roles while playing with two or more children* / *Practices nurturing behaviors*	Literacy/ Library/ Writing	Create a "shopping list" for baby supplies. Provide magazines and newspaper ads and flyers, markers, colored paper, pencils, etc.	*Copies simple words*
Blocks	Put baby-related props in block area and encourage children to build cribs, play areas, or high chairs	*Reproduces block designs*	Table toys	Add puzzles about families and homes	*Puts together simple puzzles*
Art			Computer	Provide story-writing software and encourage children to write stories about their families	*Writes to express meaning*
Sand/ Water/ Sensory	If weather precludes taking water table outside, add props for washing baby dolls to water table inside	*Shares toys with other children*	Science	Set out plastic food and food pyramid posters. Have children plan a week's worth of healthy snacks.	
Cozy Corner	Add baby doll and infant board books		Music	Add cassette player with tapes of baby songs	

USING CHILDREN'S LITERATURE

Bibliotherapy is the art of using children's literature to help children understand difficult experiences and resolve developmental issues that interfere with growth. Books can be read to children to reflect a range of cultural issues, developmental concerns, life experiences, and emotional dilemmas. A wide range of books that cover these topics is now available. (See list of children's books at the end of this chapter.)

Some of these books are appropriate to read to groups of children—those reflecting topics relevant to many children's lives (such as the birth of a new baby or moving to a new home). For situations that apply to an individual child (such as the death of a parent or a chronically ill sibling in the home) and may be uncomfortable for others, teachers and caregivers can read to just that child.

On occasion, early childhood educators make books to help children deal with situations that make them feel afraid, angry sad, or worried. Teachers with whom the authors have worked have made simple books (with hand-drawn figures or photographs) related to issues including:

- Fear of the dentist
- Fear of haircuts
- Fear of the dark
- Fear of thunderstorms
- Worry about daddy or mommy in the Army
- Sadness over the death of a pet
- Missing Daddy who is in jail
- Disturbing news event that many children have heard about

These books are read in small-group class meetings or to children individually as is appropriate to the situation. Often a second copy of the book is made to send home with the child.

Before reading or creating a book for an individual child related to a sensitive topic, consult with the child's family to obtain their approval. It has been the experience of the authors that many families welcome ideas for helping their child cope with a difficult situation. Other families prefer to handle it in their own way at home.

For more information on making books for children, see Suggested Readings and Resources for description of "Struggle Books" (McCord, 1995) and "Social Stories" (Gray & White, 2002).

KEY TERMS AND CONCEPTS

Emotionally responsive curriculum: curriculum centered on the emotional needs of children and that reflects and responds to experiences and issues in children's lives

Developmental change: experiences that are a normal part of growing up and are experienced by all children as they develop

Critical change: common events, not experienced by every child, that impact a child's life and tend to cause some temporary stress

Catastrophic change: sudden, unexpected, and often life-threatening events that happen only to some children and result in significant stress, often requiring the help of professionals not available in the typical early childhood classroom

Bibliotherapy: the use of children's literature to help children understand difficult experiences and resolve developmental issues that interfere with growth

LEARNING IN ACTION: SMALL GROUP ACTIVITIES AND FIELD ASSIGNMENTS

1. In small groups, consider interests and topics that are concrete, real, and relevant to most children's lives. Make a list of class meeting topics appropriate for the beginning of the school year, the middle of the year, and the end of the year. Compare your ideas with the *Sequence of Introduction of CARES Strategies* presented in Appendix E: Getting Started in Your Classroom.
2. Given the following summary of the developmental and experiential histories reported by the parents of the children in your class, what would be some topics you would choose to focus on as a curriculum theme?

Birth history	Frightening or stressful experiences	Important things to know about my child
Adopted Premature—long hospitalization after birth	Divorce Separation of parents Foster care Moved recently	Sensitive Slow to warm up Mother expecting new baby Easily frustrated

3. Separate into groups of three to four. Select an emotion-centered theme and complete a blank lesson planning form copied from Appendix F. With the large group, share three activities or changes to the environment based upon your theme.
4. Consider the following scenario: Suddenly the fire alarm went off in a large child care center. The teachers rushed all the children into lines and hurried them outside and lined up in their assigned locations. Several of the children were clearly terrified. (No one explained anything to anyone.)

- What would you do differently during the fire drill to be responsive to the children's fears?
- What would you do after returning to the classroom?
- What would you do if children persisted in talking about fire drills or fires?

RELATED CHILDREN'S BOOKS

Alexander, M. (1971). *Nobody asked me if I wanted a baby sister*. New York: Dial Books. (feelings about new sibling)

Asch, F. (1986). *Goodbye house*. New York: Aladdin Paperbacks. (moving, separation)

Birnbaum, B. (1992). *My school, your school*. Austin, TX: Steck-Vaughn Co. (school experience)

Bonnet-Stein, S. (1974). *That new baby: An open family book for parents and children together*. New York: Walker. (new baby)

Carlson, N. (2001*)*. *My best friend moved away*. New York: Penguin Putnam Books for Young Readers. (moving, separation)

Carlstrom, N. W. (1999). *I'm not moving, Mama!* New York: Aladdin Paperbacks. (moving, separation)

Civari, A., & Cartwright, S. (1996). *Going to school*. Tulsa, OK: EDC Publishing. (school experience)

Clifton, L. (1983). *Everett Anderson's goodbye*. New York: Henry Holt. (death)

Cole, J. (1998). *The new baby at your house*. New York: Morrow Junior Books. (birth of a sibling)

Corey, D. (1976). *You go away*. Chicago: Albert Whitman. (separation)

Corey, D. (1980). *Everybody takes turns*. Chicago: Albert Whitman. (sharing)

Crary, E. (1986). *Mommy don't go*. Seattle, WA: Parenting Press. (separation)

Davol, M. (1993). *Black, white, just right!* Morton Grove, IL: Albert Whitman & Co. (interracial family)

Drescher, J. (1980). *Your family, my family*. New York: Walker. (different types of families)

Fassler, J. (1983). *My Grandpa died today*. Springfield, IL: Human Sciences Press. (death of loved one)

Hazen, B. S. (1995). *Goodbye hello*. New York: Atheneum Books for Young Readers. (moving, separation)

Hickman, M. (1990). *When Andy's father went to prison*. Niles, IL: Albert Whitman. (feelings about father in prison)

Hill, E. (1982). *Where is Spot?* New York: G. P. Putnam's Sons. (separation)

Howe, J. (1994). *When you go to kindergarten*. New York: Mulberry Books. (new school)

Johnson, D. (1998). *What will Mommy do when I'm at school?* New York: Aladdin Paperbacks. (separation, new school)

Johnson, J., & Johnson, M. (1982). *Where's Jess?* Omaha, NE: Centering Corporation. (death of a sibling)

Jonas, A. (1982). *When you were a baby*. New York: Greenwillow Books. (birth of sibling)

Kline, S. (1989). *Ooops*. New York: Puffin Books. (concern about messes)

Lawrence, M. (1987). *My life: Melinda's story*. Alexandria, VA: Children's Hospice International. (child's illness, hospital)

McQuade, J. (1999). *At preschool with teddy bear*. New York: Dial Books for Young Readers. (new school, routines)

Oxenbury, H. (1983). *First day of school*. New York: Dial Books for Young Readers. (beginning school)

Prestine, J. S. (1993). *Someone special died*. Carthage, IL: Fearon Teacher Aids. (death)

Relf, P. (1981). *The first day of school*. New York: Golden Press. (beginning school)

Rockwell, H. (1973). *My doctor*. New York: Macmillan. (mastering fear)

Rockwell, H. (1975). *My dentist*. New York: Macmillan. (mastering fear)

Rogers, F. (1988). *When a pet dies*. New York: G.P. Putnam Sons.

Simon, N. (1969). *What do I do?* Chicago: Albert Whitman. (waiting, controlling impulses)

Simon, N. (1976). *Why am I different?* Morton Grove, IL: Albert Whitman. (similarities and differences in people)

Szaj, K. C. (1996). *I hate goodbyes!* Mahwah, NJ: Paulist Press. (loss and separation)

Tester, S. R. (1979). *We laughed a lot, my first day of school*. Mankato, MN: The Child's World. (new school)

Tompert, A. (1988). *Will you come back for me?* Chicago: Albert Whitman. (separation)

Vigna, J. (1991). *Saying goodbye to Daddy*. Niles, IL: Albert Whitman. (death and healing in weeks afterward)

Williams, V. (1987). *More, more, more, said the baby*. New York: Greenwillow Books. (waiting, controlling impulses)

Wise-Brown, M. (1947). *Goodnight moon*. New York: Harper & Row. (night-time fears)

Wolde, G. (1974). *Betsy's baby brother*. New York: Random House. (birth of sibling)

Wolde, G. (1976). *Betsy's first day of day care*. New York: Randome House. (new school, separation)

Zelonky, J. (1992). *My best friend moved away*. Austin, TX: Steck-Vaughn Publishers. (moving, loss, separation)

SUGGESTED READING AND RESOURCES

Cantor, J. (1998). *"Mommy, I'm scared": How TV and movies frighten children and what we can do to protect them*. San Diego: Harcourt Brace.

Carlson-Paige, N., & Levin, D. (1990). *Who's calling the shots? How to respond effectively to children's fascination with war play, war toys, and violent TV*. Philadelphia: New Society Publishers.

Christian, L. G. (1997). Children and death. *Young Children, 52*(4), 76–80.

Close, N. (2002). *Listening to children: Talking with children about difficult issues*. Boston, MA: Allyn & Bacon.

Crosson-Tower, C. (2002). *Understanding child abuse and neglect*. Boston, MA: Allyn & Bacon.

Donovan, D., & McIntyre, D. (1990). *Healing the hurt child*. New York: W. W. Norton.

Ernes, J. (1991). *Connecting: Meeting the needs of formerly homeless preschool children—A curriculum for child care*. Staff, NY: Child Care.

Frieman, B. B. (1993). Separation and divorce: Children want their teachers to know. *Young Children, 48*(6), 58–63.

Garrity, C., Jens, K., Porter, W., Sager, N. & Short-Camilli, C. (1996). *Bully-proofing your school: A comprehensive approach for elementary schools*. Longmont, CO: Sopris West.

Goldman, L. (1994). *Life and loss: A guide to help grieving children*. Muncie, IN: Accelerated Development Inc.

Gray, C., & White, A. L. (2002). *My social story book*. London: Jessica Kingsley Publishers.

Jervis, K. (Ed.) (1984). *Separation: Strategies for helping two to four year olds*. Washington, DC: National Association for the Education of Young Children.

Koplow, L. (1992). *The way home: A child therapist looks at the inner lives of city children*. New York: Dutton.

Klein, T. P., Wirth, D., & Linas, K. (2003). Play: Children's context for development. *Young Children, 58*(3), 38–45.

Levin, D. (1998). *Remote control childhood? Combating the hazards of media culture.* Washington, DC: National Association for the Education of Young Children.

Levin, D. (2003). *Teaching young children in violent times.* (2nd ed.). Cambridge, MA: Educators for Social Responsibility.

McCord, S. (1995). *The storybook journey: Pathways to literacy through story and play.* Upper Saddle River, NJ: Merrill/ Prentice Hall.

Molnar, J. (1988). *Home is where the heart is: The crisis of homeless children and families in New York City.* New York: Bank Street College of Education.

Olweus, D. (1993). *Bullying at school: What we know and what we can do.* Cambridge, MA: Blackwell.

Powell, J. (1999). *Talking about bullying.* Austin, TX: Raintree Steck-Vaughn.

Prestine, J. S. (1993). *Helping children cope with death.* Carthage, IL: Fearon Teacher Aids. (guide to accompany children's book Someone Special Died)

Wolfelt, A. (1983). *Helping children cope with grief.* Muncie, IN: Accelerated Development Inc.

Wortham, S. C. (2002). *Early childhood curriculum.* Upper Saddle River, New Jersey: Merrill/Prentice Hall.

REFERENCES

Devall, E. L., & Cahill, B. J. (1995). Addressing children's life changes in the early childhood curriculum. *Early Childhood Education Journal, 23*(2), 57–62.

Koplow, L. (1996). *Unsmiling faces: How preschools can heal.* New York: Teachers College Press.

Oehlberg, B. (1996). *Making it better: Activities for children in a stressful world.* Beltsville, MD: Redleaf Press.

Chapter 11

INTERVENTION FOR CHILDREN WITH BEHAVIOR CHALLENGES

After the last child leaves for the day, Martina collapses into the nearest chair. As she reflects on the day, she pictures in her mind what seems to be an endless cycle of dealing with Nicola's challenging behaviors: hitting, screaming, throwing toys, even biting other children. She feels as if she has spent the whole day putting out fires, consoling the victims of Nicola's aggression, and neglecting the needs of other children because of the attention she devotes to Nicola. Martina feels resentful, guilty, overwhelmed, and inadequate.

Like many teachers, Martina faces the difficult task of dealing with a child with challenging behavior. This chapter presents several strategies for responding to challenging behavior including:

- preventive practices and teaching strategies
- understanding the function of challenging behavior
- conducting an "ABC analysis" to describe the behavior, events triggering its occurrence, and consequences that maintain the behavior
- creating a positive behavior support plan
- seeking outside assistance
- working with families to use positive behavior support.

WHAT IS CHALLENGING BEHAVIOR?

Challenging behavior is any behavior that:
- interferes with children's learning and development
- isolates the child from peers
- causes harm to the child, other children, or adults
- causes damage to the physical environment
- puts a child at risk for later behavior problems or school failure (Kaiser & Rasminsky, 1999; Klass, Guskin, & Thomas, 1995; Neilsen, Olive, Donovan, & McEvoy, 1998).

Common challenging behaviors include tantrums; aggression; defiance, destructive behavior, bullying; and inappropriate language, touch, or gestures. These acting-out behaviors cause distress to teachers, parents, and other children. At the opposite end of the behavior continuum are children who are extremely shy, withdrawn, passive, or unresponsive to others. These behaviors may be overlooked by teachers who are busy dealing with the demands of more active or disruptive children, or they may not be viewed as "challenging" behaviors. Yet children whose behavior results in social isolation are equally at-risk in terms of their development (Koralek, 1999).

BASIC PREVENTIVE PRACTICES AND TEACHING STRATEGIES

The early childhood educator's first response to a child with challenging behavior should be to reflect on her own practice. Am I providing a safe, organized environment and a predictable routine for this child? Do I use positive guidance techniques? Have I attempted to establish a caring relationship with the child? Am I planning activities to teach social skills and enhance emotional competence?

To assist you with the process of self-reflection, a review of preventive practices and teaching strategies to promote positive social behavior and emotional competence presented in prior chapters is provided in the form of a self-assessment in Appendix G.

Next, the caregiver can focus on the needs of each individual child about whom she has concerns regarding challenging behaviors and create an individualized plan for that child based upon these basic classroom preventive practices and teaching strategies. Caregivers should consider the following questions when creating an individualized classroom strategies plan:

1. What do I know about the child's background (e.g., birth history, health, family supports, culture)?
2. What is the child's behavior of most concern?
3. What are my goals for this child?
4. What changes in the classroom physical environment or in routines might help this child?
5. How will I apply the Safety Rule to this child?
6. What positive guidance techniques will I use with this child?
7. How will I use responsive language with this child?
8. How will I help this child identify and express his feelings?
9. What will I do to help this child feel a sense of belonging in the classroom?
10. Which prosocial skills does this child need to build?
11. What will I do to help this child with problem solving?
12. What will I do to help this child with managing anger and calming down?
13. What activities will I plan for stress reduction for this child?
14. What are the needs, interests, and life experiences of this child that should be considered when planning curriculum themes and classroom activities?
15. How will I engage the child's family and consult with members of the early childhood team?

Often such careful attention to basic preventive practices and teaching of social and emotional skills geared to the needs of children with challenging behaviors is all that is needed to reduce problem behaviors in the classroom. However, there are times when an individual child requires more intensive intervention to address challenging behavior.

UNDERSTANDING FUNCTIONS OF CHALLENGING BEHAVIOR

Every challenging behavior meets a need or serves a function for a child. Problem behavior may also be viewed as a form of communication—children use behavior to communicate what they want or do not want (Artesani, 2001; Kaiser & Rasminsky, 1999).

The **function** of most challenging behavior typically falls under two general categories (Kaiser & Rasminsky, 1999; Neilson, Olive, Donovan, & McEvoy, 1998):

- Obtaining an outcome (access to an object or activity, gaining attention from an adult or peer, sensory stimulation)
- Avoiding or escaping something (difficult task, disliked activity, unwelcome demand, uncomfortable social interaction or sensory stimulation)

With these points in mind, we see that challenging behaviors represent the child's attempt to communicate a variety of different messages such as:

- You're asking me to do something that is too difficult and I'm frustrated and want to quit.
- I cannot cope with being part of a group right now.
- I want that toy, and I don't know how to ask for it.
- I'm bored, pay some attention to me.
- I'm not comfortable sitting here so long.

Focused observation of challenging behavior results in a better understanding of the reasons behind problem behavior, when it happens and with whom, and the function it serves for the child. (Artesani, 2001; Kaiser & Rasminsky, 1999; Strain, McConnell, Carta, Fowler, Neisworth, & Wolery, 1992). Direct observation provides essential information about the possible functions of a child's behavior through an "**ABC analysis**"–documenting antecedents, behavior, and consequences (Bijou, Peterson, & Ault, 1968; Kaiser & Rasminsky, 2003).

Antecedents are events that occur immediately before a challenging behavior and seem to trigger it. Some examples of antecedents that might trigger challenging behaviors are adult demands and requests; activities or tasks that seem difficult to the child; transitions; interruption;, age-inappropriate expectations such as waiting for long periods of time; lack of attention; and peer actions such as teasing, bullying, intrusion on a child's activity or space, or exclusion from play (Kaiser & Rasminsky, 2003; Neilson, Olive, Donovan, & McEvoy, 1998).

Behavior needs to be described clearly and specifically so that all observers can identify it (not "Bianca is stubborn." but "Bianca throws herself on the floor and refuses to move." or "Bianca grabs a toy from another child and refuses to give it back.") (Durand, 1990).

Consequences are what happens immediately following the challenging behavior. Consequences that reinforce the child (serve the purpose of obtaining or avoiding) are called *maintaining consequences*. Typical consequences for Bianca include gaining the teacher's attention (giving a verbal reprimand, moving closer to Bianca, or redirecting her behavior), another child relinquishing a favorite toy, or Bianca's successful avoidance of clean-up time by being removed from the group (Kaiser & Rasminsky, 2003; Neilson, Olive, Donovan, & McEvoy, 1998).

In addition to observation, information to assist in understanding challenging behavior can also be gathered from a review of a child's health records and program files or from interviews with parents and people who have worked with the child (teachers, child care providers, or therapists). Interviews can help provide a complete picture of the challenging behavior and the environmental conditions and events that surround it. Interview questions usually include the following (Boulware, Schwartz, & McBride, 1999; Kaiser & Rasminsky, 2003):

- Which of the child's behaviors do you consider to be challenging?
- What does the behavior of concern look like?
- When and where does the behavior occur?
- When and where does the behavior *not* occur?
- Who is present when the behavior usually occurs?
- What activities, events, and interactions occur just before the behavior?
- What happens right after the behavior occurs?
- How does the child communicate?

(For information on a more structured interview format—called the Functional Assessment Interview—see O'Neill, Horner, Albin, Sprague, Storey, & Newton, 1997.)

CREATING A POSITIVE BEHAVIOR SUPPORT PLAN

When faced with challenging behaviors, adults too often:
- ♦ Perceive the behavior as deliberate noncompliance, "being difficult or manipulative"
- ♦ Attempt to "control" or "punish" the child
- ♦ Neglect to address the needs of the child
- ♦ Engage in a power struggle with the child that maintains or increases the problem behavior or results in the substitution of a new, equally problematic behavior.

A more constructive approach is to create a **positive behavior support plan**. Positive behavior support does not focus on eliminating the "problem" behavior, but "focuses on prevention by identifying the purpose of the challenging behavior, acknowledging and building on the strengths and preferences of the child, reinforcing appropriate behavior and teaching the child functionally equivalent replacement behavior" (Boulware, Schwartz, & McBride, 1999, p. 29). Following is the process for creating and implementing a positive behavior support plan:

1. Make careful observations and interview parents and caregivers to conduct an ABC analysis: Describe the problem behavior, its predictors (antecedents), probable purpose (how the behavior "works" for the child), and maintaining consequences (behaviors of adults or peers that fulfill the purpose for the child).
2. Modify the environment to reduce events and interactions that predict problem behavior and trigger its occurrence.
3. Teach **replacement skills** to replace the challenging behavior with appropriate behavior that serves the same purpose for the child.

Ideally, the positive behavior support plan is created by a team-either the classroom team of teacher and assistant teacher along with parents, or a larger team consisting of parents, teacher, aide, and specialists (early childhood special education consultant, physical therapist, occupational therapist, psychologist, and/or speech therapist).

ABC Analysis Examples

Case 1: 2-year-old Erika
Description of problem behavior: Erika attempts to obtain desired toys and food by grabbing, often pulling objects from the hands of the other toddlers in the room. If playmates resist, Erika screams "mine!"

Antecedents/Predictors: This is especially likely to occur when several other toddlers are playing in the same area.

Probable purpose: Erika obtains an object or desired food.

Maintaining consequences: The other toddlers tend to allow Erika to keep the object. Teachers rarely intervene unless a child is injured when Erika grabs or begins to cry when Erika screams.

Case 2: 4-year-old Dwayne
Description of problem behavior: During small-group, teacher-directed activities, Dwayne fidgets in his chair, plays with the activity materials without following directions, and frequently asks to go get a drink of water. If teachers press him to participate, Dwayne reacts by throwing objects, screaming, or falling on the floor.

Antecedents/Predictors: Teacher-directed, structured activities requiring sustained attention and sitting still for long periods.

Probable purpose: Dwayne avoids the demands of activities that he finds difficult by resisting or withdrawing.

Maintaining consequences: When Dwayne engages in these behaviors, teachers often give up their efforts to engage him or allow him to leave the activity.

Modifying the Environment to Prevent Problem Behaviors

Modifying the environment is an attempt to prevent or reduce the occurrence of challenging behavior by changing events and interactions that trigger the behavior. The objective is to select modifications that fit in the natural routines and structure of the classroom.

When the purpose of a behavior is to obtain attention, object, or activity, successful prevention/modification strategies include:

- Provide enough materials (add duplicates).
- Provide choice of activity, materials, and/or partner.
- Provide more frequent attention and reinforcement.
- Provide frequent offers of assistance.
- Arrange time for interaction with adult or peer.
- Arrange access to desired activity/object.
- Interpret and verbalize need of child ("Jackson, do you want a turn?").
- Assist the child with peer entry or turn-taking ("Donny, can Angie play with blocks too?").

When the purpose of a behavior is to avoid or escape activity, demands, or social interaction, successful prevention/modification strategies include:

- Reduce distractions and level of stimulation.
- Modify task length.
- Modify task expectations to accommodate differing levels.
- Modify instructions to make sure child understands.
- Provide adapted materials.
- Demonstrate activity before encouraging child to begin.
- Provide choice of alternate, desirable activity or materials or partner.
- Provide warning of change or transition.
- Modify seating arrangements.
- Use visuals, photos, or object to represent next activity.
- Eliminate wait time.

(Source: Adapted from Fox, Lentini, and Dunlap, 2002)

Teaching Replacement Skills

We can teach children many appropriate responses to use instead of engaging in challenging behaviors. As a general guideline, replacement skills must provide an alternate behavior to the problem behavior that serves the same function for the child (work quickly and require same effort) and utilize skills that the child is already capable of performing. Replacement skills are taught during regular routines and activities during time the child is *not* displaying problem behavior.

Many replacement skills involve teaching children to use a form of communication (spoken words, gestures, or use of symbols) to obtain the same outcome they achieved through use of challenging behaviors. Teachers then cue the child to use the communication option *before* the challenging behavior occurs

When the purpose of a behavior is to obtain attention, object, or activity, possible replacement skills include:

- Request help using words such as "Help me please" or signing "help."
- Request a turn using words or signing "turn.".
- Request a toy using words such as "mine" or "I want that toy" or signing "mine."
- Request a hug (or other forms of attention).
- Identify and express feelings.
- Request adult intervention.

To be most successful, requests to peers should be made in the form of a statement "I want a turn, please" or "I'd like to play with you" versus a question. Adults often suggest to children that they ask, "Can I play?" yet it is one of the least effective entrance strategies, as peers are prone to answer "no" (Hazen, Black, & Fleming-Johnson, 1984.)

When the purpose of a behavior is to avoid or escape activity, demands, or social interaction, possible replacement skills include:

- Request a break.
- Say or sign "all done" or "finished."
- Request help.
- Identify and express feelings.
- Say or sign "no," "stop," "wait," or "move."
- Request another choice.

American Sign Language for infants and toddlers has been used successfully to meet communication needs of hearing infants and toddlers before they can speak and with preschool-age children with language deficits to convey simple messages to adults and peers. (See Suggested Reading and Resources.)

To create symbols (a chart of commonly used communications can be laminated and kept readily available in the classroom), teachers often use Boardmaker© or PECS (Picture Exchange Communication System). (See Suggested Reading and Resources.)

A Positive Response to Challenging Behavior

The overall objective of a positive behavior support plan is to develop procedures that will make the problem behavior unnecessary. Specifically, teachers and teams:

- Modify the environment to reduce events and interactions that trigger problem behavior
- State exactly what is expected of the child
- Teach replacement skills
- Cue children to use appropriate replacement skill
- Praise/reinforce the child when the replacement skill is performed
- Respond in a way that does *not* maintain problem behavior (inadvertent reinforcement)

(Fox, Lentini, & Dunlap, 2002)

As noted in Chapter 3, occasionally a teacher must respond to a child who is in danger of harming himself or others using crisis intervention strategies such as:

- Removing the child from the area.
- Moving the other children away from the child.
- Assigning an adult to remain with the child until he is calm.
- Insisting the child sit in time-out.
- Holding the child until he is calm.

These actions are considered crisis intervention strategies, not strategies designed to promote positive behavior change.

BEHAVIOR SUPPORT PLANS IN ACTION

Consider the following classroom scenarios depicting challenging behaviors and the behavior support plan developed by the teacher based upon a functional assessment.

Function for the Child Is to Obtain an Outcome

Two-year-old Jared frequently pushed classmates aside to sit on his teacher Dawn's lap, threw toys or banged them loudly on a hard surface (for example, he banged his spoon on the table if Dawn was speaking to another child at the snack table), and cried any time Dawn did not immediately respond to him. Dawn determined that the function of these behaviors was to get her attention.

She also learned to recognize antecedents which tended to trigger Jared's challenging behaviors—busy times of the day when her attention was devoted to other things or any time she gave sustained attention to another child. She recognized that she tended to respond to Jared's behaviors by giving him attention.

She decided that one means of prevention would be to identify and verbalize Jared's probable feelings for him. If she was reading a book to another toddler and Jared started to approach, Dawn would say to him, "It looks like you want me to read to you, too. Do you want to sit next to me here?" For replacement skills, she began to teach Jared simple phrases to use, such as "my turn" and "help me."

Once Jared was able to use these phrases with prompting, she was careful to cue Jared to use these phrases *before* any challenging behavior occurred, knowing that if she asked Jared to request a turn *after* he pushed another child, she might inadvertently be teaching Jared to engage in the challenging behavior first and then request a turn.

Dawn's behavior support plan is represented in chart form in Figure 11.1

FIGURE 11.1

Positive Behavior Support Plan for Jared

Triggers: Antecedent events	Behaviors	Maintaining consequence
Dawn giving attention to other child Dawn busy with other things like setting up snack table or washing table after painting activity	Push peers; bang or throw objects; cry loudly	Dawn gives attention; she moves closer to Jared, speaks to him, reprimands him, or tries to redirect his behavior
Function: Gaining attention from teacher Dawn		
Preventions	**New Replacement Skills**	**New Responses by Adults**
Provide more frequent attention and reinforcement Provide frequent offers of assistance Interpret and verbalize need of child "Jared, it looks like you want a turn."	Request help Request a hug (or other forms of attention) Request a turn Identify and express feelings	Anticipate need for attention and cue Jared to use replacement skill Praise/reinforce performance of replacement skill Ignore inappropriate behavior unless it is harmful to others

Source: Adapted from Fox, Lentini, & Dunlap, 2002.

After creating the above outline of the positive behavior support plan, Dawn elaborates by:
- Describing more precisely the preventions planned
- Describing specifics related to replacement skills—what will be the words and actions Jared will use and how they will be taught to him
- Describing in detail the new responses by adults, including types of praise and reinforcement to be used

Function for the Child Is to Avoid or Escape

Three-year-old Catrina was notorious for throwing toys when asked to clean up. More often than not, she would endanger other children and her teacher Michael would lead Catrina to a corner of the room for a time-out. Over time, Michael noticed that time-out did not reduce the incidence of toy-throwing. Analyzing the function of toy-throwing as avoidance of clean-up, he realized he was probably inadvertently reinforcing Catrina's behavior by allowing her to "escape" from clean-up and sit by herself in the corner. He decided to find another way for Catrina to achieve the same purpose—avoiding cleaning up the toys she had been playing with—while finding ways to encourage Catrina to engage in some aspect of clean-up time.

The next day, Catrina was pretending to feed her baby doll during center time. Before clean-up time, Michael asked Catrina if she and her doll would help him blink the lights to announce the start of clean-up. She shook her head "yes" and he lifted her up to the light switch. Then he asked if she would help him put away the Legos™ so they could get ready for snack at the tables. Although Catrina did very little actual assistance, and was allowed to keep her baby doll until it was time to wash her hands for snack, at least Catrina did not throw any of the Legos™. Michael was content to work in stages—first give Catrina a more appropriate way to avoid cleaning up toys she had been playing with, and later work on ways to encourage Catrina to put away toys during clean-up.

First-grader Jonah had difficulty persisting with independent tasks. As part of a readers and writers workshop each day, he was expected to write and draw pictures in his journal for 15 minutes. Typically, after about 5 minutes, Jonah would begin to fidget and disturb the children working next to him. At that point, Mr. Stevens often had Jonah move to a corner of the room, but frequently Jonah continued to play with his pencil or stare out the window instead of resuming writing in his journal.

Noting this pattern, Mr. Stevens decided to give Jonah an option to "take a break" from the journal writing. He told Jonah that whenever he felt wiggly and needed a break from writing, he could go to the "squiggle square" and move around for awhile, and then return to his desk. (The squiggle square was a two-by-two-foot square made out of masking tape on the linoleum—in a spot away from the desks.) When Mr. Stevens noticed Jonah going to the squiggle square, he gave Jonah about two minutes to spin and shake in the square, then approached him. "That was a nice job taking a break from writing and not bothering your classmates. Thank you. Now that you've had some time away, let's go look at your journal together. I'm interested to see if you are still writing about hot-rod cars."

MONITORING EFFECTIVENESS OF BEHAVIOR SUPPORT PLANS

Teachers often collect data in a systematic way to monitor the effectiveness of a behavior support plan. In Jared's case, Dawn created a data collection chart focused on the times of day that Jared typically required a lot of attention. She completed the chart during one week before implementing the behavior support plan and for two weeks after implementation to evaluate the success of the plan. (See Figure 11.2.)

Using this frequency chart, Dawn discovered that Jared's problem behaviors diminished from an average of 7.4 times per day during the week *before* implementing the plan to 1.6 times per day in the second week *after* implementing the plan—clearly an improvement!

FIGURE 11.2

Frequency Chart to Evaluate Jared's Behavior Support Plan

Week before implementation of behavior support plan:

	Monday	Tuesday	Wednesday	Thursday	Friday
Reading books	11	111	11	1111	111
Playtime	111	11	111	1	11
Snack	1	11	1	1	11
Cleanup	1	1		1	11
Total per day	7	8	6	7	9

Week one after implementation:

	Monday	Tuesday	Wednesday	Thursday	Friday
Reading books	111	11	1	11	1
Playtime	1	1	11	1	1
Snack	1	1			
Cleanup	1		1	1	1
Total per day	6	4	4	4	3

Week two after implementation:

	Monday	Tuesday	Wednesday	Thursday	Friday
Reading books		1		1	
Playtime	1		1	1	
Snack					
Cleanup	1	1			1
Total per day	2	2	1	2	1

Another way to monitor the success of a behavior support plan is to meet as a team to determine the team's follow-through with the plan, successes with preventing or changing the problem behavior, and possible revisions needed. Teams can answer questions such as:

1. What positive changes in the child's behavior have you observed?
2. What procedures have you followed on the plan to
   a) modify the environment to prevent the problem behavior?
   b) teach new replacement skills?
   c) reinforce the appropriate skills?
3. Do you believe that your original hypothesis about the purpose of the behavior was accurate? If not, what do you think is the purpose of the behavior and why?
4. Which strategies/procedures of the plan should be revised?

(Adapted from Fox, Lentini, & Dunlap, 2002)

WHEN TO SEEK ASSISTANCE

All children go through periods of emotional and behavior difficulties in the early years. The difference between normal difficulties and more severe problems is one of degree in terms of frequency, severity, persistence, and resistance to change (Schaefer & Millman, 1981). Sometimes, it is helpful to use a standardized norm-referenced assessment of social/emotional competence to determine if a child's behavior is of concern as compared to age-appropriate norms. See Appendix H for a summary of social skills inventories designed to help care and education professionals who may be concerned about a child's behavioral and emotional difficulties.

When faced with a child with challenging behaviors that are so frequent and severe that they impair the child's ability to form positive relationships with peers or adults, disrupt the classroom, pose danger to others, or place the child in an at-risk category as measured by a standardized assessment of social/emotional development, care and education providers should seek outside professional assistance. (Contact local Department of Human Services or mental health agencies. See Suggested Readings and Resources for related web sites.)

In addition, certain behaviors and physical symptoms may indicate that a child is experiencing severe stress or serious psychological difficulties requiring professional intervention. (See Chapter 9 for behavioral and physical reactions to stress.)

WORKING WITH FAMILIES TO USE POSITIVE BEHAVIOR SUPPORT

Family members should be part of the team whenever care and education providers are developing a behavior support plan. Keep in mind that it is often difficult for parents to hear about behavior problems, even when they are painfully aware of them (Webster-Stratton & Herbert, 1994). Parents may be surprised and anxious to discover that positive behavior support involves changing the environment and adult behavior as part of the plan to prevent challenging behavior rather than focusing on changing the child to eliminate problem behavior. When involved in the positive behavior support process, parents can give important clues related to the circumstances and functions of behavior. They can brainstorm preventive procedures in the care or education setting and adapt their own family routines to help their child function more successfully.

> At a parent conference, Mr. and Mrs. Andresen expressed concern with a persistent problem at home with their 3-year-old son. Carl, who has a receptive language disorder, frequently resisted when required to stop what he was doing and transition to a new activity. He would throw himself on the ground, refuse to move, and scream and kick if his parents attempted to move him. This happened when Carl was asked to stop playing to come to the table to eat, when it was time to take a bath, get ready for bed, get dressed in the morning, or get in the car to go to school. After some discussion leading to an ABC analysis, Mr. and Mrs. Andresen agreed that Carl's behavior was not a lack of compliance due to sheer defiance, but rather a lack of understanding.
>
> Since Carl demonstrated similar behaviors at school during transitions, Carl's teacher and parents decided to use photographs during transitions to help Carl understand what was coming next. At school, Carl was given a miniature version of the Pictorial Daily Schedule. At home, his parents created a flip-book with photos of a plate and spoon to represent eating, a bathtub, his closet door open with clothes visible to represent dressing, and a car next to a picture of his classmates and teacher to represent going to school.
>
> Carl rapidly learned to associate the photos with the activities they represented. When his parents presented a picture and told Carl what was going to happen next, he usually said "okay" (one of his few words) and followed his parents. Carl responded in a similar way when teachers pointed to the pictorial schedule and explained what was going to happen next.

KEY TERMS AND CONCEPTS

Challenging behavior: any behavior that interferes with a child's learning, development, and success at peer relationships and play; is harmful to the child, other children, or adults; causes damage to the physical environment; or puts a child at risk for later behavior problems or school failure

Function of behavior: how a behavior works to fill a need for the child to obtain an outcome or avoid something

ABC analysis: a process of determining the antecedents and consequences of a specific behavior

Antecedent: event that occurs immediately before a challenging behavior and seems to trigger it

Consequence: event that happens immediately following the challenging behavior—consequences that reinforces the child (serve the purpose of obtaining or avoiding); also called *maintaining consequences*

Positive behavior support plan: an individualized plan to reduce problem behavior by identifying its purpose, teaching the child alternative replacement behaviors, and reinforcing appropriate behavior

Replacement skill: an alternate behavior to the problem behavior that serves the same function for the child and utilizes skills that the child is already capable of performing

LEARNING IN ACTION:
SMALL GROUP ACTIVITIES AND FIELD ASSIGNMENTS

1. Consider the behaviors exhibited by Nicola in the opening vignette of this chapter. In groups of two to three, answer the questions on page 1 to create an individualized plan for Nicola utilizing preventive strategies discussed in previous chapters of this book.
2. Assign teams of two to three students to each of the common problem behaviors listed at the bottom of this page.
    Create a behavior support plan for the assigned problem behavior by completing the chart below.
    Determine a method for monitoring the effectiveness of your behavior support plan.

Triggers: Antecedent events	Behaviors	Maintaining consequence
Function:		
Preventions	New Replacement Skills	New Responses

Behavior problems to consider:
- biting
- hitting or pinching
- throwing objects at others
- swearing
- name-calling
- tattling
- refusal to share or take turns
- disrupting circle/group time
- running around the classroom
- throwing tantrums
- whining
- nonparticipation in social play

RELATED CHILDREN'S BOOKS

Ancredolo, L., & Goodwyn, S. (2002). *Baby signs for mealtime*. Harper Collins Publishers Inc.
Ancredolo, L., & Goodwyn, S. (2002). *My first baby signs*. Harper Collins Publishers Inc.
Early Sign Language Series. (2002). *Signs for pets and animals*. Eugene, OR: Garlic Press.
   An alphabet of animal signs
   Food signs
   First signs

SUGGESTED READING AND RESOURCES

Acredolo, L., & Goodwyn, S. (1996). *Baby signs: How to talk with your baby before your baby can talk*. Chicago: Contemporary Books.
Bahan, B., & Dannis, J. (1990). *Signs for me: Basic sign vocabulary for children, parents, and teachers*. San Diego, CA: Dawn Sign Press. Presents American Sign Language in a clear, accessible format. Illustrations for 24 emotion words. Information available at http://www.dawnsign.com
Boardmaker by Mayer Johnson. Boardmaker is a graphics database containing over 3,000 Picture Communications Symbols in bitmapped clip art form. Information and catalog available at http://www.woodlaketechnologies.com
Center on the Social and Emotional Foundations for Early Learning. University of Illinois at Urbana-Champaign, Champaign, IL. A national center focused on strengthening the capacity of child care and Head Start to improve the social and emotional outcomes of young children. Provides information to help early childhood care and education professionals meet the needs of children with challenging behaviors. What Works Briefs and Training Modules and Materials available at http://www.csefel.uicu.edu
Essa, E. (2002). *Practical guide to solving preschool behavior problems* (5th ed.). New York: Delmar Publishers. Easy to read book includes step-by-step instructions for dealing with 40 common behavior problems; includes a focus on working with children with disabilities.
Garcia, J. (2000). *Sign with your baby*. Bellingham, WA: Stratton-Kehl Publications. Easy American Sign Language signs that represent simple ideas babies and toddlers can understand. Parents report reduced frustration for them and their baby, a stronger parent/child bond, and accelerated verbal language development. Also used with older toddlers and preschoolers who are language-delayed. Books, videos, and reminder cards for "Sign with Your Baby" are available at http://www.sign2me.com
Picture Exchange Communication System (PECS). Using PECS, children learn to spontaneously initiate communicative exchanges. Children are taught to approach and give a picture of a desired item to a communicative partner in exchange for that item. Information available at http://www.bbsautism.com/pecs_contents.htm

Websites:
http://www.dec-sped.org: Division for Early Childhood of the Council for Exceptional Children. DEC support the work of professionals who work with or on behalf of young children with special needs and their families.

http://www.zerotothree.org: Zero to Three website contains resources for families and professionals who work with infants and toddlers and their families.

http://www.nimh.nih.gov: National Institute of Mental Health. Valuable information on specific mental disorders, diagnosis, and treatment.

http://www.ffcmh.org: Federation of Families for Children's Mental Health. National parent-run organization focused on the needs of children with emotional, behavioral, or mental disorders and their families.

REFERENCES

Artesani, A. J. (2001). *Understanding the purpose of challenging behavior: A guide to conducting functional assessments*. Upper Saddle River, NJ: Merrill/Prentice Hall.

Bijou, S. W., Peterson, R. F., & Ault, M. H. (1968). A method to integrate descriptive and experimental field studies at the level of data and empirical concepts. *Journal of Applied Behavior Analysis, 1*, 175–191.

Boulware, G., Schwartz, I., & McBride, B. (1999). Addressing challenging behaviors at home. In S. Sandall & M. Ostrosky (Eds.), *Young Exceptional Children monograph series: Practical ideas for addressing challenging behaviors* (pp. 29–40). Longmont, CO: Sopris West.

Durand, V. M. (1990). *Severe behavior problems: A functional communication training approach*. New York: Guilford.

Fox, L., Lentini, R., & Dunlap, G. (2002). *Individualized intensive interventions: Developing a behavior support plan*. Champaign, IL: University of Illinois at Urbana-Chamapign Center on the Social and Emotional Foundations for Early Learning. Project funded by the Child Care and Head Start Bureaus in the U.S. Department of Health and Human Services. Available at http://www.csefel.uiuc.edu

Hazen, N., Black, B., & Fleming-Johnson, F. (1984). Social acceptance. *Young Children, 39*, 26–36.

Kaiser, S., & Rasminsky, J. S. (1999). *Meeting the challenge: Effective strategies for challenging behaviors in early childhood environments*. Washington, DC: National Association for the Education of Young Children.

Kaiser, S., & Rasminsky, J. S. (2003). *Challenging behavior in young children*. Boston, MA: Allyn & Bacon.

Klass, C. S., Guskin, K. A., & Thomas, M. (1995). The early childhood program: Promoting children's development through and within relationships. *Zero to Three, 16*, 9–17.

Koralek, D. (1999). *Classroom strategies to promote children's social and emotional development*. Lewisville, NC: Kaplan Press.

Neilson, S., Olive, M., Donovan, A., & McEvoy, M. (1998). Challenging behavior in your classroom? Don't react, teach instead! *Young Exceptional Children, 2*(1), 2–10.

O'Neill, R., Horner, R., Albin, R., Sprague, J., Storey, K., & Newton, J.S. (1997). *Functional assessment and program development for problem behavior* (2nd ed.). Pacific Grove, CA: Brooks/Cole.

Schaefer, C. E., & Millman, H. L. (1981). *How to help children with common problems*. New York: New American Library, Inc.

Strain, P., McConnell, S., Carta, J., Fowler, S., Neisworth, J., & Wolery, M. (1992). Behaviorism in early intervention. *Topics in Early Childhood Special Education, 12*(1), 121–141.

Webster-Stratton, C., & Herbert, M. (1994). *Troubled families—Problem children: Working with parents: A collaborative process*. Chichester, England: Wiley.

Appendix A: Lesson Plan Form for "Friends" Theme

	Monday	Tuesday	Wednesday	Thursday	Friday
Group Time (songs, stories, etc.)	Read *Friends in the Park* (This book depicts young children of varying abilities and ethnicity playing in the park.)	Fingerplay: Five Little Friends (Hold up five fingers, subtract one with each action. See bottom of next page for words.)	Read book: *Friends* by Helme Heine. Motto of the book is "Friends always stick together." Ask open-ended questions about their experiences with friends as you read. *Responds to a read-aloud story with questions and comments*	Notice missing friends, talk about why they are absent. Announce materials will be available in art area today to make notes and cards for friends at school or a get-well cards for sick friends.	Read *Making Friends* (This book defines friendship, sharing, turn-taking, caring, and feelings.) Announce that "buddies" from fourth grade will come to read to children at the end of class today.
Small Groups (teacher-directed)	Make a graph about the friends in our class (color of hair or color of eyes). Talk about how friends are alike and different. *Sorts and classifies objects by attributes; Interprets simple graphs; Compares similarities and differences of objects*		Create class book about friends at school. Have each child complete a page with these words pre-printed at the top: "Friends stick together" Children may draw a picture, add words, and "sign" their page. *Labels drawings; Prints first and last name*		
Class Meeting	Create a concept web about friendship. Begin the conversation with questions: How do friends act? What do friends do together? Where can you make friends?	Use puppets to act out friendship scenarios—what friends do for each other. Allow children to suggest the scenarios. *Verbalizes feelings and shows empathic concern for others*	Engage children in discussion about when it is hard to be a friend – problems friends sometimes have (problems with sharing, taking turns)	Read *My Friends*. This predictable book begins each line with "I learned to . . from my friend the . . ." Have children discuss things they have learned from their friends at school. *Verbally completes a simple predictable pattern*	Revisit concept web on friendship. Ask children if they have more ideas to add to the web.

154

			Objectives
Outdoor Activities	Jump the river	Play "The Limbo" game using a broomstick.	Play "We're All Winners" from *Peaceful Classroom* **Follows simple rules**
Special Activities (field trip, visitors)	Cooking: Make "friendship" cookies for snack	"Buddies" from fourth grade to come to read to children for 15 minutes prior to departure time	
Family Involvement	Ask families to bring in pictures of family and friends	Encourage families to invite their child's friend over to play	*CARES for Families* newsletter focusing on sharing, friends.

Environmental Changes and Objectives for Children

Center	**Changes to the Environment**	**Objectives**	**Center**	**Changes to the Environment**	**Objectives**
Dramatic Play	Encourage children to use puppets to act out friendship scenarios. Set out "Tea Party" sets and model having a tea party with friends	**Assumes simple roles while playing with two or more children. Sustains interactions with familiar adults and other children.**	Literacy/ Library/ Writing	Feature new books: *Friends* *Friends in the Park* *Making Friends* *Will You Be My Friend?* *My Friends*	Looks at books, pictures, and other printed materials **Imitates reading behavior.**
Blocks	Add block play people with differing abilities Model how to build houses for these "friends"	*Recognizes basic geometric shapes*	Table toys	Kids at Play puzzle set (Lakeshore)	
Art	Materials to make get-well cards for friends	*Writes to express meaning.*	Computer	Story-writing software Encourage children to write stories about friends	*Writes to express meaning*
Sand/ Water/ Sensory	Soap and four eggbeaters in water table		Science	No changes	
Cozy Corner	Book *Friends at School*				

Appendix B: Problem Solving in Action

Preschool Classroom: This example depicts a teacher and two 4-year-olds.

Jamal grabs the truck that Micah was using. Micah screams and swings at Jamal, attempting to hit him. Their teacher, Rhonda, quickly approaches placing herself between the children and gently restraining Micah. "Micah, stop. I can tell that you are angry that Jamal took your truck. But hitting is not okay. It is not safe." As Micah and Jamal calm somewhat, Rhonda proceeds with mediating the problem solving steps. "I'll hold the truck while we talk."

1. What Is the Problem? Rhonda asks, "What happened here? What's the problem?" Rhonda knows that it is best to begin questions with *what* rather than *why*. "Why" questions sound accusing and make children defensive ("Why did you take the truck?" "Why did you hit him?"). Even adults sometimes have difficulty explaining <u>why</u> they did something, especially in the heat of the moment.

Micah says, "Jamal took my truck. I was playing with it." Jamal responds, "Yeah, but I told you I wanted to see it go down the ramp!"

Rhonda says, "I see from your faces that you are both angry. Jamal, look at Micah. Do you see that his face is kind of red and angry looking? He did not like it when you took his truck. Micah, Jamal looks angry too. Maybe he was waiting for a long time to use the truck. You said Micah had the truck. But Jamal wanted to see the truck go down the ramp. The problem is, you *both* want to play with the truck." Jamal looks at her and nods. Micah looks at the truck.

2. What Can I Do? Rhonda proceeds. "What can you do to solve this problem?" The boys squirm, and Micah reaches as if he is ready to grab the truck again. Jamal says, "We could share the truck." Rhonda says, "That's one idea. Micah, do you have another idea?" Micah shakes his head negatively. Rhonda notes Micah's reluctance and suggests, "I have another idea. Jamal could find another truck or car to roll down the ramp."

3. What Might Happen If . . . ? The boys look at her but don't answer. Rhonda asks, "What do you think will work? Can two boys share the truck and use it at the same time?" Micah says, "I don't want to share." "Micah doesn't like the idea of sharing," repeats Rhonda. "What about finding another truck? Would that work? I see another truck on the shelf that is about the same size."

Jamal looks at the shelf and says, "Yeah, I guess I could use the blue truck over there." Rhonda looks at both boys, "Is that a fair solution? Jamal can use the blue truck on the ramp, and Micah can use this truck where he wants to play." Both boys nod.

4. Choose a Solution and Use It. Rhonda senses that the boys need continued support, so she rephrases the chosen solution, "So you've decided that Jamal will get the blue truck and Micah can use this one" as she holds out the truck in her hand. "Micah, walk over to the shelf to help Jamal get the blue truck. Then you can play with this truck." Rhonda takes this extra step to ensure that the plan will work.

5. Is It Working? If Not, What Can I Do Now? Rhonda and Micah go with Jamal to the shelf, who picks up the blue truck and proceeds to roll it down the ramp nearby. Micah accepts the truck from her hand and goes back to his play. Rhonda watches both boys play for a moment, separately but contentedly. Then she approaches Jamal. "I see your truck rolling down the ramp. It worked to talk about the problem and find another truck." Jamal smiles and talks about how fast the truck goes. Rhonda moves over to Micah. "You look happy. Did it work to talk about the problem and help Jamal find another truck?" Micah nods his head.

Toddler Classroom: This example depicts a teacher (Anne) assisting two toddlers with some verbal skills.

Lakisha and Noriko are together in the dramatic play center. Lakisha is wrapping a doll in a blanket while Noriko takes plastic dishes out of the cupboard. Noriko looks at Lakisha and suddenly grabs the doll and from her arms. Lakisha begins to scream and tries to pull the doll back. Anne moves to the area and says, "Lakisha, you look angry. You were playing with the doll. Can you tell Noriko something? Say, 'mine.'" Lakisha stops crying long enough to shout, "Mine!"

The teacher proceeds. "Noriko, do you hear Lakisha? She is saying 'mine.' Do you want the doll, too? Do you want to say, 'I want it'?" Noriko still clings to the doll saying, "I want it."

Now the teacher helps the children restate the problem. "Good talking, girls. Lakisha said 'mine' and Noriko said 'I want it.' Sounds like you both want the doll. What can you do when two girls both want the doll?" Neither girl responds. Anne guesses that both girls are firmly focused on the doll, and she says calmly, "I'll hold the doll while we decide what to do," gently takes the doll from Noriko's arms, and repeats, "What can you do when two girls both want the doll?"

Noriko looks over at the crib holding two other dolls, but doesn't move or say anything. Anne takes the cue and asks, "Noriko I see you looking at the crib. Do you want to get another doll?" Noriko longingly looks at the doll in Anne's arms, moves over to the crib, takes a doll, and hands it to Lakisha.

Anne reinforces Noriko's actions and checks to make sure that it is an acceptable solution for Lakisha. "Noriko, that was a good idea. You got another doll for Lakisha. Is that okay with you, Lakisha?" Lakisha nods her head. "Noriko, Lakisha is happy with the doll you gave her. Now you may play with this doll," Anne says while handing over the original doll to Noriko.

Appendix C: Lesson Plans for "Beginning School" Theme

	Monday	Tuesday	Wednesday	Thursday	Friday
Group Time (songs, stories, etc.)	Teach children a "hello" song. Each child says his/her name. Introduce pictorial Daily Schedule. *Says first name; Follows classroom routines; Sequences two or three items*	Introduce Safety Rule; show poster. Talk about examples of safety in classroom as you walk children around the room, pointing out centers and bathrooms	After singing "Hello" song, do "Roll Over" activity from *The Peaceful Classroom*, page 28. Introduce "Choosing Centers" chart. *Follows classroom routines; Demonstrates a plan for play.*	Introduce attendance chart. When taking attendance, always note who is missing as well as who is present. Play "Missing Person" game from *The Peaceful Classroom*, page 48.	Introduce Cozy Corner. Read *Evan's Corner*, shortening number of words read on each page to adapt to age level of children.
Class Meeting	Read what *Will Mommy Do When I'm at School?* Ask children what they think their parents will do while they are at school. Talk about separation, fears, what school is like. *Identifies front and back of book; Identifies title and title page*	Repeat previous day's Class Meeting with second half of class.	Review pictorial Daily Schedule.	Have each child draw a picture of the people in their family. Assist each child to count up how many people in her family. Assist children to fill in a simple graph depicting the number of people in their family. *Interprets simple graphs.*	Repeat previous day's Class Meeting with second half of class
Outdoor Activities		Talk about Safety Rule before and after going outside.	Take a walk around the school grounds and neighborhood.	Create obstacle course. This might include climbing over, under, around objects. *Demonstrates spatial relationships using position words.*	
Family Involvement	Establish ritual for greeting parents. Allow flexible plan for parents to stay in classroom as children adapt to school.	Send home newsletter on Safety Rule.		Create Parent Information area and/or bulletin board.	Show Cozy Corner to parents.

Environmental Changes and Objectives for Children

Center	Changes to the Environment	Objectives	Center	Changes to the Environment	Objectives
Dramatic Play	Organize attractive housekeeping area using child-sized objects and furniture, fabrics, dress-ups for both boys and girls, multicultural dolls, and telephones to promote conversations.	*Participates in dramatization. Plays at more than one role. Sustains interactions with familiar adults and other children. Interacts positively with all children.*	Literacy/ Library/ Writing	*Going to School Buenas Noches Luna Michael's First Day at School. Will You Come Back for Me? Edward Unready for School Will I Have a Friend?.*	*Looks at books, pictures, and other printed materials. Imitates reading behavior. Demonstrates that print has meaning.*
Blocks	Organize graduated sized wooden blocks on shelves with clear labeling. Add a few trucks and/or cars. Stand up multi-ethnic family figures on top of shelves. Hang a small Safety Rule poster.	*Makes comparisons of objects. Sorts and classifies by shape and size, using more than one attribute. Recognizes basic geometric shapes. Compares objects by size and height.*	Table toys	Puzzles about routines or school.	
Art	Prepare attractive and functional art area with daily open-ended art options. Introduce easel. Create neat bulletin board for display of children's art.	*Draws simple pictures.*	Computer	Add computer software about beginning school and the routines of school.	*Demonstrates skills through technology.*
Sand/ Water/ Sensory	Partially fill sensory table with warm water. Add toys: funnels, small pitchers, measuring cups. Put a chair at sensory table so teacher can sit and chat with children.	*Makes comparisons of objects. Sustains interactions with familiar adults and other children. Compares objects.*	Science		
Cozy Corner	Organize Cozy Corner with pillows, stuffed animal, book about starting school.				

159

Appendix D: Lesson Plan for "Bullying" Theme (primary grades)

	Monday	Tuesday	Wednesday	Thursday	Friday
Group Time (songs, stories, etc.)	Read *Why Am I Different?* Talk about the ways friends in this class are the same and ways they are different, and how that is "okay."	Talk about things children can do if they make a mistake and treat someone in a hurtful way. Make a list of ideas, which could include: • Say you're sorry • Make that person a card to apologize • Do something nice for that person	Read *Chrysanthemum* (a story about name calling.) Involve children in a discussion, asking questions such as, Has anyone ever made fun of your name? How did you feel? What did you do about it? What should you do if it happens again?	Read *King of the Playground* (a story about a bully) Lead a discussion, asking the children: What was Kevin's problem? How do you think Kevin was feeling? How did Kevin stand up for himself? Do you like how Kevin solved his problem?	Read *The Big Bad Bully Bear* Lead discussion about book, integrating concepts talked about this week
Small Groups (teacher-directed)	Each child makes book about his favorite activities, favorite toy, favorite book, favorite flavor ice cream, etc. Use cutout pictures from magazines or draw illustrations.	Read aloud the books children made on Monday. Talk about each person's strengths and what he contributes to class community.	Design covers for books	Have children write in a journal. Topics could include: • a time when they were bullied • how it feels to be bullied • ways to respond to bullies • a time when they helped a child who was being bullied	Finish journal stories
Outdoor Activities	Play cooperative games	Pair "unpopular" children with friendly, helpful buddies during games	Reward outdoor caring behaviors: start a Caring Caterpillar outdoors.	Plan a cooperative activity to benefit the school, such as clean up the playground or wash the windows	

160

Class Meeting	Define bullying as when someone is repeatedly treated unkindly by one or more people. With children, make a list of ways that sometimes children are unkind. Include name calling, making fun, picking on, hitting, kicking, shoving, pushing, pinching, damaging belongings, and excluding someone from group activities.	Develop list of ways to respond to bullying: • Tell them to stop • Tell them to leave you alone • Tell them how you feel "I don't like it when you call me names." • Play with other friends • Ask an adult for help	Read Stop Picking On Me. Have puppets and children act out similar situations and discuss consequences.	Have children dramatize the story King of the Playground. First, act out the story as read. Then, have children decide on other ways Kevin could have responded and dramatize.	Do assertiveness role-plays. Start with teacher using two puppets. Move on to teacher puppet interacting with one child. Children practice standing tall and saying: • Leave me alone. • No. • Stop that. • Yes, you're right. I am slow. (putting bully off guard by agreeing)

Adult Resources:

Bosch, C. W. (1988). *Bully on the bus.* Seattle, WA: Parenting Press Inc.

Garrity, C., Jens, K., Porter, W., Sager, N., & Short-Camilli, C. (1996). *Bully proofing your school: A comprehensive approach for elementary schools.* Longmont, CO: Sopris West.

Powell, J. (1999). *Talking about bullying.* Austin, TX: Raintree Steck-Vaughn.

Sheanh, G. (1996). *Helping kids deal with conflict.* Winnipeg, CA: Peguis Publishers

website:http://www.colorado.edu/cspv/publications/factsheets/safeschools/FS-SC10.html

Appendix E: Getting Started in Your Classroom

Since 1992, the authors have been conducting workshops for early childhood care and education professionals and teaching college guidance strategies courses. Often, having been presented with the many strategies summarized in this book, teachers-in-training express a uniform cry of "Where do I start?" We presented this question to a group of teachers who had completed the *CARES Model* training and were mentored by the authors in their classrooms for an entire school year to assist in the implementation of *CARES Strategies*.

At the end of the school year, based on their successes and frustrations with attempting to implement a myriad of *CARES Strategies*, these teachers developed a sequence to follow for the next school year (Figure E.1). The sequence was successfully followed by this group of teachers in the following year and has been used by many early childhood professionals since then.

FIGURE E.1   **Sequence of Introduction of Cares Strategies**

September	Room arrangement and labeling Cozy corner set up and explained to children Pictorial schedule posted and explained to children frequently Safety rule introduced and explained with concrete examples daily Introduce class meeting concept Read and discuss books about going to school Discuss feelings involved around transition and separation Practice responsive language with children and families CARES for Families Newsletter: Safety Rule

October	Class meetings
	Identifying feelings with facial expressions and words to label
	    Use emotion posters, feelings charts, happy/sad sticks, feeling dolls, *Second Step* curriculum, mirrors, books
	    Begin to include empathy, care, and concern for others in discussion
	    Display picture books about emotions throughout the classroom
	    Use puppets to demonstrate feelings and prosocial skills
	    Identify "helpful" vs. "hurtful" actions
	Use encouragement instead of repetitious praise statements
	CARES for Families Newsletter on emotions

November	Plan and implement activities to build a sense of community and promote prosocial skills Plan emotion-centered lesson plans relevant to the needs of children in your classroom including lots of expressive activities CARES for Families Newsletter on prosocial skills

December	Introduce calming-down steps in class meetings and small groups
	Teach assertiveness behaviors
	Introduce stress reduction activities in class meetings or small groups
	    Model tense/relaxed using Barbie and Raggedy Ann
	    Teach back rubs, feather painting, etc.
	    Practice deep breathing
	    Connect all of the above with how it makes children feel
	CARES for Families Newsletters on calming down and stress reduction

January	Introduce five steps to problem solving gradually in class meetings Use puppets to suggest scenarios. Ask "what is the problem?" Identify feelings. Brainstorm ideas and write them down. The next day, quickly review scenario and read list of possible solutions. Evaluate solutions and pick one viable solution for the puppets to act out. Practice steps to calming down in class meetings and small groups Assist children to practice the steps in real-life situations Continue activities on feelings, prosocial skills, and sense of belonging. Continue stress reduction activities CARES for Families Newsletter on problem solving
February	Practice five steps to problem solving in class meetings and small groups Assist children to practice the steps in real-life situations requiring problem solving or calming down
March and April	Introduce voting in class meetings and small groups. Allow children to make decisions related to their own classroom. Practice steps to calming down and problem solving in class meetings and small groups Assist children to practice the steps in real-life situations Continue stress reduction activities Continue activities on feelings, prosocial skills, and sense of belonging CARES for Families Newsletter on media effects
May	Class meetings on "saying goodbye," plans over summer, and what will happen for children next year (return to preschool or go to kindergarten) CARES for Families Newsletter on "goodbyes"

Appendix F: Blank Lesson Planning Forms

	Monday	Tuesday	Wednesday	Thursday	Friday
Group Time					
Small Groups)					
Class Meeting					
Outdoor Activities					
Special Activities (field trip, visitors)					
Snack					
Family Involvement					

Environmental Changes and Objectives for Children

Center	Changes to the Environment	Objectives	Center	Changes to the Environment	Objectives
Dramatic Play			Literacy/ Library/ Writing		
Blocks			Table toys		
Art			Computer		
Sand/ Water/ Sensory			Science		
Cozy Corner					

Appendix G: Basic Classroom Preventive Practices

Strategies to Promote Positive Social Behavior and Emotional Competence:
A Self-Assessment

Self-Scoring Code: For each item, indicate if it is not yet implemented (N), occasionally implemented (O), or consistently implemented in your classroom (C)	Code
ENVIRONMENT	
Clear physical boundaries define activity areas	
Noisy areas separate from areas for quiet activities	
Materials suited to age, interest, and abilities of children	
Labeled materials and shelves encourage independence	
Space provided for each child to store belongings	
Duplicates of favorite materials provided	
Materials and space for indoor active, gross motor play	
Cleanliness maintained on all materials and equipment	
Room decorations minimal and posted at child eye level	
Relaxing, comfortable, home-like environment	
Materials reflect families, cultures, and language	
Cozy corner set up with tension relieving materials	
CLASSROOM ROUTINES	
Maintain consistent and predictable schedule	
Post pictorial schedule with simple words and illustrations children can understand and refer to often	
Adjust schedule as needed to respond to children's needs and special circumstances	
Provide a balance of indoor/outdoor, quiet/active, and large group/small group/independent activities	
Minimize transitions, provide advance notice, and explain what happens next	
Conduct group routines in a consistent manner	
Eliminate excessive waiting or sitting for long periods	
Practice rituals for arrival and departure to help children and families cope with separation	
SAFETY RULE	
Safety rule clearly posted using words and pictures	
Identify and demonstrate "safe" and "not safe" actions in concrete situations	
Help children use safety rule to decide on appropriate behavior	
POSITIVE GUIDANCE TECHNIQUES	
State rules in positive terms	
Make requests and give directions in respectful ways	
Validate children's feelings	
Clarify classroom rules and give reasons for the limits	
Model behavior you want children to follow	
Reinforce appropriate behavior	
Ignore non-disruptive inappropriate behavior	
Offer choices to children	
Redirect and offer acceptable substitutes	
Use logical consequences	

	Code
EMOTIONAL EXPRESSION	
Create environment where children feel safe to express feelings	
Plan activities for identification and labeling of emotions	
Offer materials that encourage children to explore and express their feelings	
Display pictures and books about emotions throughout the classroom	
PROSOCIAL SKILLS	
Help children develop positive, trusting relationships with one or more teachers	
Help children develop positive relationships with peers	
Teach children how to initiate play with another child	
Plan activities to promote group identity and sense of belonging	
Plan activities to teach specific social skills in class meetings or small groups	
Plan activities and experiences that encourage cooperation and peer interaction	
Conduct class meetings with a prosocial theme	
Validate and reinforce prosocial actions by children	
PROBLEM SOLVING	
Conduct class meetings to teach problem solving using role plays, puppets, and children's books	
Involve children in making decisions and solving problems that come up in the classroom	
Coach child through steps in problem solving in actual conflict situations (adapted to age and ability of child)	
Introduce children to voting to make class decisions	
MANAGING ANGER AND AGGRESSION	
Acknowledge and accept anger but not aggressive acts	
Teach assertiveness behaviors (protecting own rights while respecting rights of others)	
Provide immediate practice of alternative behavior after aggressive behavior	
Teach and practice calming-down steps	
Limit exposure to violent media and toys in classroom	
STRESS REDUCTION	
Teach children relaxation and stress reduction techniques	
Include tension relieving materials in cozy corner	
CURRICULUM PLANNING	
Develop emotion-centered themes based on the needs, interests, and life experiences of the children	
Include a section for class meetings on lesson plan form	
INTERACTIONS WITH TEAMS AND FAMILIES	
Use a variety of communication methods to keep families informed about the program and its philosophy	
Learn about each child's family, culture, and community	
Involve families in the program design and classroom activities	
Practice active listening and five steps to problem solving with teams and families in the case of conflict	
Create a caring community for teams and families	

Appendix H: Social Skills Inventories

Social Competence and Behavior Evaluation (SCBE), Preschool Edition
P.J. La Franiere & J.E. Dumas ;Western Psychological Services
Age 2 ½–6
Administration: 15 minutes, individual

The SCBE measures social competence, affective expression, and adjustment in children 2 ½ to 6 years of age. The primary objective of the SCBE is to describe the child's behavior for purposes of socialization and education, rather than diagnosis. It focuses on the child's adaptation to and functioning within his or her environment. It includes 80 items that can be completed by a preschool or kindergarten teacher. There are eight basic scales (Depressive-Joyful; Anxious-Secure; Angry-Tolerant; Isolated-Integrated; Aggressive-Calm; Egotistical-Prosocial; Oppositional-Cooperative; Dependent-Autonomous) and four summary scales (Social Competence; Externalizing Problems; Internalizing Problems; General Adaptation).

Devereux Early Childhood Assessment (DECA)
Devereux Foundation
Age 2–5
Administration: 10 minutes, individual

The DECA is a standardized, norm-referenced behavior rating scale evaluating within-child protective factors in preschool children aged 2 to 5 completed by family members or early care and education professionals. The DECA evaluates the frequency of 27 positive behaviors including three scales (initiative, self-control, and attachment) and a total protective factors scale. The DECA also contains a 10-item behavioral concerns scale which measures a wide variety of challenging and problem behaviors seen in some preschool children.

Burks' Behavioral Rating Scale (BBRS)
Harold F. Burks
Grades Preshool–9

The BBRS helps you diagnose and treat children with behavior problems. Widely used by school psychologists and teachers, the BBRS is an effective way to evaluate disruptive or troubled children. The BBRS includes 110 items, each describing a behavior infrequently observed in normal children. A parent or teacher simply indicates, on a 5-point response scale, how often the behavior is seen in the child being evaluated.

The BBRS gives you a profile of scores covering 19 problem behaviors: Excessive Self-Blame, Anxiety, Withdrawal, Dependency, Suffering, Sense of Persecution, Aggressiveness, Resistance, Poor Ego Strength, Coordination, Intellectuality, Academics (not included on Preschool Edition), Attention, Impulse Control, Reality Contact, Sense of Identity, and Social Conformity. The BBRS offers a practical and proven way to identify problem behavior in children.

Social Skills Rating System (SSRS)
Frank M. Gresham, Stephen N. Elliot
Age 3–18
Administration: 10–25 minutes

SSRS measures positive social behaviors: Cooperation, Assertion, Responsibility, Empathy, Self-Control, and problem behaviors: Externalization/Internalization Problems, and Hyperactivity, to obtain a more complete picture from teachers, parents, and even students themselves. Academic Competence Scale provides a quick estimate to academic functioning. Ratings include reading and mathematics, performance, general cognitive functioning as well as student relationships, peer acceptance, academic performance, and parental support.

SSRS yields standard scores and percentile ranks for scales and subscales. Use the Assessment-Intervention Record (AIR) for frequency and importance ratings. The SSRS is backed by extensive research and was standardized on a national sample of over 4,000. It is also the first rating scale to provide separate norms for boys and girls ages 3-18 and for elementary students with or without disabilities.

Preschool Behavior Checklist (PBCL)
Jacqueline McGuire, Naomi Richman
Age 2–5

This quick 22-item screening tool is designed to help preschool professionals who may be concerned about a child's behavioral and emotional difficulties. The checklist consists of a series of items within specific areas, including soiling, temper, fears, worries, and moods. The examiner describes the degree of usually observed behaviors. Scoring is completed quickly. The PBCL provides an objective assessment of behavior, and thereby helps to decide when intervention is necessary.

The total score can be compared to criterion cut-off scores that indicate the possibility of behavioral or emotional problems. Individual items scores give information regarding specific behavior areas. Results from the PBCL assist with the planning of management programs for the individual child. It is then possible, at an early age, to identify children who may be at risk of later developing serious behavioral problems.

Preschool and Kindergarten Behavior Scales (PKBS)
Kenneth W. Merrell
Age 3–6
Administration: 12 minutes, individual

The PKBS is a behavior rating scale. With 76 items in two separate scales, it provides an integrated and functional appraisal of the social skills and problem behaviors of young children. The scale can be completed by a variety of behavioral informants, such as parents, teachers, and other caregivers.

The PKBS is designed to be used as a screening tool for early detection of developing social-emotional problems, as part of a multimethod assessment battery for classification and eligibility purposes, to develop intervention programs and gauge subsequent behavioral change, and as an early childhood research tool.

Index

ABC analysis, 138, 140–142
Abdominal breathing, 116, 119
Activity reinforcers, 41, 47
Affective guidance, 15, 17
Affective reflections, 54, 59, 60
Aggression, 7, 60, 80, 89, 92, 101, 103, 106, 108, 113, 125, 138, 167
Anger, 7, 14, 60
    assertiveness skills, 103
    causes of, 101–102
    calming-down steps, 104–108
    dealing with, 105–106, 167
    defined, 101, 108
    reducing, 101
    secondary emotion, 101
Antecedents, 140–145, 149
Assertiveness (*see also* Anger), 103–104

Behavior, challenging (*see* Challenging behavior)
Bibliotherapy, 132–133
Brainstorming, 83, 96
Buddy system, 72–73
Bullying, 44, 102, 138, 140, 160–161

Calming-down steps (*see also* Anger), 104–108
Catastrophic change, 126, 133
Challenging behavior, 4, 39
    antecedents, 140
    consequences, 140
    defined, 138
    functions of, 139
    interviews, 140, 141
    positive behavior support plan, 141–146
    prevention of, 138–139
    replacement skills, 141–143
    seeking assistance, 148
Child-rearing practices, 16, 103
Children's literature, 85, 132, 133
Choosing chart, 29, 31
Class meeting(s)
    defined, 12–14
    scheduling, 14
    topics, 14, 38, 53, 54, 58, 70, 84, 105, 106, 115, 124, 125, 127
Clean-up, 36, 140, 146
Code of ethical conduct, 16, 18, 47, 50

Conflicts, kinds of, 80–82, 88–89
Conflict resolution (*see* Problem solving)
Consequences
    and function assessment, 140–142
    logical, 44
    maintaining, 140
Cooperation (*see also* Prosocial), 68, 70, 72, 167
Cozy Corner (*see also* Environment), 4, 20, 21–23, 29, 31, 45, 101, 104, 105, 106, 114, 116
Critical change, 126, 132
Culture
    respecting family, 6, 14, 16, 27, 47, 73, 103, 125, 166, 167
Curriculum planning (*see* emotionally responsive curriculum)

Developmentally appropriate curriculum, 15, 17
Developmental change, 126, 132
Direct guidance, 15, 16
Discipline (*see also* Guidance techniques), 39–40, 45, 47
Diversity, 71, 127
Domestic violence, 2, 3, 102

Effective praise, 41–42, 43, 47
Encouragement, 41
Emotional intelligence, 52, 60
Emotional literacy, 52, 53, 55, 60
Emotional regulation, 6, 53, 59–60, 61
Emotional self-awareness, 53
Emotional vocabulary, 52, 54, 83
Emotionally responsive curriculum
    bibliotherapy, 132, 133
    defined, 124, 132
    planning themes, 127-131
Emotions, 6, 14, 52, 91, 102, 108, 124, 162, 167
    affective reflections, 54, 59, 60
    identifying and labeling, 53–57
    recognizing in others, 57–59
    managing emotions, 59–60
Empathy, 6, 52, 57, 58, 60, 66, 68, 74, 162, 169
Environment , 5, 166
    and anger, 102, 105
    and challenging behavior, 139, 141, 142, 144
    and stress reduction, 21, 144
    Choosing Chart, 29, 31
    Cozy Corner, 21–23
    lighting, 28
    organization of, 25–26
    outdoor, 23–25
    predictable, 28–30
    relaxing and personal, 26–28

space for active play, 23–24
structuring space and materials, 20–21
Externalizing behaviors, 60

Family disruption, 2, 3, 5, 40
Family (*see also* Parents)
    and culture, 14, 16, 26, 47, 71, 104
    collaborating with, 16, 39, 69, 73, 93, 94, 107, 126, 131, 132, 139, 148, 155, 158, 167, 168
    involvement, importance of, 15–16
    newsletters, 74, 94, 107, 162
Feelings (*see* Emotions)
Feelings vocabulary, 53, 58, 61
Fight or flight response, 113, 144, 119
Friendship, 6, 69, 71–73, 127, 154
Function of behavior, 140, 142, 144, 145, 146, 148, 149, 150, 159

Group association and belonging (*see also* Prosocial), 72
Group entry, 69, 81
Guidance
    affective, 15, 17
    defined, 15, 16
    direct, 15, 16
    indirect, 15, 16
    physical, 15, 16
    verbal, 15, 16
Guidance techniques
    activity reinforcers, 41, 47
    effective praise/encouragement, 41–42, 43, 47
    facilitate problem solving, 43
    ignore non-disruptive behavior, 43
    logical consequences, 44
    modeling, 41
    offer choices, 43
    redirect, 43
    reinforce appropriate behavior, 41
    responsive language, 40
    restraint (holding), 46
    Safety Rule, 40
    sequence of response, 46
    social reinforcers, 41, 45, 47
    tangible reinforcers, 41, 47
    time-out, 45–46

Holding, 46
Indirect guidance, 15, 16
Ignoring, 43
Internalizing behaviors, 59

Logical consequences, 44, 166

Maintaining consequences, 140, 141, 142, 149
Materials, selection of, 20
Media violence, 67, 102, 118
Modeling, 15, 41, 47, 66, 73, 84

Neurotransmitters, 101, 117

Observation, 140, 141
Offer choices, 43, 166
Open-ended activities, 106
Outdoor environment, 23–25

Parents (*see* Family)
Partner chats, 13, 108
Peer rejection, 100, 102, 103
Physical guidance, 15, 16
Pictorial Daily Schedule, 29, 31, 149, 158
Play
    competitive, 72
    superhero, 125
    symbolic, 125
    themes, 124
Positive behavior support plan, 141–148
    and families, 148–149
    defined, 141
    process for creating, 141–144
    monitoring effectiveness, 146–148
Positive guidance *(see* Guidance techniques)
Positive reinforcement, 41
    praise vs. encouragement, 41–42, 43, 47
Praise, 41
    effective vs. ineffective, 42, 47
Predictable schedule, 28–29, 168
Primary grades
    activities for, 13, 23, 44, 71, 84, 85, 88, 160–161
Problem Solving (*see also* Guidance), 81–93
    model for, 82–84
    modification for special needs, 91
    solution list, 86–87
    teaching, 84–88
    win-win solution, 82, 96
    with toddlers, 91
Prosocial behaviors
    defined, 66
    importance of, 66–67
    teaching, 67–73

Protective factors, 5, 7, 15, 21, 168
Puppets, use of, 13, 38, 58, 59, 69, 83, 84, 85, 89, 96, 106, 154, 161, 162, 163, 167

Redirection, 43, 105, 125, 140, 145, 166
Reinforcement
    activity reinforcers, 41, 47
    social reinforcers, 41, 45, 47
    tangible reinforcers, 41, 47
Relaxation response, 114, 116, 119
Replacement skills, 141, 142–142, 144, 145, 148, 150
Resilience, 5, 6, 7
Responsive language, 40–41, 47
Restraint, 45
Risk factors, 5, 7
Routines, 28, 29, 38, 40, 114, 138, 139, 142, 149, 151, 166

Safety Rule, 5, 6, 36–39, 40, 44, 47, 48, 105, 106, 114, 124, 139, 158, 162, 166
    introducing to children, 36–38
    introducing to families, 39
    Spanish version, 38
School readiness and social competence, 4
Secondary emotion, 101, 108
Self control skills (*see also* Anger), 4, 7, 20, 40, 100, 108, 168, 169
Self-esteem, 2, 6, 41, 44, 92, 101
Self-reflection, 139
Self-regulation, 2, 104, 108
Sequence of response, 46–47
Sharing, 6, 14, 21, 43, 60, 66, 68, 73, 74, 75, 85, 154, 156
Sign language, 57, 92, 106, 110, 143, 151
Social competence
    enhancing, 5, 14, 66
    evaluating, 168
    importance of, 4, 66
Social reinforcers, 41, 45, 47
Stress, 4, 6, 7, 112
    defined, 113
    reducing, 21–30, 104–105, 114–115
    relaxation response, 114
    signs of, 113
    teaching stress reduction, 115–118

Taking turns, 66, 68, 70, 75, 85, 94, 154
Tangible reinforcers, 41, 47
Teachable moment, 15, 17
Teasing, 3, 6, 81, 89, 102, 105, 140
Television, 2, 67, 73, 80, 118
Temperament, 5
Time-out

defined, 45, 48
    disadvantages of, 44–45, 80, 82, 146
    procedures for, 45–46
Toddlers, 23, 24, 57, 68, 69, 70, 91, 92, 94, 96, 105, 106, 107, 125, 126, 141, 143, 151, 157
Transfer of training, 15
Transitions, 5, 26, 29, 31, 118, 126, 140, 149, 166
Trauma, 2, 40, 53, 102

Verbal guidance, 15, 17, 40–41
Violence, 2, 3, 52, 67, 82, 102, 112, 124
Visualization, 115, 116, 119

Win-win solution, 82, 85, 86, 88, 96